AGADA:

The Language of Jewish Faith

ALUMNI SERIES OF THE HEBREW UNION COLLEGE PRESS

AGADA:
The Language of Jewish Faith

Samuel E. Karff

Hebrew Union College Press
CINCINNATI, OHIO 1979

Library of Congress Cataloging in Publication Data

Karff, Samuel E.
Agada: the language of Jewish faith.

(Alumni series of the Hebrew Union College Press)
Includes bibliographical references.
1. Judaism—20th century—Addresses, essays, lectures.
2. Aggada—Addresses, essays, lectures. 3. Jewish the-
ology—Addresses, essays, lectures. I. Title. II. Series:
Hebrew Union College, Cincinnati. Alumni publication
series.
BM565.K355   296   79-15610
ISBN 0-87820-114-9
ISSN 0192-2904

MANUFACTURED IN THE UNITED STATES OF AMERICA

This book is published under the auspices of the Rabbinic Alumni Association of Hebrew Union College-Jewish Institute of Religion. A quinquennial fund to which its members contribute is set aside for the specific purpose of encouraging members of the Association to pursue studies in Judaism with the prospect of publication.

NORMAN KAHAN
President, Rabbinic Alumni
    Association

WALTER JACOB
Chairman, Publications Committee
    of the Rabbinic Alumni
    Association

For Joan
whose love has sustained me and whose critical
judgment has helped me grow

Contents

Preface

THIS VOLUME stems from a lifelong love affair with agada. These Jewish myths by which biblical writer and rabbinic sage sought to articulate the religious experience of our people have held me in their spell for as long as I can remember.

However, the more serious my Jewish education became the more I was conditioned to regard agada as a pleasant but hardly pivotal aspect of our heritage. These stories, I was led to believe, represented a comforting diversion from Judaism's primary concern with the rigors of halacha or Jewish law.

Since ordination I have come increasingly to regard agada as the primary language of Jewish faith. Within these pages some basic issues of faith are examined and the insights and idiom of classical agada are reappropriated.

In form this extended essay lays claim to a middle ground between homiletics and the scholarly monograph. Its content has been shaped by more than two decades in the congregational rabbinate.

I am grateful to the members of Chicago Sinai Congregation and Congregation Beth Israel of Houston for the questions they asked and the challenge they offered for the refinement of my theological understanding.

My thanks also to Catherine Beer who not only typed the various drafts of this manuscript but encouraged me to believe that it was worth sharing with others.

May this volume help colleagues and thoughtful laymen clarify the role of agada as the language of Jewish "God-talk." May the reader find my love for agada contagious.

Samuel E. Karff
Houston, Texas

I · Defender of the Faith

MEN AND WOMEN in our culture do not speak about God or address Him in prayer nearly as much as their forefathers. This is one of the defining characteristics of a "secular age."

The American Jew is regarded as the prototype of the unreligious American. He is reported to worship much less regularly than his Protestant or Catholic neighbor, and he is usually in the vanguard of efforts to remove "God-talk" and religious symbols from the public domain. If challenged on the latter score, he may insist that he is merely championing the separation of church and state provided for in the Constitution, or protecting himself (and his children) from the tendency of American God-talk to adopt a Christian accent. (After all, no American President has yet kindled a Chanukah Menorah on the White House lawn, nor has the Post Office issued a Chanukah stamp.)

Such protestations notwithstanding, the Jew has appeared to be especially uncomfortable with God-talk, an impression reinforced by that popular refrain, "I'm not religious but I'm proud to be a Jew." The rabbi has been in a unique position to observe the secularization of the American Jewish community. If worship "turns off" his people, they do not hesitate to become "Seventh-Day Absentists," and the empty pews bear the mark of their conviction.

The decline of formal religious affirmation must be taken quite personally by one who has chosen to become a professional "defender of the faith." At times a rabbi may see himself as a man caught in the backwaters, cut off from the main drift of contemporary culture. We traffic in sacred stories while our people seek their "bigger-than life" images in the sports arena or the cinema. We preach to a full house on High Holidays and at Bar Mitzvahs,

1

but must usually defer to the competing networks of TV, golf course, ballet, and similar cultural attractions.

The rabbi's authority as interpreter of a covenant people's obligations appears to have been profoundly eroded by the acids of modernity. Liberal Jews no longer believe they are held accountable for the observance of a divinely revealed tradition requiring rabbinic interpretation. Even the professedly Orthodox negotiate their individual settlements with Jewish law, often without benefit of rabbinic counsel. Is the rabbi answering questions his people are not asking?

Although the American rabbi could never comfortably appeal to the revealed will of God (especially in ritual matters), there was a time when he possessed a special source of authority as the chief advocate of an insecure people's claim to full equality in this land. In pressing that claim, the liberal rabbi was expected to refute the theological canards dispersed by benighted Christian clerics, and he was admired for the skill with which he rose to the occasion. How many sermons were delivered on the theme "Who crucified Jesus?" How many reassurances given that we Jews did not do it. Rabbinic stature was often measured in those days by the rabbi's successful defense of his ancestors' innocence and more generally by the skill with which he cultivated the good will of the Gentile community.

By now even the role of rabbinic apologist has diminished considerably. For one thing the American Jew has come of age and feels less obliged to submit to such demeaning tests of virtue. For another the level of overt anti-Semitism has considerably ebbed.

The above considerations may not be summarily dismissed. They do affect rabbinic self-esteem and may precipitate, periodically, a vocational identity crisis. Such issues provide the grist for many symposia on "the rabbi's role" or "the future of the rabbinate."

The Three-Dimensional Covenant

Before permitting himself the luxury of despair, however, the rabbi must explore further the nature and challenge of his vocation. The Zohar, a medieval mystical work, declares that *God, Torah,* and *Israel* are inextricably intertwined. These are the three dimensions in the classical covenant consciousness of the Jew. Today the rabbi remains the primary "professional" in Jewish life who is committed to the proclamation and defense of that three-dimensional covenant. He is pledged to maintain the link between three questions: Who are we? (Israel); What must we do? (Torah); and, Why may we hope? (God). The rabbi is a specialist committed to helping his people regain the wholeness, the integrity of Jewish life.

Although a secular culture does not formally support or encourage such a religious orientation, there are impressive signs that the threefold covenant (God, Torah, Israel) is still operative in the life of the contemporary Jew.

Most adult Jews will acknowledge that the Jewish people (Israel) is a small, vulnerable people whose pilgrimage through history is in some special sense their own. For all but the most obtuse son of the covenant, Auschwitz continues to evoke a private meaning which it does not possess for the most empathic Gentile. Nor is even the marginal Jew spared constant reminders that our secular society remains more Christian than neutral. At Yuletide, if he is honest, every Jew must admit to being far more of a cultural outsider than the most secular Christian, and for most Jews Israel's rebirth is a source of visceral pride and Israel's peril a source of personal anxiety. The contemporary Jew has not lost the sense of Jacob's common destiny.

Neither will the claims of Torah be totally denied. In the past the people Israel's fate yielded special obligation. "You were strangers in the land of Egypt." Therefore "you shall not oppress the stranger." In one of Bernard Malamud's novels Morris Bober, a Jewish grocer schooled in suffering, is asked to define Torah. He replies: "For everybody should be the best, not only for you and me . . ."

With all his vaunted affluence, his purported defection from the ranks of liberalism and the fastidious frippery of the gilded ghetto, the son of Jacob continues to feel the claim even when he fails to respond to it. All too often he does fail to respond, but the echo of Pharaoh's whip lingers in the collective unconscious of the Jew, and its mark has not been erased from his heart or life.

The claim of Torah is also felt even more deeply in the primary experiences of life. Birth requires circumcision or a naming ceremony, puberty requires Confirmation or Bar Mitzvah—which despite its occasional vulgarization remains a way of binding the individual's search for identity to the norms of his elders. Love seeks consecration: even the so-called secular Jew wishes the blessings to be uttered, the vows spoken, and not only for the sake of the parents. Death remains a time to deny absurdity and oblivion by reciting or hearing the Kaddish in the presence of the congregation of Israel.

One could add the persistent, magnetic power of Rosh Hashanah, Yom Kippur, and the Passover Seder to the common-core Torah claim upon the modern Jew. Admittedly, this paltry pattern of observance falls far short of that all-pervasive regimen which was to enfold the Jew from the moment of his waking to the moment of slumber. But the rabbi perceives that the Torah continues to press its claims most compellingly when it provides the form, the sacred scenario, by which a Jew may best express the pathos and glory of life.

So much for the remnants of Israel and Torah consciousness. What of the third dimension of the covenant and the rabbi's role? Is God dead? Are we entering a totally postreligious age in which the rabbi will be numbered among a stalwart band of resisters to an inexorable trend? I do not think so. As long as we remain human, we will be conscious of our great but finite power in a universe of inexhaustible depth. We will deny our nothingness in the presence of death, and seek to affirm the abiding significance of our life. This quest for meaning will remain inescapably a quest for God.

Intimations of transcendence abound in the tents of contemporary Israel. They may not be emblazoned on our people's shirtsleeves or always verbalized, but no sensitive rabbi has failed to note signs of irrepressible wonder at the mystery of being, a throbbing gratitude for unearned gifts, a soul-searing accountability for the quality of one's life, a relentless drive to understand fed by faith in an ordered universe, a trembling trust that man is not alone in his struggle against evil, a stubborn belief in the primal and potential value of existence.

Even after many agonizing and exhausting conversations with "devout nonbelievers," we may find that they are at best "atheists with an ache." They may want us to win the argument even when they will not permit us to do so. They need someone against whose honest affirmation they can press their doubt and pursue their quest for faith.

The secular drift of American culture is itself by no means irrevocable. Such shrewd observers of religious trends as Martin Marty of the University of Chicago note a marked hunger for sacredness, a desire for personal religious experience among the churched and the unchurched in America today. Indeed America may well be in the process of discovery or rediscovery that man cannot live by bread and technology alone.

My college generation of several decades ago was far less responsive to religious questions than today's students. Some of the quest for the sacred among the young assumes bizarre forms and may grate on our sensibilities, but this much seems relatively clear: militant secularism or atheism has inspired little enthusiasm on campus or in the larger American Jewish community. Jewish collegiates, once regarded as the aggressive champions of atheism, are often considerably more "turned on" by religious symbols than their parents, and those few synagogues organized around the principle that a Jewish people and culture lives but God is dead have not mobilized widespread support.

Three Challenges in a Secular Age

Spiritual hunger is not absent from the contemporary scene, but our age does present the rabbinic defender of the faith with a threefold challenge.

The first stems from the scientific-technological mind-set of our time. Langdon Gilkey observes that many in our culture are uneasy with "all . . . types of discourse . . . referring to what is transcendent to and yet active in nature and history."[1] Stories of a God who speaks to men and women from beyond the heavens or who splits the sea to rescue His people from their pursuers are, at the very least, problematical.

Hence the popular joke about the lad who returned from religious school and described the Israelite exodus from Egypt as if he were a military historian: "The Hebrew engineers built a bridge over the Sea of Reeds and the people of Israel crossed over. When the Egyptians began pursuing them the Hebrew engineers blew up the bridge and the Egyptians drowned." The lad's father asked: "Is this the way the rabbi told the story?" The son replied: "No, but if I told it his way you'd never believe it."

The biblical account declares that God liberated the Hebrews. It focuses not on a scientific level of explanation (changes of tides or wind patterns) but on God's activity in nature and history to redeem the oppressed. Technological man is culturally predisposed to believe that science exhausts the explanation of an event—that once you have spoken of man-made and man-destroyed bridges or high and low tides, you have said all there is to say about Israel's escape from Egypt.

This point is important enough to warrant further elaboration. The Bible speaks of drought or flood as God's way of testing and punishing a sinful people. God withheld water from a generation in the wilderness, or much earlier brought a great flood upon Noah's age as a way of chastening a corrupt world. We turn for our understanding of climatic conditions not to the preacher but to the meteorologist. He speaks in terms of high- and low-pressure systems as the immediate cause of climatic change. In any case, a weatherman who thanked God for good weather or invited us to repent in order to avert a hurricane would leave us amused if not offended. Modern man is less prone to discern the threads of divine power and purpose in nature or history.

The second characteristic of a secular age which affects the rabbi's role as defender of the faith is the changing concept of personal identity. There was a time when a man's particular history and faith, mediated by ritual and myth, totally defined his place and purpose in the cosmos. In such a time a Jew could not conceivably ask: "Which am I first, a man or a Jew?" *The covenant of Abraham was his way of being human.*

To be sure, the Jew was always tempted by strange fruit and on occasion succumbed. Many a Christian today has ancestral roots in the covenant of Abraham. But the threat of assimilation or apostasy was different from the peculiar blandishments of the modern age. Premodern man perceived his personal identity in terms of an all-encompassing, particular folk-faith. Modern man uniquely perceives himself as a person (a human being) who *uses* faiths singularly or in combination to find fulfillment in life.

The covenant consciousness of Moses ben Maimon (Maimonides), who died in 1204, was deeply shaped by Muslim and Aristotelian thought, but Maimonides could not conceivably have asked: "Which am I first, a person or a Jew?" For him the Jewish convenant and his personhood were inextricably bound together. On the other hand, Moses ben Mendel (or Mendelssohn), who died in 1786, and whom many have called the first modern Jew, once wrote a letter to a Christian friend in which he claimed that "Moses, the human being [*mensch*] is writing to Herder the human being and not the Jew to the Christian preacher."[2] Mendelssohn implied that his Jewishness and his personhood were separable. That statement charts the identity crisis of the postemancipation Jew. Arthur Cohen correctly observes that "the age which Mendelssohn epitomizes made possible for the first time the real distinction of the public and the private. The public domain . . . became the secular and neutral. . . . the European enlightenment was turned toward the secularization of the public order."[3]

The fruits of that development are very much with us. Thus the contemporary rabbi will frequently encounter Jews— especially under thirty—who perceive themselves not primarily as Jews gripped by an all-encompassing destiny and an inescapable claim, but as men and women on a universal shopping expedition who feel free to pick and choose that which may satisfy their spiritual hunger. The Jewish tradition must display its wares on the same basis as Zen Buddhism or Christianity, with no compelling claim to priority. One of the hallmarks of a secular age is the affirmation, "I am a person before I am a Jew."

A third characteristic of our secular age is its brokenness. The premodern Jew experienced God, Torah, and Israel in their interdependence. These three terms formed part of a coherent life story:

> I am a son of Abraham, Isaac, and Jacob. God called my people (Israel) into being when he redeemed us from bondage and entered into a covenant with us at Sinai. The terms of that covenant (Torah) are the touchstone by which I must measure my faithfulness to God. By observing the Torah I become what God intended me to become and fulfill my part of Israel's vocation in the world. The God who appeared unto my fathers is present in my experience. The God who commanded my fathers commands me. The God who redeemed them will redeem me.

Today the individual elements—God, Torah, Israel—may still be present in Jewish self-consciousness, but their *interdependence* has been shattered. Many who acknowledge the Jewish fellow-ship of fate ("we are part of this people Israel") may see no relation between our fate and our divine vocation ("the *world* may remind us of our common destiny, but we are not singled out by God for a special role"). Many Jews who acknowledge the special ethical burden of our people and who observe some traditional rituals (Torah) may not do so in response to a divine command-ment (God). Finally, many who experience personal intimations of God's presence in their lives may not necessarily link this personal God to the ONE Israel encountered in Egypt, or at the foot of Sinai. This is an age of brokenness and of fragmentary visions.

Halacha and Agada

The ancient rabbinic sage used two kinds of speech: halacha and agada. Halacha is the language of Jewish law. It asks and answers the question: What must a Jew do to fulfill the covenant? Agada was the language of Jewish faith. It tells the story of God's relation to man through his relation to the people Israel.

Halacha defines the proper conduct of a Jew. Agada proclaims the transcendent meaning and significance of living as a Jew. Its common form is not legal but narrative.

The terms *halacha* and *agada* are talmudic, but they may be applied, and in this volume will be applied, to the text of the Hebrew Bible as well. The Ten Commandments are halacha, but the encompassing story of an invisible, commanding presence who summoned Moses to Mount Sinai and gave him the Torah is agada. The biblical commandment to eat unleavened bread is halacha. The story of God redeeming Hebrew slaves from Egyptian bondage is agada. We call the prayerbook used at the Passover Seder the Haggadah (same root as agada) because it tells the story of a God active in nature and history to make men free.

Most laments on the decline of rabbinic authority in the modern world focus on the rabbi's loss of legal (halachic) authority. Although the traditional ordination certificate defines him as one authorized to make judgments on questions of Jewish law, the contemporary rabbi is not extensively consulted to establish whether or not a chicken or a business deal is kosher. The lapse of his authority in defining mitzvot (commandments) has much to do, however, with the lapse of Jewish faith in a divine commander—a God who communicates His will or "speaks" to man. *Thus the validity of halacha and agada are interrelated.* As agadist the rabbi seeks to affirm the *reality* of a covenant between God and Israel.

Long before I knew I would become a rabbi I had developed a love for agada. My first Hebrew teacher introduced me to the anthology of rabbinic stories compiled by the great Hebrew poet Chaim Nachman Bialik. I was entranced by those stories in which God carried on an extended, impassioned dialogue with men— especially Jews. I knew that these were "fables," but I did not ask in what deeper sense they might be true. My inchoate faith was not *consciously* mediated by the language of Jewish God-talk.

Only after ordination did I come to appreciate the significance of agada. If mathematics is the symbolic language of science, agada is the primary language of Jewish faith. Mathematical equations symbolize a relationship between various parts of the physical universe. Agada's stories symbolize a relationship (covenant) between man and God. More specifically, agada is the stories we tell to express and confirm the reality and meaning of the people Israel's relation to God.

Agada: The Language of Worship

At one time or another, we and our children may wonder as did the son in the Passover ritual: "What mean ye by this service?" He was asking in effect: "What do you mean when you celebrate the escape of an ancient group of slaves from Egypt by eating matzoh? I was not a slave with them. What claim does that story have upon me?"

The Passover ritual regards such a son as wicked. Because he says "ye" rather than "we," he excludes himself from the fellowship of Israel. We are told that had he been in Egypt, he would not have been worthy of being redeemed.

The "wicked son" does indeed illuminate the need for agada. Through agada we seek to *evoke a sense of continuity between the past and present, and between the individual Jew and the covenant community of fate-faith*. The function of the Passover story itself (Haggadah) is to provide a script for our annual reenactment (in words, gesture, and symbolic diet) of a people's liberation from bondage. If the medium is successful, the message we receive is this: "I am part of that people. Their experience is mine. Their life story is mine."

Agada proclaims that the story which invests our individual lives with transcendent meaning is a story which links us to God's covenant with the people Israel. In Deuteronomy we find a poignant agada which describes Moses bidding farewell to the children of Israel. He reminds the people of their past and their present.

> You stand this day, all of you, before the Lord your God . . . that you may enter into the sworn covenant of the Lord your God . . . that He may establish you this day as His people, that He may be your God as He promised you and as He swore to your fathers, to Abraham, to Isaac, to Jacob. Nor is it with you only that I make this covenant, but with him who is not here with us this day.[4]

Whenever this story is read, its intent is to evoke in the listener a sense of participation in the covenant between God and Israel. We were not there that day, but the covenant has a claim upon us. It remains part of the greater story of our lives.

In the synagogue we regularly recite these words: "Hear O Israel, the Lord our God, the Lord is one. Praised be His name whose glorious kingdom is forever and ever."

An ancient rabbi once pondered the meaning of this declaration and spun the following story: When Jacob (his name changed to Israel) grew old and was preparing to die, he summoned his twelve sons (the children of Israel) to his bed and asked: "What will happen after I die? Will you remain faithful to the covenant of your fathers?" The sons answered: "Hear O Israel (our father), the Lord is our God, the Lord is One." Reassured that the covenant would be preserved, Israel closed his eyes and responded: "If that be true, then 'Praised be His name whose glorious kingdom is forever and ever.' "[5]

As rabbi I tell this agada to each Confirmation class. At the conclusion of the year they will be invited to share in a covenant-renewal ceremony. On or near the festival of Shavuot, which commemorates the giving of the Torah at Sinai, these young people will be asked to confirm their involvement in a story that reaches back to the misty past and will attain its goal when "the Lord shall be One and His name shall be One."

Public worship generally is an occasion when we proclaim that we are part of the fellowship of Israel in covenant with God. *The prayerbook is liturgical agada. Its words are designed to evoke, express, confirm that we individuals—with all the personal agendas and histories which distinguish us from each other— share a common story that is the key to our life's transcendent meaning.* The peak moments of authentic worship are moments when we feel that the words of Moses to the children of Israel, or of Jacob to his sons, are words addressed to us. Liturgical agada is the language through which the children of Israel in each generation reaffirm the convenant of their fathers.

Agada: The Language of Preaching

Agada remains not only the language of worship, but the language of preaching. Some years ago my Passover sermon coincided with the first anniversary of the assassination of Martin Luther King, Jr. Memorial observances were held, and ominous disturbances broke out on the West Side of Chicago. I titled my sermon "The Haggadah and the Horoscope." I retold the agada of Moses' confrontation with Pharaoh, of Pharaoh's initial reliance on the power of his astrologers, and of his ultimate submission before the "mighty hand of God."

> There are essentially two ways of interpreting the black-white confrontation in the American city today. We may use a horoscope, curse our stars, and pinpoint the malicious forces that have disturbed our serenity: mass immigration from the South, provocation by outside agitators, irreverence for law and order, etc. . . . Or we may take our perspective from the Haggadah and say, "In every generation each person must act as if he went forth out of Egypt." In every generation God says to the Pharaoh within us, "Let my people go.". . . The Haggadah affirms that the decisive power outside ourselves belongs . . . to a loving, caring God who . . . supports man's efforts to fulfill the moral promise of creation. . . . Therefore "even if all of us were wise and well versed in the Torah, it would still be our duty from year to year to tell the story of our deliverance from Egypt. Indeed to dwell at length is accounted praiseworthy."

Preaching is agada if the rabbi invokes the authority of Jewish tradition to illuminate a contemporary human situation. Whether or not the rabbi formally quotes the biblical story of God's confrontation with Pharaoh, the preacher remains an agadist if he declares that oppression must yield because there is a transcendent power active in our time as in ages past to make men free.

The agadist most differs from the editorial writer when he explicitly declares that the God who challenged, loved, and judged our ancestors addresses us in our situation also. Essentially the preacher retells old stories with new names and places.

Agada: The Language of Consolation

Agada remains not only the language of worship and preaching, but also of consolation or reassurance. When experience threatens our confidence in God's power and love, we need stories which may help to restore trust. *Agada is the story we tell to confirm our faith in life's primordial meaning even in the presence of suffering and death.*

The Book of Job is such a biblical agada. The storyteller bitterly rejects the notion that only the wicked suffer. On the basis of grim personal experience, Job has discovered otherwise. Though grievously afflicted, he scorns the consolation of his comforters; he refuses to relate his suffering to his presumed sin; he rejects the covential defense of life's meaning. But Job does not reject God. He yearns to believe that despite contradictions beyond man's power to comprehend or resolve, God is worthy of trust. Job's yearning for vindication is achieved and his faith confirmed. God reveals his presence to Job. Speaking "out of the whirlwind," God does not deny Job's innocence. He denies only that finite man may expect fully to comprehend God's ways. "Where were you when I laid the foundations of the earth? . . . Have you ever in your life commanded the morning? . . . Have the gates of death been laid bare to your sight?"[6]

Job is at once humbled and reassured. The experience of God's presence sustains his confidence that "there is a plus at the heart of the mystery." The Book of Job is a classical biblical agada, *a story about God's trustworthiness even in the presence of innocent suffering.*

A talmudic agada tells the story of the death of Rabbi Meir's two sons. The sons died while the father was engaged in Sabbath study. When Meir returned home and asked for his sons, his wife, Bruriah, equivocated at first but then replied: "I was once given a valuable treasure to guard until it would be called for. Today the owner came to claim his treasure. Should I return it?" Meir responded: "Of course you must return that which was given you to guard. I do not understand why you have to ask me such a question." Bruriah then led Meir to the bed where his dead sons lay. "This is the treasure which God gave me to guard, and today he claimed it." Rabbi Meir wept bitterly. Bruriah said: "Did you not say it was necessary to return a treasure which was given me to guard?"[7]

All comfort is agada if its goal is to restore or confirm a Jew's faith that God's love and power are worthy of trust. Whether or not the rabbi uses the words of biblical or talmudic literature, his words and gestures are agada whenever he seeks to deny that life is absurd.

A Death in the Family

It was Father's Day. I received a call from a family who were not members of my congregation. The parents had just been told that their daughter, stricken some weeks earlier with a chronic illness, was dying. She had been in a coma for eight days. The parents met me at the temple. The mother told me the medical history and broke down, shouting: "I gave enough life already." The husband explained that his wife was a survivor of Auschwitz. Forty-one members of her family had perished there. The mother continued her story. She had always tried to believe in God and taught her daughters to believe. She reported that last week in the hospital her daughter turned to her, saying: "I don't think I can pray to Him any more. He's let me down."

The mother added: "What did I do wrong? . . . She was so good, maybe she was too good for us. . . . Did we wait too long for a diagnosis? . . . I have had enough life. Why couldn't it be me?"

We walked into the chapel. The bitter irony of meeting here on Father's Day was compounded as we stared at the remnant of Saturday night's chapel wedding. The bridal canopy had been removed just before we entered. We opened the Ark. The mother cried: "Forgive me God, I said what I shouldn't." I was tempted to tell the agada of a God who weeps for the pain of his children and who struggles with them to redeem the world of evil—but instead I led them in prayer.

The mother was far more comfortable with God-talk than many of her more "secularized" contemporaries, yet any mother so stricken would in some way raise the same questions and seek the same deliverance. We prayed, wept, and parted. A few days later I received a call from the father. Jane had died. Would I conduct the funeral service?

What can one say to such mourners? How rekindle trust in life's promise? How declare that Jane's life, though snuffed out before the bud could fully blossom, was more than a flower dashed to bits by an unseasonable storm?

How can words mirror the bitterness, the anger, the helplessness, the gaping void? At such times I often feel that there is an impossible silent challenge hurtled from the pews of the funeral chapel, a barrage of pointed arrows bearing a common message: "Well, Rabbi, where then is God? We dare you to declare your trust in your friend now."

And yet I also hear, amid the stunned fellowship of family and friends, an irrepressible yearning for a sign that could rekindle trust. When death strikes, even before high noon, we are especially in need of grounds to affirm the abiding significance of a human life. We huddle together for comfort and seek to trust God in the presence of mystery.

In part these were the words spoken at the funeral:

We have assembled here to give words to our sorrow, mindful that all we say cannot fully express the pain and yearning of our hearts. We know that life is suspended on a fragile thread. The first cry of the newly born, the last gasp of an anguished soul, remind us of life's pain. There is no more poignant sign of the pain we may be called upon to bear than the occasion which brings us together this day. Jane, a young girl radiant with the promise of life, poised between the reveries of a little girl and the dreams of a young woman, has been taken from us.

Why, we ask, why so soon? There are some answers but none which fully satisfy our deepest longings. There are those who will say with humble resignation and trust, "The Lord giveth, and the Lord taketh away, praised be the name of the Lord." There may be others among us who will see this tragedy of life as the price of life's blessings. That marvelous miracle of sensitivity which enabled Jane to love and laugh and think and care makes her and us especially vulnerable to the assault of dread disease and untimely death. Others among us may turn to that strand of Jewish faith which speaks of man as God's partner. God is in need of us to help Him fulfill the latent promise of creation. He needs our help in combating the disease which struck down our beloved. How many lives will be lengthened if man were as diligent in waging war against disease as he has been in waging war against man. . . . In Anne Frank's Diary a young girl who experienced life's tragic dimension at first hand nevertheless and in spite of everything affirmed her confidence in life's goodness. She wrote: "I simply can't build my hopes on a foundation consisting of confusion, misery and death. I must uphold my ideals, for perhaps the time will come when I shall be able to carry them out." Anne did not live long enough fully to carry out her ideals, neither did Jane, neither do any of us really. But they lived long enough to love and to laugh and think and dream. Let us remain hostages to Jane's dreams. Let us build on the foundations of our sorrow a world with a bit more goodness and beauty than we have inherited. Let us spread that sunshine which was the hallmark of Jane's life. Let us be inspired by the memory of a precious, charming young girl to return to life with love in our hearts and dreams in our souls. Then shall her spirit continue to shed its light upon us and bless us.

At the cemetery I recited the words which the agada reserved for that moment of parting:

Praised be Thou, O Lord, our God . . . Ruler of the Universe, who dost form us in Thine image, who dost nourish and sustain us in Thy goodness, who causest us to die in accordance with Thy law, and who hast implanted within us immortal life. Blessed art Thou, O Lord, Judge of Truth.[8]

Agada is the language of Jewish faith. From biblical narrative and rabbinic stories to contemporary worship, preaching, and consolation, agada is *that form of speech through which the Jew has expressed his consciousness of life as a covenant between God and man.* The problematic of Jewish faith or of the rabbi as defender of the faith is very much a question of agada.

The Agenda of This Volume

Agada has been the classical language of Jewish self-understanding. Through stories of God's covenant with Israel, agada helped the Jew understand and experience the meaning of

Jewish life. We too still ask: Who is a Jew? Can agada mediate our understanding of an authentic Jewish life?

Agada has been the language of reassurance. Through its words the Jew has expressed his doubts and his yearning for renewed faith despite the traumas of his personal and communal life. In an age when the innocent still suffer and God's apparent silence still torments the anguished soul, can agada mediate our quest for faith?

Agada offered the Jew the ''gift of meaning'' in a prescientific age. Man's intellectual horizons have widened immensely. Is it possible for a Jew who takes seriously the claims of modern thought and experience to interpret his life in the language of agada?

Agada points to a world in which religious experience is real. It is the story of God's presence in the life of man. Does the contemporary Jew experience intimations of God's presence?

Even if the sense of the sacred has not departed from our world, can the ''traditional'' agada adequately embody and express our religious experience? Do we need a new agada?

The present volume is intended to explore such issues. Essentially we ask: Is the religious language we have inherited a treasure or an albatross? Does the story of the Jew's covenant with God illumine our experience as Jewish persons in an age of space travel?

The reader should be forewarned (if that were necessary) that I approach these issues as a lover of biblical and rabbinic God-talk and as a teacher of Jews who appear at times to question its validity. I write as a Jew who, though not immune to the brokenness of our time, still cherishes the agada's vision of wholeness.

II · Who Is a Jew?

*I will betroth thee unto me forever.
Yea, I will betroth thee unto me in
righteousness and in justice, in loving
kindness and in compassion. And I will
betroth thee unto me in faithfulness, and
thou shalt know the Lord.*

(Hosea)

I SAT NEXT to the groom's parents at the bridal table. The bride was a confirmand of mine; the groom, a Jewish boy from a town in Iowa. The father of the groom expressed delight that his son had found a "nice Jewish girl." A native of that town in Iowa, he had watched the relentless contraction of its Jewish community. The young left for the larger cities. Many who remained married outside the faith. The separate congregations were on the verge of a merger of necessity. The father of the groom observed wryly: "When you get these different elements in our community to unite, you can be sure there is a crisis."

The "enemy" came not to persecute but to absorb the remnant of Israel in its Iowa diaspora. What of the future? The father of the groom shrugged his shoulders in serious doubt. Some minutes earlier the groom had turned to his bride and recited the traditional vow: "Be thou consecrated unto me as my wife according to the law of Moses and Israel." I had uttered the prescribed benedictions, including the petition: "May they build a home amidst the people Israel worthy of Thy praise." I had united them under the covenant. They were called and pledged to become a new link in that millennial chain of fidelity which binds Israel to God.

Did they feel such a mandate? What would they have answered had I asked: "Why preserve Judaism?" Would the father of the groom have been any less jolted by the question? They were indeed part of the people Israel, but did they feel this people's sacred calling? Did the bride and groom feel their convenant with each other as part of a larger convenant which bound them to Israel and to God? And what would the father of the groom have responded to the suggestion that his son and daughter-in-law were "called by God to remain part of this people"?

The rabbi ministers to people who call themselves Jews. Biblical agada is the language in which our ancestors first spoke of the origin and meaning of their covenant with God. It offers the traditional answer to the question, Who is a Jew? Or, Why be a Jew?

Man is a newcomer in the world. As the recorder of written stories about himself, man is only five thousand years old. For four thousand of these years, the Jew (Hebrew, Israelite) has maintained a sense of historical continuity. Our children still read stories which bind them to an ancestor, Abraham, who is believed to have lived some four thousand years ago. We and our children may read of laws (Exodus 20:19–23:10) which governed the lives of our kinsmen in the second millennium before the common era.

If we were to compare that "covenant code" with another code from the same period—the Babylonian law code of Hammurabi—impressive similarities and differences would be evident. The biblical Hebrews were influenced by, but also resisted and reshaped, the cultural traditions surrounding them. But there is one overriding distinction between Exodus and Hammurabi which we ought to ponder. The code of the Babylonian lawgiver was lost in antiquity. For thousands of years it lay interred in the bowels of the earth until rediscovered by archaeologists in the twentieth century. No people alive today has, in unbroken continuity, considered itself descendants of Hammurabi and the custodians of the laws which his god, Shamash, commissioned him to promulgate.

By contrast, no archaeological spadework was required to

acquaint us with the biblical covenant code. In unbroken sequence the words of Exodus 20 were transcribed on parchment and taught by descendants of those ancient Hebrews from antiquity to our day. There is a people alive today which continues to regard itself in some special sense as an heir of that Torah.

The words on the Torah scroll were read, studied, interpreted, and transmitted by generations of Jews, from ancient Palestine to the mellahs of North Africa and the shtetls of Europe, to the frontier towns of the American West, the gilded ghettoes of suburbia, and synagogues in the Third Jewish Commonwealth of modern Israel.

That Torah scroll contains a story (agada) of how the first Hebrews came into being.

> Now the Lord said unto Abram, "Get thee out of thy country and from thy kindred and from thy father's house unto the land that I will show thee. And I will make of thee a great nation, and I will bless thee and make thy name great. And be thou a blessing; and I will bless them that bless thee, and him that curseth thee will I curse, and in thee shall all the families of the earth be blessed." [1]

Rabbinic agada elaborates upon the events which launched this people on its unique destiny. Hardly a Jewish child has escaped hearing the agada which speaks of an ancient generation gap between Terach and his son Abram—whose name was later changed to Abraham.

> Terach was a manufacturer of idols. He once went away somewhere and left Abraham to sell the idols in his place. A man came and wished to buy one. "How old are you?" Abraham asked the man. "Fifty years old," was the reply. "Woe to such a man," Abraham exclaimed. "You are fifty years old and worship a day-old object." At this the man became ashamed and departed. On another occasion a woman came with a plate full of flowers and requested him to take this and offer it to them. He [Abraham] took a stick and broke the idols and put the stick in the hand of the largest one. When his father returned he demanded: "What have you done to them?" Abraham replied: "I cannot conceal it from you. A woman came

with a plate full of fine meal and requested me to offer it to them [the idols]. One claimed: "I must eat first," while another claimed: "I must eat first." Thereupon the largest [idol] took the stick and broke them." Terach cried out: "Why do you make sport of me? Have they any knowledge?" Abraham responded: "Should not your ears listen to what your mouth is saying?"[2]

That is the agada's account of the distinction between Abraham and Terach. There were indeed radical differences between the Hebraic and pagan religions of the ancient world, between Abraham and Terach. What constituted the difference? Was it simply a matter of numbers: the exclusive worship of one God versus the promiscuous worship of many? Was it that Abraham's God could not be represented in images, or did the Hebrews also usher in a radically different view of the divine nature and of God's relation to the world?

The twentieth century has made great strides in the scientific study of ancient cultures. Archaeologists have uncovered long-lost artifacts. Linguists have decoded ancient languages. We need not rely solely on biblical and rabbinic sources to discover the difference between the faith of Terach and the faith of Abraham. We may turn to the stories which non-Hebraic peoples told of gods and men, stories which emerged from about the same time as those found in the Hebrew Bible.

Ancient man, be he pagan or Hebrew, perceived a relation to a transcendent reality beyond his senses. Ancient man used words to speak of his religious experience and share it with others. The religious language (God-talk) of pagan and biblical man reveals substantial differences. We may assume that their perceptions of life's ultimate reality and purpose differed also. We shall designate pagan religious stories as *myth* and biblical tales of God's relation to Israel as *agada*. Neither myth nor agada can be proved true or false by scientific test. They are different *faiths*— or proclaim different views of man's place in the world.

Pagan myths speak of a multiplicity of gods closely identified with nature and possessing many of the limiting qualities of men. Compare the biblical agada's story of creation with the central

Babylonian creation myth. The biblical tale tells that "in the beginning God created the heaven and the earth." The Babylonian *(Enuma Elish)* myth declares that in the beginning there were only the male and female waters of chaos, Apsu and Tiamat. These cohabited ("mingled their waters") and gave birth to various deities. Tiamat then sought to destroy her divine offspring, but Marduk, the dominant god, subdued and killed Tiamat and proceeded to create the world out of her corpse.[3]

The great historian of religion Yehezkel Kaufmann reminds us that "the [pagan] gods themselves are subject to evil forces and impulses, and, having sinned, they too must suffer for their guilt. Thus, the guilty Kingu is slain for his part in Tiamat's attack upon the Babylonian gods. Gilgamesh rebukes Ishtar for her wantonness and cruelty. . . . The sinning god is . . . another characteristic manifestation of the pagan idea."[4]

Pagan gods not only share the moral fallibilities of man but, like men, they are dependent upon a power or powers greater than themselves. The gods are also born and die. They may be created and destroyed. By contrast the God of biblical agada is perceived as *the ultimate power in the universe*: "In the beginning, God."

Pagan God-talk focuses on the deities' relations to each other—their loves, jealousies, hostilities. Biblical agada focuses on God's relation (covenant) with man in the world.

Pagan myth summons man to escape from time; it knows no sense of history. Man can do nothing new in the world nor do the gods act to bring about what has never been. Before the beginning of time, the gods already provided a model for all human events and acts. Man simply reenacts what the gods have done before him. Every act—from sowing seeds in the ground to human copulation—is an imitation of divine acts performed before the beginning of time. These acts, when ritually reenacted by persons become ways of identifying with the realm of the sacred and living in an eternal present.

In his book *Cosmos and History* Mircea Eliade contends that "interest in the . . . new 'in history' is a recent discovery in the life of humanity." More specifically Eliade contends that "the Hebrews were the first to discover the meaning of history as the epiphany [revelation] of God, and this conception . . . was taken up and amplified by Christianity."[5]

The biblical God acts in human events to bring about that which has never been. Human life moves toward a new goal. God and man collaborate to bring about a new reality. That new reality is perceived by the prophets as a world in which all men will acknowledge God's sovereignty and live in accordance with His will. This biblical sense of the "not yet" culminates in a vision of the goal of history. "And it shall come to pass in the end of days . . . they shall beat their swords into plowshares and their spears into pruning hooks. Nation shall not lift up sword against nation. Nor shall they learn war any more."[6]

The vision finds this expression in Jeremiah: "Behold the days are coming . . . when I will make a new covenant with the House of Israel and with the House of Judah. . . . I will put my law within them, and will write it on their hearts . . . and they shall teach no more everyone his neighbor and everyone his brother saying 'know the Lord,' for all of them shall know me, from the least of them to the greatest of them.'"[7]

The agada of the Hebrew Bible is also more modest than pagan myth in its claims to penetrate the mystery of God. God may not be depicted in a physical image. Neither may He be completely frozen in a verbal image. In Exodus 3, when Moses wishes to know the name of God, he "hears" God say, "I am as I am," or "I shall be as I shall be." This is the traditional etymology for the Hebrew word for God (Yahweh), which, we learn from the rabbis, was not even to be uttered except by the high priest in the holiest chamber of the Temple on Yom Kippur. Moses' request and God's response reflect the agada's awareness that our words are, at best, finite instruments which point to, but cannot fully capture, the glory of God. Pagan God-talk knows no such restraint either in verbal or physical imagery. Leo Baeck expressed the difference between myth and agada thus:

> It is crucial for religion to preserve the feeling that everything it thinks and says about the divine is merely a metaphor between God and the world, between God and man . . . . But when its metaphors

purport to be definite answers giving an account of the 'divine nature' or of divine fate and experience and presuming to describe the life of the Godhead, then the symbols crystallize into conceptions and the mythological becomes dominant.[8]

The "generation gap" between Terach and Abraham was indeed a major faith gap. To appreciate the difference, one need only juxtapose ancient Near Eastern texts with the narratives of the Hebrew Bible. The results of such comparison (which we have but sketchily alluded to) reveal that the Bible does in fact represent a radical turning point in religious perspective.

The God emerging from the pages of biblical agada is the one ultimate power in the universe, devoid of biography or moral flaw—an imageless reality worthy of man's trust, who calls the world into being, summons man to covenant with Him, and acts in human life to reveal and fulfill the goal of history.

History and Agada

Is the Bible a "true story"? If we mean, Did God really reveal Himself to the people Israel? that is a question of faith. No independent authority can prove or disprove the faith-affirmations of biblical agada. But the question "Is the Bible true?" may also mean: Did a man called Abraham live? Were a people called Israelites slaves in Egypt? Did this people occupy the land of Canaan? Were they exiled by the Assyrians? In other words, can a modern "secular" historian—armed with the scientific tools of archaeology and linguistics—discover independent evidence for the reliability of the Bible as history?

The historical evidence is suggestive but by no means conclusive. Biblical chronology places the Patriarchs in the second millennium B.C.E. (more specifically, the 19th–16th cent.). Near Eastern documents from that period, such as the cuneiform tablets found at Tell el-Amarna, refer to a class of people, Habiru (Apiru), who apparently served as administrators and mercenaries in the region extending from Egypt to Mesopotamia. They lived apart and were designated foreign by the native population. Some respectable scholars have associated the Habiru with the biblical Hebrews. Other scholars are less certain. [9]

Biblical names and places are also found in other contemporary sources. Variants of the name Abraham have been discovered around the biblically named cities of Ur and Haran. Illuminating parallels also emerge between customs described in the Bible and in Near Eastern documents. Archaeologists have unearthed ancient (15th-cent. B.C.E.) marriage contracts at Nuzi in northern Mesopotamia which stipulate that if a wife does not bear children she is obligated to provide her husband with a handmaid. This, of course, parallels the biblical story of Abraham's wife, Sarah, and her handmaid, Hagar. [10]

According to the biblical Book of Exodus, the Egyptian cities of Pithom and Rameses were built by Hebrew slaves. Egyptian documents on the reign of Rameses II speak of that Pharaoh employing Habiru to build the great city of Rameses. There is, however, no explicit identification of the Habiru with "children of Israel" who were slaves and later managed to escape under the leadership of Moses.

Biblical accounts of later events are often more explicitly certified by external sources. In Second Kings we read: "And the King of Assyria came up throughout all the land and went up to Samaria [northern Israel] and besieged it three years . . . and carried Israel away into Assyria . . ." The annals of the Assyrian monarch Sargon II (721–705) contain this account: "I besieged and conquered Samaria, led away as booty 27,290 inhabitants of it . . ." [11]

More than a century later, according to the Bible, Nebuchadnezzar overcame the southern kingdom of Judah and destroyed the Jerusalem Temple. King Jehoiachin was taken captive and languished in a Babylonian prison. The Bible records, however, that after thirty-seven years, during Evil-Merodoch's reign as king of Babylon, Jehoiachin was released from prison and given much honor.

At the beginning of the twentieth century, the Kaiser's Museum in Berlin received cuneiform tablets unearthed by a

German archaeologist digging near the Ishtar Gate in Babylon. Decades later, during the Nazi period, the curator of the museum studied and deciphered the tablets. Much to his astonishment, these texts directly paralleled the biblical account of Jehoiachin's captivity and release. [12]

Is the Bible historically reliable? The skillful scholar may find much useful material in the biblical text which, together with other sources, will help him to reconstitute that ancient Near Eastern era. In writing his volume *The Rise of the West,* the historian William H. McNeill doubtless used biblical sources. He writes that a group of Hebrews

> had sojourned in Egypt, departing for the desert some time in the Thirteenth Century B.C. under the leadership of Moses. Their abrupt change in mode of life from forced labor on public works to wandering in the wilderness—reversion though it undoubtedly was to an ancestral nomadic pattern—required explicit law giving. The years in Egypt must have eroded ancient customs and Moses' followers were probably of varied origins lacking any single traditional leadership and organization. It was natural, indeed inevitable that Moses' law-giving should take religious form and there is no reason to doubt the essential accuracy of the biblical account, how after making good the escape from Egypt, Moses ascended Mt. Sinai to commune with Yahveh and return with a single code of law, the Ten Commandments. The people's formal acceptance of the Commandments constituted their covenant with Yahveh whom they recognized henceforth as their divine guardian and supreme authority. [13]

Note the difference between McNeill's history and biblical agada. McNeill the historian speaks of Hebrews "making good their escape from Egypt." The biblical writer views the exodus as an act of divine deliverance. God acted in history to make men free. Moses told his people, "with a strong hand hath the Lord brought thee out of Egypt." [14]

Did a people Israel dwell in Egypt as slaves and subsequently experience freedom? Yes, concludes McNeill, the historian. Was Israel's escape an act of divine deliverance? McNeill the historian is silent. The issue cannot be decided by scientific research or skillful conjecture. It remains an issue of faith.

Did a people Israel *believe* it had entered into a covenant with Yahweh and feel obligated to observe certain laws and loyalty to their God? McNeill says yes and adds that it was natural for such a law "to take religious form." Did God truly reveal a way to the people Israel? Does God communicate with man? Is God a giver of Torah? Those questions are not within the purview of McNeill, the historian.

Now we begin to see more clearly the distinction between history and agada. At best historians seek to document and explain man's acts and beliefs from a biological, psychological, economic, or political perspective. The agadist, a religious storyteller, adds another dimension. He sees history as a covenant between man and God. The historian wishes to understand the "natural" or proximate causes of human events. The religious chronicler (agadist) seeks to perceive and proclaim the ultimate context, the transcendent meaning, of human events.

In other words, the primary concern of the agadist is to express his conviction that God is creator, guide, and redeemer of man in history. Prompted by this motive, he will at times consciously or unconsciously embellish his account of events, or even spin stories out of his imagination. Thus Samson is endowed by God with the power to crush barehandedly the pillars of the Philistine temple. Sarah gives birth to a child, Isaac, at age ninety. Such biblical narratives, which stretch or defy our sense of reality, may be understood as *agadic exaggerations for theological effect*. The crucial difference between agada and history arises from different concerns and perspectives. The agadist sees life as a drama in which God plays the principal role.

A historian may also be a believing Jew. When he addresses his professional peers, he will seek to understand the Israelite escape from Egypt by pointing to internal weaknesses in the Egyptian establishment or the presence of favorable tides, and so on. When he worships in the synagogue, he may perceive the exodus as a sign that there is a God *active in nature and history* to make men free, and as believing Jew he declares: "Who is like unto thee, O Lord, among the mighty, who is like unto Thee working wonders?" In a later chapter we shall have more to say about the various levels on which an event may be understood by the same person under differing circumstances.

The God-talkers of the Bible saw history as revelation. They perceived God's presence in human events. The God-talk of the prophets is a first-person account of a compelling personal religious experience ("thus saith the Lord," or, "the Lord spoke unto me saying"). The agada of the biblical narrators is a third-person account of a religious experience ("the king did that which was evil in the sight of the Lord"). Together the prophets and narrators leave us a record of how biblical man perceived his life as covenant between God and Israel. Let us now briefly summarize the story that is told.

Who Is a Jew? The Testimony of Biblical Agada

Who are we? We are a people whom God first called into being by his revelation to Abram (later Abraham). The covenant is at once a gift, a command and a promise.

> I am God Almighty. Walk before Me and be thou wholehearted . . . and I will establish My covenant between Me and thee and thy seed after thee through their generations for an everlasting covenant to be a God unto thee and to thy seed after thee. [15]

Generations thereafter, when Abraham's great-great-grand-children (the children of Jacob-Israel) became slaves in Egypt, God appeared unto Moses and promised to redeem the Israelites from bondage. The promise is kept. Following the deliverance God summons Moses, saying:

> Thus shall ye say to the House of Jacob and tell the people of Israel: "You have seen what I did to the Egyptians and how I bore you on eagle's wings and brought you to myself. Now, therefore, if you obey My voice and keep My covenant ye shall be My own possession among all peoples. For the earth is Mine, and you shall be to Me a kingdom of priests and a holy nation." [16]

The Torah itself (of which the Decalogue is a sample) constitutes also a gift, a command, and a promise. This people, the children of

Jacob, the great-grandchildren of Abraham, are capable of betraying the demands of the covenant. They question God's promises at the very foot of Mount Sinai as they dance around the golden calf, shouting: "These be thy gods, O Israel, which brought thee out of the land of Egypt." [17]

Once they enter the land, gratitude and fidelity alternate with assimilation and betrayal. The Israelites do not enjoy being "a people dwelling apart." They imitate the idolatry of their neighbors and flout the moral demands of the covenant. In time they are exiled from the land. The prophets *perceive* the exile as a consequence of Israel's infidelity. In the name of Yahweh Amos warns: "I hate, I despise your feasts, and I will take no delight in your solemn assemblies . . . but let justice well up as water and righteousness as a mighty stream." [18]

The ten northern tribes were exiled by Assyria (722 B.C.E.) and disappear from the pages of history. The southern kingdom was conquered one hundred years later by Babylonia, but these exiles endure and their survival is understood by the prophet as a sign of God's steadfast love. Though deferred, the promise remains intact. God chastens His people but will not abandon them.

> Thus saith the Lord: Yet again there shall be heard in this place, whereby you say it is waste without man, without beast, even in the cities of Judah and the streets of Jerusalem . . . the voice of joy and the voice of gladness, the voice of the bridegroom and the voice of the bride, the voice of them that say "Give thanks to the Lord of Hosts, for the Lord is good, His mercy endureth forever." . . . For I will cause the captivity of the land to return as of the first, saith the Lord. [19]

Over the years the prophets came to understand God's refusal to abandon His people as a sign of unconditional love. Hosea had earlier expressed God's hope for reconciliation through the image of a husband wooing back his faithless wife.

> Therefore, behold, I will allure her and bring her into the wilderness and speak tenderly unto her . . . and she shall respond there as in the days of her youth and as in the days when she came up out of the land of Egypt. . . . And I will betroth thee unto me forever. Yea, I

will betroth thee unto Me in righteousness and in justice and in lovingkindness and in compassion. And I will betroth thee unto Me in faithfulness, and thou shalt know the Lord. . . . And I will have compassion upon her that had not obtained compassion, and I will say to them that were not my people: "Thou art my people," and they shall say: "Thou art my God."[20]

More than a century later the prophet Ezekiel conveyed a different motive for God's unconditional covenant. This people had become a witness for God. If He forsook them, what would the pagan nations say? God has a stake in the people Israel. Their presence in the world bears testimony to the power and purpose of a God who seeks the acknowledgment of all nations.

And when they came unto the nations . . . they profaned My holy name, and men said of them: "These are the people of the Lord and are gone forth out of His land!" [Is that what happens to a people who are bound to Yahweh?]. . . .Therefore, say unto the House of Israel: "I do not do this [return you from exile] for your sake, O House of Israel, but for My holy name."[21]

A later prophet (Second Isaiah) understood Israel's suffering as the price for being God's witness. The nations confess: "He [Israel] was wounded because of our transgressions. He was crushed because of our iniquities. The chastisement of our welfare was upon him . . . and with his stripes were we healed."[22] When the Persian Empire conquered Babylon, this prophet perceived Judah's impending restoration under the Persian ruler Cyrus as an act of God. Israel has suffered too much already. She pays a price for being God's servant unto the nations. God will now restore her that she may continue to witness to His power and love.

Behold My servant, whom I uphold, Mine elect in whom My soul delighteth. I have put My spirit upon him. He shall make the right to go forth to the nations. . . . he shall not fail nor be crushed till he have set the right on the earth, and the coastlands shall wait for his teaching.[23]

God's special relation with Israel abides, for Israel is God's servant, bearing witness to His sovereignty until the day when God's exclusive rule will be universally acknowledged and his plan for history fulfilled. Greater than Israel's return to a land of promise was the promise which, through Israel, is offered to all men.

> It shall come to pass in the end of days that the mountain of the Lord's house shall be established as the top of the mountains, and shall be exalted above the hills, and all nations shall flow unto it, and many people shall go and say: "Come ye, and let us go up to the mountain of the Lord, to the house of the God of Jacob." . . . And they shall beat their swords into plowshares and their spears into pruning hooks. Nation shall not lift up sword against nation, neither shall they learn war any more.[24]

When that day dawns, God's sovereignty will be recognized throughout the world, and all persons will proclaim their common kinship under God. One formulation of this ultimate hope is found in the eighth chapter of Zechariah.

> Thus says the Lord of Hosts: People shall yet come, even the citizens of many cities, and the citizens of one city shall go to another saying: Let us go at once to propitiate the Lord and to seek the Lord of Hosts. . . . In those days ten men, from nations of every language, shall lay hold of him who is a Jew, saying: Let us go with you, for we have heard that God is with you.[25]

Zechariah also envisages a day when "the Lord shall become king over all the earth, on that day the Lord shall be One and His name One."[26]

Who is a Jew? The answer of biblical agada is clear: we are a people whom God called into being and singled out as special witnesses to His reality, power, and purpose. We are a people to whom God revealed Himself as Creator of the World, Teacher of the Way, and Sovereign of History. We are a people who has experienced the power of God's judgment and love. We continue to bear witness that the Source of Life has ordained a goal for history. By living within the covenant we make known and may help to advance God's goal for His creation.

The Jewish and Christian Stories

Biblical agada was contrasted with pagan myth, but we have not yet considered other stories of God's relationship to man which have been passed on across the centuries. The alternate story which American Jews most frequently encounter is that of the Christian faith. The Christian understanding of God's relation to man is embodied essentially in the narratives of the New Testament.

Jesus was, by all accounts, a Jew, bound to the same imageless God who had called Israel into being as His people. But the Christian faith tells a new story about the meaning of Jesus' life and death. Certain elements of that story served increasingly to distinguish Judaism from Christianity.

In biblical agada the prophets of Israel (including Moses) perform wonders by God's grace to certify the power of God and bear witness to His word. In the New Testament, Jesus' wondrous acts become a sign of his own uniqueness, of his own role as a savior of men. The prophets of Israel were human spokesmen for God. Jesus was in his person a unique part of God's truth, an incarnation of the divine. From the standpoint of biblical agada, such a concept raises the danger of the worship of man; for the Christian the incarnation offers a fuller understanding of God's presence in human life. This is part of the enduring theological argument between the synagogue and the church.

In biblical and rabbinic agada the Messiah is always in the future. In the New Testament Jesus is the Messiah and he has come. In biblical agada the Messiah's principal role is to usher in a righteous kingdom of justice and to deliver his people and all people from the yoke of oppression. In the New Testament Jesus emerges as the savior of man from sin and death. His death atones for the sins of men in all generations if they believe in him.

Agada underscores man's capacity and inclination to sin, but sin does not become, as in the Christian story, an all-pervasive condition from which man must be cleansed by a dramatic act of divine intervention in history. Abraham Heschel, in his last book, made this distinction between the Jewish and Christian stories of man's place in the world.:

There are two basic concepts with which we attempt to decipher what is at stake in our existence, final possibilities beyond which we cannot go in trying to order our lives. . . . one is that man must atone for guilt; the other that he has a task to carry out, an expectation to fulfill. The first has found expression in the fall of man, his sinful nature, while the second has laid stress upon the mitzvot (the human response to God's commandment).[27]

In biblical and rabbinic agada, there is no once-and-for-all act by which man must be saved from sin or death. Rather it is man's dignity to live in an abiding relationship to a God who says: "You can be my partner, you are worthy to share with me in redeeming the world, I love you even when you sin, but never forget that you are capable of more and better."

In agada God's greatest revelation is Torah, a way of life. In the Christian story God's primary revelation is a man who is in some sense more than a man. In agada God's greatest gift to His people, and through them to all mankind, is not a Savior who died for their sins but an ongoing covenant. This covenant commissions Israel to bear witness to the value of life (the goodness of creation), to the human task of serving God in the world, and to the steadfast hope that God's kingdom will be established on earth.

The Jewish story celebrates events in a people's life with God: exodus from Egypt (Passover), receiving the Torah (Shavuot), wandering in the wilderness under God's guidance (Succot). The Christian story celebrates the events in Jesus' life with God, his birth (Christmas), death (Good Friday), and resurrection (Easter Sunday).

The Jew is reconciled to God through the symbol of one who is both "our Father and our King," and to whom we are bound in an abiding covenant. The Christian is reconciled to God through the symbol of Jesus' death on the cross.

In agada Israel's sacred task has not been fulfilled. God's kingdom of righteousness has not yet dawned. In the Christian story, Israel's mantel belongs to the new Israel, to those who have accepted the special role of Jesus and believe in him.

Across the centuries Jews have been enticed and at times

compelled to accept Christian faith as the primary story of their lives. For most of their history, faithful Jews have had to live in a world in which other religious stories were culturally dominant. In Muslim lands the Jew encountered a still different understanding of God's relationship to man. In America today Jews still encounter a society which is more Christian than neutral. There remain Christians who wonder why Jews have not seen the light, and there are Jews who wonder if it really matters that the Jewish people continue to survive as Jews.

The Wedding as Covenant-Renewal Ceremony

Let us return, for a moment, to the groom from Iowa and his bride from Chicago. If Judaism is to survive in America, it will be primarily because a goodly number of Jews maintain the bond and transmit the faith to their offspring. To what extent is this being done?

The historian might report that in America today almost six million persons consider themselves Jewish. Most feel that some pattern of belief and conduct inherited from the past (Torah) retains a claim upon them. This claim includes the obligation to establish a Jewish family and transmit a heritage to the children. Most continue to believe that the Jewish people is worth preserving. They take pride in its past and wish to secure its future. They feel a solidarity of fate with Jews in other parts of the world and a deep commitment to the survival of the State of Israel. Even if they are not religious they add: "I am proud to be a Jew." (We shall explore the implications of such a declaration in a later chapter.) Even many Jews who marry a non-Jewish spouse still want their offspring to be Jewish and provide accordingly.

How much longer will this pattern persist? How much longer will most Jews marry Jews or converts to Judaism? How long will the majority of children in "mixed marriages" be raised as Jews? This question may take on added poignancy when we realize that there are only six million Jews in a country of over two hundred million people, and that these Jews represent almost half of the Jewish population of the world. The question of Jewish continuity in America is even more sobering because our culture appears to call into question all historical particularity, all demands for loyalty to historic traditions maintained through marriage. Indeed liberalism commends that people be joined together, not by accident of birth or common historical destiny, but by open personal covenants freely arrived at. In the context of contemporary courtship and marriage, this means that lovers and friends choose each other as persons, not as Christians or Jews.

The defenders of mixed marriage contend that a couple may blend the best of each tradition or that the traditions have a common ethical core; if the matter is pressed, they may protest that the commitments of past generations may not bind the present.

Alternately, those who claim the virtue of marrying "one's own kind" may argue: (1) Marriage is complicated enough, why add other sources of disharmony? (2) Why confuse possible children? Or (3) There are values we want to preserve.

Those in search of a deeper framework for a Jewish marriage will find it in the agada recited at a traditional wedding. Indeed the benedictions recited at the wedding of that bride from Chicago and the groom from Iowa were liturgical agada.

We began the wedding service by celebrating the divine gift of love between man and woman as part of God's creative purpose: "Praised be Thou, O Lord our God, King of the Universe, Creator of Man; Praised be Thou, O Lord our God, King of the Universe, who has made man in Thine image, after Thy likeness, and out of his very self Thou has prepared for him a steadfast companion. Praised be Thou, O Lord, who has created man."

This couple stands under the canopy of consecrated wedlock, as lovers and friends whose bond to each other is at the very heart of God's creative purpose. But almost at once the liturgy reminds us that they are bound together as son and daughter of a particular covenant. Their common fate and yearning have a covenantal dimension. They are involved in the people Israel's joys and sorrows. The *personal* and *covenantal* dimensions are beautifully intertwined as allusions to the joy of physical love are immediately followed by the expression of hope for the restoration of the people Israel.

Praised be Thou, O Lord our God, King of the Universe, who has created joy and gladness, bridegroom and bride, rejoicing, song, pleasure and delight, love and brotherhood, peace and fellowship. Soon may there be heard at the gates of Judah and in the streets of Jerusalem the voice of joy and gladness, the voice of the bridegroom and the voice of the bride. . . . Praised be Thou, O Lord, who gladdenth the bridegroom and the bride.

Similarly the prayer that invokes God's joyous blessing upon bride and groom ("as Thou didst gladden Thy creatures in the Garden of Eden in time of yore") is followed by the hope that they "may build a home amidst the people Israel worthy of praise." They are called to be *both* (1) lovers and friends, and (2) transmitters of a unique covenant to the next generation.

In classical Judaism covenant consciousness and person-hood are intertwined. Thus the groom from Iowa and the bride from Chicago are united according to the "laws of Moses and Israel." They are bound to each other, to the people Israel, and to the God of a covenant who has called man and woman for steadfast love and singled out the people Israel for special witness.

The agada transcends the modern "secular" rationale for discarding or retaining one's Jewish particularity. The agada bids all generations, including our own, to reaffirm the need for a Jewish presence in God's world and to accept that need as a personal, irrevocable mandate.

The ultimate justification for Jewish particularity remains the convenant. One who has plumbed the depths of Jewish authenticity will hear the echoes of an ancient summons: "I the Lord have called thee . . . you are my witness . . . in thee and thy seed shall all the nations of the earth be blessed."

To live within the framework of classical agada is to perceive one's life as rooted in the covenant and to regard with utmost seriousness the words addressed to ancient Israel: "Not with you only do I establish this covenant, but with those who stand here with us this day and with those who do not stand with us this day."[28] We are the heirs of those who stood there that day.

III · Israel: A People with a Passion for Meaning

Your name shall no longer be called Jacob but Israel, for you have struggled with God and man and prevailed.

(Genesis)

WE SAT IN the interdenominational Army Chapel nestled in the forbidding bosom of the Bavarian Alps. We were Jewish survivors of the madness concocted near the very ground on which we prayed. My congregation had come from various parts of Germany, and I from the United States, to participate in a Torah Convocation for Jewish Armed Forces personnel. The place of meeting was Berchtesgaden, Hitler's favorite retreat—the scene where he completed *Mein Kampf* and plotted his rise to power on a platform of Aryan supremacy and hatred of the Jew.

The irony of meeting at Berchtesgaden was not lost on any of us. We knew that the Nazi Holocaust, though an event in world history, held a special place in the chronicles of our people. Had we been there we probably would not have survived. To be singled out for the "final solution," a Christian needed to be virtually a saint; a Jew needed only to be a son or daughter of the convenant or the great-great-grandchild of a Jew. In the midst of our convocation, I gazed at the words on a cigarette pack and found myself saying: "Caution, being Jewish may be hazardous to your health."

We were indeed singled out, but by whom and for what? Many members of our group at Berchtesgaden found it difficult to raise the question and even more difficult to offer a traditional answer.

In the introductory chapter we spoke of the rabbi as defender of the faith, as one called upon to affirm the worthwhileness of life even in the presence of suffering and premature death. Agada, we said, was the language in which our predecessors affirmed that in spite of everything, there is a "plus at the heart of the mystery."

The contemporary rabbi also confronts persons with a distinct Jewish consciousness. The Iowan father of the groom was concerned not only that his son marry a "nice girl" and bring him the joy of grandchildren but that his grandchildren be Jewish. He was concerned not only that his native town survive but that there be a Jewish presence in Iowa.

The persons assembled at Berchtesgaden contemplated the horror of Hitler not simply as individuals pondering man's inhumanity to man. They were Jews, members of a group singled out by Hitler for total extinction. The ghosts of Dachau threatened their confidence in the meaning of life and the nobility of man. Might they not also question the validity of a Jewish existence in this world?

A Visit to Israel

A year after the journey to Berchtesgaden I would face similar questions closer to home. We were traveling in Israel. It was our first trip as a family. My two older daughters were visibly impressed by the landscape and the people. Being Jewish here seemed even more fun than in America. After a few days in the Jewish state they began to savor the special pleasure of membership in the majority. Each Chanukah in the States my oldest daughter (Rachel, then age ten) would ask wistfully: "Why do most people celebrate Christmas?" Our magnification of Chanukah at home did not fully compensate for the dominant cultural tone, which remained more Christian than neutral. Hence the notion of celebrating Chanukah or the Sabbath in a country where most people were Jews struck a delightful chord.

It should be added, however, that my children have not felt seriously disadvantaged living as a minority in America. The historic cost of being Jewish was hardly familiar to them. Being a daughter of the covenant meant pleasant Passover Seders (with prizes for finding the Afikomen), kindling the Chanukah Menorah (in expectation of a gift for each of the eight nights), and prefacing one's personal prayers with specifically Jewish words addressed to that mysterious and powerful Spirit at the core of life (Hear, O Israel, the Lord our God, the Lord is One). Being Jewish was fun in America, but it could be special fun to be a Jew (so my oldest daughter perceived) in a country where even the dogs understood Hebrew.

In Israel, of all places, my children were to personally apprehend the darker aspects of Jewish life: that sons and daughters of the covenant have at times been singled out for special suffering. We visited a kibbutz called "The Fighters of the Ghetto." It was founded shortly after the creation of the state by a core of Holocaust survivors determined to remember and memorialize the heroism of brothers and sisters who fell victims to the Nazi scourge.

One of the kibbutz leaders tried to discourage us from visiting the museum with our children. Upon hearing this my oldest daughter insisted that we should, arguing with a compelling wisdom beyond her years that children need to be prepared by their parents to confront the "unhappy side of life."

The museum documented in grisly detail the story of those years by singling out the martyrs who mobilized valiant if futile defiance among their brothers. That night the children complained of nightmares. My own sleep was troubled by the persistent question Rachel had asked earlier in the day and for which I seemed to have no answer appropriate for a ten-year-old: Why? Why were the Jews picked on? Had they done anything wrong? The concept of a people subjected to such a devastating, undeserved onslaught could not be rendered digestible simply by attributing the harm to a madman called Hitler. Why *this* people?

Suddenly the agada recounting Pharaoh's acts against Hebrews in Egypt or Haman's plot against Jews in Persia (Book of Esther) loomed as part of a diabolical web which could periodically engulf this people. Suddenly my oldest daughter perceived, if only for an instant, the price of being Jewish. Though less discerning, the younger ones also asked with some trepidation: Could it happen again?

In the introductory chapter we observed that agada was the language in which ancient Hebrews sought to confirm their confidence in God's power and love even in the presence of anguish and suffering.

The need for such reassurance stemmed not alone from the *personal tragedies* which at one time or another confront every individual member of the human family, but also from those catastrophes which befell men and women *because they were members of the people Israel*. The Jews deported from their homes by Nebudchadnezzar (586 B.C.E.) experienced their misfortune as members of the household of Israel. They must have asked: How can we believe in a God who permits our enemies to overwhelm us? If the Babylonian gods are more powerful, we shall worship them.

Under prophetic tutelage the Hebrews were taught to accept exile as punishment for their faithlessness. Far from being a sign of Yahweh's weakness, their exile was a confirmation of His power and justice. But He who chastens His people loves them and will in time restore them to their land. Thus spoke Jeremiah, seeking to sustain his brethren and restore their hope in the promise of the covenant.

As we have already seen, not all the prophets interpreted exile as punishment for Israel's sins. The Second Isaiah proclaimed that Israel was "a suffering servant" for God in a world that did not yet acknowledge his sovereignty. Isaiah spoke in God's name: "Comfort ye, comfort ye, my people."[1] He hears the nations admit: "Verily he [Israel] has borne grief inflicted by us and suffered sorrows we had caused, yet we did esteem him stricken, smitten of God, and afflicted though he was wounded through our transgression, bruised through our iniquities."[2]

Wherever we find words of comfort and reaffirmation, we may discern a prior crisis of faith. Often the stronger the reaffirmation, the more persistent the doubt. Thus the same Jeremiah who affirmed the time when the "voice of bridegroom and bride shall again be heard in the Gates of Jerusalem'' also exclaimed: ''Wherefore doth the way of the wicked prosper? Wherefore are all they secure that deal very treacherously?''[3]

The Great Disaster

One of the greatest crises in Jewish history was the destruction of the Second Temple by the Romans in 70 C.E. To this day the victory of Titus is commemorated by an arch bearing his name which stands across from the Roman Forum. A relief on the arch depicts legionnaires bearing booty, including a Menorah snatched from the burning Temple. Titus' father, the Emperor Vespasian, minted coins with the inscription *Judea capta*—''Judah vanquished.''

The searing rubble of a sacred place bore terrible witness to years of turmoil and pain. The Jewish masses had suffered for more than a century, not only from the rapacious Roman governors, but from avaricious, venal Jewish leaders who at times murdered their own kin to seize the reins of kingship. Ironically the Romans were first invited to rule Judea by one of the Jewish factions in a brutal civil war which threatened to devastate the community.

Even during the years immediately preceding the futile revolt against Rome, which culminated in the Temple's destruction, the Jews were bitterly divided on the best strategy for coexistence with Roman power. The Zealots counseled uncompromising resistance, while men like Johanan ben Zaccai abjured the use of force. They counseled a turning inward and were willing to render unto Caesar the vessels of political power until such time as God would usher in His kingdom. Even during the years of battle with Rome, Jews frequently fought each other with no less vehemence than they fought the Roman oppressor.

Nevertheless, the destruction of the Temple was for all a bitter symbol of the Jewish people's degradation. That edifice which, in its various incarnations, had served not only as the primary focus of worship but as a symbol of Jewish unity and a sign of the covenant between God and Israel now lay in utter ruin.

Many thousands of Jews lost their lives, thousands more were sold into slavery by their captors.

The modern historian could reflect upon the defeat of Judah in 70 C.E. and rattle off an impressive barrage of causal factors: the superior military prowess of Rome, the draining effect of massive poverty on the Judean masses' capacity to wage war, the comparative absence of trained military leadership, the internal dissension which stalked the ranks of Judah. But the people required another framework of understanding. They were children of Israel bound to a God who was Sovereign of the World. How could God permit such a catastrophe to befall his people? The survivors of 70 C.E. required reassurance that the covenant remained intact, that the God who had revealed Himself in Egypt and Sinai, who had borne them to and from exile, was still worthy of trust. This challenge was faced and met by the rabbinic agadists of the subsequent centuries.

Josephus: Historian and Agadist

Before we turn to their response let us pause to consider an eyewitness to that era, a fascinating and controversial man named Josephus, who was both historian and agadist. He has left us the most extensive account of the Jewish war against Rome. He claims to be writing an objective account though he played an active part in those events and openly regarded the Jewish revolutionaries as misguided fools.

He narrates his account of those frenetic days not only in terms of the political, psychological, and economic factors which explain their outcome but from the perspective of one who affirms that God acts in history, and that God's presence was decisively manifest in Rome's triumph over Judah. Hence we have called him both an historian and an agadist.

Josephus was born in Jerusalem in 37 or 38 C.E. His father was of priestly descent and his mother kin to the Hasmoneans, the last royal house to govern an independent Judea. Josephus was a privileged Jew, relatively untouched by the oppressive burdens borne by the masses and on good terms with the Roman ruling power. In the year 64 C.E., after returning from a diplomatic mission to Rome, he saw his countrymen swept up by the fervor of revolution. He opposed this mood and sought to subdue it.

When the activists gained control and war broke out, Josephus participated in defending the Judean fortress at Jotapata against Vespasian. Clearly, he found himself forced to play a subtle game. He acted the part of a loyalist Jewish patriot to prevent his murder at the hands of his own people, but was also deeply resentful that such a role had become necessary.

When Vespasian overran the garrison, Josephus was taken captive. He curried favor with the general by predicting his succession to the imperial throne and spent the rest of the war period advising the Romans and urging his people to bow before their invincible foe to prevent the needless destruction of the Holy City.

When the city fell to the Romans in 70 C.E., Josephus accompanied Titus to Rome. Emperor Vespasian conferred Roman citizenship upon Josephus and rewarded him with a generous pension.

Josephus began writing about the "greatest war of all time" in the year 81. His principal motive may well have been to vindicate his own role in the catastrophe. Josephus quotes the words he purportedly spoke to the beleaguered garrison defending Jerusalem. As they hurled missiles against him, he reminded his brothers that Jerusalem had fallen at other times and that no efforts on the part of its defenders had availed.

> Thus when the king of Babylon laid siege to the city, Zedekiah our sovereign, having, contrary to the prophetic warnings of Jeremiah, given him battle, was himself taken prisoner and saw the city and the Temple leveled to the ground. Yet how much more moderate was that prince than your rulers, and his subjects than you! For though Jeremiah proclaimed aloud that they were hateful to God for their transgressions and would be carried away captive if they did not surrender the city, neither the king nor the people put him to death. But you . . . heap abuses on me who exhort you to save yourselves and assail me with missiles . . .[4]

Josephus argues that once again it is God's will that Jerusalem fall, not only because of the stupidity of its defenders, who by their resistance compelled Titus to wreak destruction, but because of the "secret sins—theft, treachery, and adultery . . . and murder . . ." which have characterized the political life of Judah in recent times.[5]

Noting the triumphal progress of the Roman onslaught, Josephus draws this inference: "So I am sure the Almighty has quitted your holy places and stands now on the side of your enemies."[6] Later, musing on the meaning of the fall of Jerusalem, Josephus suggests that there were certain signs in the heavens (including a star shaped like a sword) which presaged God's intent to destroy his city. Josephus the historian-agadist concludes: "Anyone who ponders these things will find that God cares for mankind and in all possible ways foreshows to his people the means of salvation and that it is through folly and evils of their own choosing that they came to destruction."[7]

Josephus' claim that he was sorely distressed "with my country destroyed" rings hollow amid the stridency of his denunciation. His exultation at the downfall of his Jewish opponents appears far stronger than his lamentations. Josephus' words provide a very valuable account of that period in history, but they could hardly give comfort or restore hope to his surviving brethren. Although he adopts the interpretive framework of the prophetic agada (Israel's defeat is an act of divine chastening), Josephus' opportunism, political cunning, and glibness set his words apart from those of the Hebrew prophets. One does not feel that Josephus shares the anguish of the people. On that score alone he is ill suited to reassure them that there is meaning to their defeat or hope for their future.

The Agada of Rabbi Johanan

The rabbinic sages, some of them Josephus' contemporaries, actually coined the word *agada* to designate the words of reassurance they spoke and the covenant faith they sought to reconfirm in the hearts of the survivors.

Among the greatest of these sages was Johanan ben Zaccai. Rabbi Johanan perceived no less than Josephus that the battle against Rome would not be won by force of arms. He too pleaded with the war parties to submit. His remonstrances unavailing, Johanan arranged to be smuggled out of the besieged city (in a coffin, according to some later agada) and petitioned the Roman commander for permission to open an academy in a coastal city, Yavneh, near what is now Tel Aviv–Jaffa.

In his academy Johanan's disciples sought to rebuild the foundations of Jewish law for a new age when, for example, atonement from sin could no longer be sought by animal sacrifice. Under Johanan and his successors the synagogue became the primary institution for Jewish worship, and when a student asked his teacher about the means for reconciliation with God now that the Temple lay in ruins, Johanan replied: "My son, do not weep. We have a means of atonement as effective as this. What is it? It is deeds of lovingkindness. As the prophet said: 'For I desire mercy and not sacrifice' [Hosea 6:6]."[8]

Johanan and his successors needed also to come to grips with the meaning of the destruction and its impact on the covenant between God and Israel. Generally Johanan agreed that the fall of Jerusalem was an act of divine chastening. Israel had proven unable to govern itself effectively and faithfully. Once when Rabbi Johanan was traveling with his students, he saw a young woman gathering wheat from amidst the dung of a horse. Rabbi Johanan pointed to the woman's lowly fate as a symbol of the people Israel's degradation. It is as if God were saying to His people: "You did not want to be subservient to heaven [God]; now you are subservient to the nations. . . . You did not wish to repair the roads which were used by the pilgrims to Jerusalem for the holy festivals; therefore you are repairing the tabernacles and towers inhabited by those who go up to the vineyards of [foreign] kings."[9]

Another agadist attributed the destruction to the "hatred without just cause" which prevailed in Judah.[10] This may well be an allusion to the internal political intrigue and strife which racked Judah in the century prior to its destruction.

In any case the catastrophe was perceived by many rabbis as an act of divine judgment. The people Israel had been unfaithful to the covenant. The prayerbook would preserve that interpretation in the phrase: "For our sins we were exiled from our land." But such interpretations, however prevalent, did not exhaust or fully satisfy the quest for renewed faith.

The Rabbis Wrestle with God

The discerning student of the agada will observe therein the shadows of a deep conflict between life-circumstance and faith. Even those sages who acquiesced in the notion of divine judgment did not affirm that conclusion without a struggle. One of the rabbis tells the story of a confrontation between Abraham and God amid the ruins of the Jerusalem Temple. God asks Abraham to explain his presence. Abraham replies that he has come to contend with God in behalf of the people Israel. Abraham is prepared to argue that the destruction of the Temple and the exile of the people should not have occurred. God accepts the challenge. Abraham is told that Israel sinned and was accordingly punished. Undaunted by this divine assertion, Abraham enumerates a list of mitigating circumstances: perhaps only a few sinned. What about the divine commitment to remember the covenant symbolized by circumcision? If God had waited for them they might have repented! God answers each of Abraham's contentions. Only *then* does Abraham bow his head in acknowledgment of divine justice and inquire yearningly of the time for Israel's redemption. Abraham receives divine reassurance that as the olive's fulfillment lies in its final end, so Israel's promise lay in a destiny yet to unfold.[11]

The author of this talmudic agada reveals his struggle for faith. Jerusalem had been destroyed, the Temple was in ruins. Many thousands of his people had been killed or sold into slavery by an alien power. How believe in the God of the covenant? The agadist responds, as did the author of the agada which depicted Abraham arguing with God on behalf of the cities of Sodom and Gomorrah (Genesis), that the evil in Jerusalem must have been all-pervasive or God would not have destroyed the city. Nevertheless, the covenant abides and God will redeem His people.

Jewish Suffering as Kiddush Hashem

The acceptance of exile and suffering as divine chastening was the primary but by no means the only rabbinic response to Israel's predicament. In the decades following the destruction of the Temple, during the two-and-a-half-year reign of Emperor Nerva and in the early years of Trajan (106–113 C.E.), relative peace prevailed. Jewish leaders were invested with a large measure of autonomy. Most Jews seemed reconciled to Rome's political hegemony. Alas, the peace was shortlived.

During the reign of Hadrian (117–138 C.E.) new repressive measures were imposed. Offended by the peculiarities of Jewish law and zealous for the undiluted fealty of all his subjects, Hadrian forbade circumcision and even proscribed the recitation of the Shema.

A monumental rebellion erupted under the leadership of Simeon ben Koseba. Initially the resistance of the rebels proved so successful that they proclaimed a Jewish state and dubbed Simeon "Prince of Israel." To multitudes, including the distinguished sage Rabbi Akiba, Simeon was the long-awaited Messiah who had come to liberate his people from their oppressors. Alas, those years of buoyant promise (132–135 C.E.) came to a dismal end. Though Hadrian sustained grievous losses he regained control, and with a rigor which made the era of Titus and Vespasian seem beneficent by comparison. Virtually all the Judean settlements were wiped out. Jerusalem was now converted into a pagan city, and on the Temple ruins a sanctuary was erected to Capitoline Jupiter.

The Bedouin shepherd who, in 1947, discovered the Dead Sea Scrolls while browsing through caves in the Judean wilderness uncovered for us poignant traces of Simeon's revolt. Apparently he and his officers took refuge in those caves during the last stages of their battle. Among the scrolls are letters signed by Simeon and coins bearing the inscription: "Simeon, Prince of Israel."

During the depths of the Hadrianic persecution, Rabbi Akiba also sought to confront the meaning of Israel's suffering.

His response differed from that of Rabbi Johanan ben Zaccai. In one agada Akiba fancies the nations of the world asking Israel why it does not abandon its God: "What is your beloved more than another beloved . . . that you die for Him and that you are slain for Him [as it says] in your own Scripture, 'for Thy sake are we slain all day . . .'?" Akiba was quoting Psalm 44:23— "Because of Thee we were slain all day, we are counted as sheep for the slaughter." Referring to an earlier period of oppression, the composer of the psalm concluded that Israel suffers not because of its sins but because it serves God in a world which does not yet acknowledge His sovereignty.

Now, centuries later, Akiba sees his people risk their lives by observing the Torah despite Hadrian's edicts. He pictures the nations questioning Israel's continuing loyalty to God, and he replies that Israel does indeed suffer *because* it resists the blandishments of the nations (including Rome) and insists on worshipping God, not Caesar.[12] Akiba himself was a martyr. During the reign of Hadrian he was put to death by slow torture. He died with the Shema on his lips.

At times rabbinic agada confirmed faith in the covenant by understanding suffering as the price paid for loyalty to God in an unredeemed world. The rabbis called such acts *Kiddush Hashem*—the sanctification of God's name. In an obvious reference to the period of Hadrianic persecution, Rabbi Nathan commented:

> "Of them that love Me and keep My commandments" [Exodus 20:6] refers to those who dwell in the land of Israel and risk their lives for the sake of the commandments. Why are you being led out to be decapitated? Because I circumcise my son to be an Israelite . . . these wounds cause me to be beloved of my Father in heaven.[13]

Thus was suffering transmuted by the agada from a badge of shame to a crown of glory.

The Boldest Challenge

On occasion the agadists of those early centuries went even

further in denying that Israel's degradation was the price of sin. They challenged God's silence as if the stake were not Israel's fidelity but divine credibility. The verse in Psalm 89 ("Who is a mighty one like unto Thee, O Eternal") is rendered by one rabbi as follows:

> Who is so mighty and strong [in self-restraint] as Thou, able to listen to the tormentings and insults of the evil man [Titus] and remain silent?[14]

Rabbi Ishmael interpreted the verse as a challenge to the Almighty.

> Who is like you O Lord among the silent, who sees the humiliation of this people and remains silent?[15]

One rabbinic sage mused that when God would seek to comfort the fallen city of Jerusalem, the city would say:

> Master of the Universe, before You gave the Torah to Israel Thou didst go round offering it to all the seventy nations, not one of which would accept it. It is finally Israel who accepted it, and since it was they who accepted it, how could Thou have done to them what Thou hast done?

God is accused of ingratitude and faithlessness. How does the Holy One, Blessed be He, respond to the indictment?

> At once the Holy One, Blessed be He, will accept the reproof of Jerusalem and will say: "I was unfortunately arbitrary with you, as is said: 'I acted in lordly fashion toward you' [Jeremiah 3:14]."

The agadist gets God to confess his unfairness! But even this verbal concession is not deemed sufficient. Israel presses God further:

> Jerusalem will reply: "Master of the Universe, is it right that what Thou art saying be kept only between us? Who will let the nations of

the earth know about me that I have done Thy will . . ." [God replies] "I shall speak to the nations of the earth about thee and make known thy works of righteousness."[16]

Here is the intrepid Jewish spirit at its most daring. God is treated by Israel as an "intimate enemy"—loved, feared, mistrusted, needed, and reaffirmed!

In the world of agada God's lofty perfection is compromised. It is almost as if God, not Israel, were in need of forgiveness. Prompted by the destruction of Jerusalem, the rabbis spin tales which attribute to God even more extreme confessions of failure. In one burst of self-deprecation God purportedly tells Israel: "Woe unto the king [God] who in his youth succeeded and in old age failed."[17]

By such stories the rabbis came to terms with the destruction of Jerusalem and confirmed their confidence in the validity of the covenant. They challenged God in order to affirm Him.

A God Who Shares Israel's Woes

The sages also imagined God sharing the suffering of His people and in need of consolation because of their exile. God's purposes are in jeopardy. Israel is God's witness in history. Israel's destruction will deter God's acknowledgment by the peoples of the world. In one agada God says to Moses: "I have been with you in this enslavement [Egypt] and shall abide with you when you are enslaved by the nations."[18] Of Israel's redemption from Egypt God says: "You and I went forth from Egypt."[19]

Similarly, the sages pictured God "weeping" over the destruction of the Temple and Israel's exile from its land. He follows his children into exile as a sign of his abiding love.[20]

Still another agadist exclaims: "The Holy One, Blessed be He, called the ministering angels and said to them, 'When a human king loses a dear one and mourns, what acts of lamentation does he perform?' They replied: 'He hangs a sack upon his door [the entrance to his palace].' So God says: 'I shall do the same.' Hence we read [Isaiah 50:3]: 'I clothe the heavens with blackness and I make sackcloth their covering.' "[21]

The rabbis were mindful that their God-talk used human images to speak of the ultimate power of the universe. They found, however, no better way to describe the God of the covenant. Lest anyone forget that such words were not to be taken literally and that all descriptions of the infinite are but imperfect figures of speech, the sages often add the word *kivyachol,* which means "as it were," or "don't take this literally." In one agada which suggests that God shares Israel's suffering, the author writes: "When Israel is enslaved, God— *kivyachol*—is enslaved with them."[22]

Hope in Future Redemption

The most significant resolution to the crisis of faith is the people's trust in God's redemptive power. We find such hope expressed often in the agada of the prophets. Thus Jeremiah says, in God's name: "I will yet build you up and you will be rebuilt, O virgin Israel. Yet will you take yourselves timbrels and go into the dance of the merrymakers. Yet will you plant vineyards in the hills of Samaria. . . . Yes, there will be a day when watchmen will proclaim in the hill country of Ephraim, 'Arise and let us go to Zion to the Lord our God.' "[23] By such words did Jeremiah seek to reaffirm the people's confidence in the covenant.

A similar reliance on future redemption is found frequently in the Psalms: "Our soul hath waited for the Lord; He is our help and our shield, for in Him doth our heart rejoice because we have trusted in His holy name. Let Thy mercy, O Lord, be a promise, according as we have waited for Thee."[24]

In the wake of the destruction of the Temple, the rabbinic masters of agada also sought to reaffirm their confidence in God's redemptive promise. They picture the nations of the earth wooing Israel to forsake the covenant of their fathers. The nations say: "How long shall you continue to die on account of your God? . . . consider all the retribution He hath inflicted upon you, how many despoilers he has brought on you. . . . Return unto us . . ." What is Israel's response? The children of Israel "enter their houses of worship and study, and they open the Torah and read therein: 'I will turn toward you and make you fruitful and multiply you. I will establish My covenant with you' [Leviticus 26:9]. And by these words the people were comforted. On the morrow, when the end [of exile] shall come, the Holy One, Blessed be He, shall say to Israel: 'My sons, I am amazed how you were able to tarry for me all those years.' Israel will reply: 'Were it not for the promises [made in] your Torah, the nations of the world would have long since caused us to defect from you!'"[25]

Thus did the messianic hope—the hope in *future* redemption—help sustain the people in the midst of suffering and oppression.

The Ways of Agada: Diversity in Pursuit of Meaning

In his precious little book on comparative religion, Huston Smith asserts that the key to Judaism is "its passion for meaning." Professor Smith writes: "What lifted the Jews from obscurity to permanent religious greatness was their passion for meaning."[26] That sense of meaning was challenged not only by the traumas of personal existence, but by the fate of the people commissioned to declare God's power and grace in history.

For the believing Jew, the issue of life's meaning was equivalent to the meaning of Jewish existence in a world where evil raged and the innocent often suffered. Israel was singled out to proclaim God's dominion in history. All too often, however, the witness struggled for reassurance that his mission was valid. His own fate challenged his faith.

Jewish fate and faith have always been inextricably intertwined. A people liberated from Egyptian slavery believed that God had redeemed them. A people exiled from their land by the Babylonians believed that God had chastened them for their infidelity to the covenant, but that God's presence had not departed from their midst. History was the stage on which this people sought continuing validation for its own existence and message. The meaning of its own life as a people was the mirror image of its faith in life's meaning.

As we have seen, agada was the language in which our ancestors' doubts, anger, and anguish were both expressed and overcome. Agada was the Jew's basic tool in his quest for meaning. One of the key questions which agada struggled to answer was this: If we are a people bearing witness to God's great power and goodness, why does our fate as His witness seem devoid of meaning?

The range of response to this question was itself significant. The agada recognized that there are times when we will need to acknowledge our responsibility ("because of our sins were we exiled"), times when we will need to understand suffering as the price of doing God's work in an unredeemed world ("for Thy sake are we slain all day"). There are times when we may need to contend with God in order to become reconciled with Him ("who is like Thee, O Lord, among the silent mighty ones?"). There may be times when we experience our anguish as a setback for God as well as man (God weeps over the destruction of Jerusalem). At all times faith in future redemption sustained the people ("were it not for the promises made in your Torah, the nations would have long since caused us to defect from you"). And there were times when explanations paled and one felt summoned, with Job, to trust in the presence of mystery.

The rabbis brilliantly intuited not only man's passion for meaning but his need for maneuverability in his quest. The only ground rule remained this: a Jew must not conclude that life is absurd. A Jew must not give up his testimony to life's value, to God's covenant with man made known through His covenant with Israel.

Note that all attempts to sustain meaning during moments of anguish were predicated upon the agadist's story of a personal God whose power and love is manifest in history. Later in this volume we shall consider the claim by some Jews in our time that this agadic framework must be radically revised. For the present, however, let us explicitly attempt to invoke the traditional agadic perspective as we confront the monumental anguish of our own time.

The Passion for Meaning: After Auschwitz

This basic framework of Jewish faith was sustained by our fathers for about two thousand years after the destruction of the Temple in 70 C.E. During those years of dispersion, centuries of prosperity and relative tranquility alternated with centuries of persecution and expulsion. Vital Jewish communities emerged and withered, in Babylonia, then in Spain and in Western and Eastern Europe. The Jew's emancipation from the European ghetto in the nineteenth century was greeted by many as the prelude to the coming of the Messiah. In our own day, however, the nation which was most closely associated with the enlightenment became the center of a madness which catapulted the world into a second global conflict and drove six million Jews to an untimely death. The ancient sages spoke of the destruction of the Temple and its aftermath as the "great disaster." The agadists of our age speak of the Nazi terror as the "Holocaust."

This trauma was too overwhelming to be confronted at first. In the 1950s, while a student in seminary, I taught in a congregational religious school on Sunday mornings. My supervisor instructed me to accentuate the positive: "Teach them that being Jewish is fun." After all, Jewish children did not want to belong to a "martyred race," and forever wear clothes of mourning.

Not only our children did we seek to shield, but ourselves; and not so much from the catastrophes of the Jewish past as from the shattering trauma of our own time. We did not seriously deal with the Holocaust until the 1960s, some twenty years after Hitler's demise. The trial of Adolph Eichmann opened the floodgates. Only thereafter did a spate of documentary books appear, detailing the immensity of the events, the indifference of the world, and the silence of God.

What agada, what stories, could we tell which would both express the depth of our anguish and reconfirm our faith in the covenant? After Auschwitz what could one say about the God whom our fathers trusted even in His silence and hiddenness, He who revealed Himself in history as an unshakable source of power and love? Could the Jew continue to bear witness to such a faith? And if not, what is the meaning of our Jewish existence?

An Agadist for Our Age

A few years ago a middle-aged man addressed a group about to be ordained as rabbis. The ordination speaker was of slight build and gaunt expression. Whenever he spoke his eyes were ablaze with pain and longing. He addressed the assemblage in low key, but as always his audience was transfixed by his presence and his message.

The man stood before those newly consecrated defenders of the faith as witness and survivor. Did they wonder what agada to proclaim? What stories to tell about God and Israel after Auschwitz? No man seemed better qualified to respond to such a question.

This man, known to the world as Elie Wiesel, had personally endured the Holocaust. In 1944 the Nazi terror reached Sighet, a small town nestled in the Carpathian Mountains. Elie was a teenager when his family was transported to the death camps. Father and son were separated from mother and daughter. Elie alone survived—bruised, haunted, imprisoned by a nightmare which shattered his world and gave him no peace.

Before the Nazis came, Elie was an extremely pious Jew who devoured the Talmud and the Hasidic tales. He lived by the mitzvot of the halacha, and he received a sense of life's meaning from the world of agada, those tales which spoke of God's covenant with Israel and of God's redemptive act in history.

Ever since Auschwitz Elie's life has been a desperate struggle to regain his faith. "Never shall I forget those moments which murdered my God and my soul, and turned my dreams to dust." Thus speaks a character in one of Wiesel's novels.[27] Wiesel remains however, a "soul on fire"—questioning, doubting, rebelling, cursing—but unwilling to surrender the gift of meaning. Like Jacob of old, like the agadists of an early age, he wrestles with God, but will not deny Him. After all, if there is no God, then Auschwitz is but an absurdity to be stoically endured. If we have no expectations, there is no faith to be challenged. Wiesel remains like Abraham and the talmudic agadists, a rebel who challenges God *because he already believes in Him*. Somewhere Wiesel has written: "One may be Jewish with God, in God and even against God, but not without God."

Wiesel has become the Jewish people's master agadist in our time. He tells the story of Gregor, a Jewish boy for whom hope turned to dust—an orphan who was so bitter at first that he could not recite Kaddish for his father. In time he regains his power to love another person. With the rediscovery of love, dust returns to renewed hope, and at the end of the novel Gregor recites the Kaddish, "that solemn affirmation, filled with grandeur and serenity by which man returns to God His crown and His sceptre."[28]

What is the key to Wiesel's struggle for reaffirmation? At an early point in his post-Holocaust agada, Gregor encounters Elijah and is told: "God's final victory, my son, lies in man's inability to reject Him. . . . You think you have emptied out your hatred and rebellion, but all you are doing is telling Him how much you need His support and forgiveness."[29]

In one of his historical vignettes, Wiesel tells of a Jewish concentration-camp inmate, Pinchas, who decided he would not fast on Yom Kippur. When he meets Pinchas afterward, and is told that he fasted after all, an explanation is required. Pinchas declares that he fasted not out of obedience but out of *defiance*. His testimony *against* God, however, becomes ineluctably a witness for God. When someone has hurt us we may continue to fulfill obligations toward him, not in love but in spite. We may wish to make him feel guilty for betraying us, but by this very act we have also shown that we care for and need the relationship. Even in defiance we reveal that we are prisoners of that need. A Jew is existentially a prisoner of God.

As he himself acknowledges, Wiesel remains within the circle of covenant faith. His cherished model is the Hasidic Rabbi Levi-Yitzhak of Berditchev, an eighteenth-century Polish Jew and a crusty rebel, who on Rosh Hashanah ascended his pulpit, directed his eyes heavenward, and in the presence of a full congregation declared: "Let Ivan blow the shofar." He meant: If You, God, treat us Jews so badly, why should we remain faithful to you and bear witness to you among the nations? Let Ivan blow the shofar.[30]

On another occasion Levi-Yitzhak declared: "O Lord, if You refuse to answer our prayers, I refuse to go on saying them."[31] But Levi-Yitzhak, for all his brashness and theological temerity, "never sulked indefinitely. Once he had spoken his mind, he came back to God," and recited the Kaddish. "The questions remain questions, but he could go on, he could begin and build on the ruins."[32]

Thus Wiesel emerges as the master agadist for a post-Holocaust generation. He too tells stories which both express his bitter doubt and reveal his hunger for faith. Like Jacob of old he will wrestle with God. He may emerge bruised, but he will not be denied the precious blessing of meaning. What did Wiesel tell those future defenders of the faith? He who had dared to speak of his own anguish told his audience of new rabbis: "All experience being transmissable, that is the very essense of Judaism—you will be called upon tomorrow to transmit yours . . . make of it a tale, a challenge, and if need be impose upon it a meaning—and a hope, for a Jew is he . . . who knows to defeat what pushes him to defeat and turn it into a promise . . ."[33]

Thus did Wiesel bid his charges to hold fast to the agada, to tell stories of their doubt and their indestructible faith in the God of the covenant. They remain part of a people whose wrestling with God began with the divine call to Abraham and will end with the coming of the Messiah. The Jew as Jew cannot proclaim the "death of God" or the absurdity of life. "One may be Jewish with God, in God, and even against God, but not without God."

A Play on Words: Seenah and Sinai

Each Jew must in his own way encounter the question, What does it mean to be a Jew after Auschwitz? The question returned to me with special force as I read from the Torah at Berchtesgaden.

A modern agada: In 1937 Hitler and Goebbels met in the Führer's Berlin apartment. Hitler described the Ten Commandments as "that curse from Mount Sinai, that poison with which both Jews and Christians have spoiled and soiled the free wonderful instincts of man. Whatever is against nature is against life itself." Goebbels interrupted: " 'Honor thy father and thy mother,' no, every boy reviles and hates his father." Hitler continued the attack: " 'Thou shalt not steal,' wrong, all life is theft.'' Hitler concluded by calling for a liberation from ''the curse of Sinai, from the dark stammering of Nomads who could no longer trust their own sound instincts. This is what we are fighting against—the curse of so-called morals, idealized to protect the weak from the strong in the face of the immortal law of battle. The great law of divine nature. Against the so-called Ten Commandments, against them we are fighting.''[34]

An ancient rabbi suggests a play on two Hebrew words: *Sinai* and *seenah* (''hostility''). The agada implies that the vulnerability of the Jew to the hazards of history is not because of what the Jew does or does not do, but because this people symbolically reminds men of a noble destiny betrayed, a vision man has yet to fulfill. In the twentieth century one individual most starkly embodied man's demonic potential, one man most poignantly reminded the West of the thin membrane which separates civilization from the jungle. Hitler's obsessive hatred of the Jew seems hardly coincidental. There may indeed be, as an ancient rabbi intuited, a relation between *Sinai* and *seenah,* between our witness and our vulnerability.[35]

The late Abraham Joshua Heschel once called attention to two contrasting concepts of man. The first is the biblical agada (Genesis 1:27), ''So God created man in his own image, in the image of God created He him. Male and female created He them.'' Commenting on this biblical agada, Heschel writes:

> Nothing is more alien to the spirit of Judaism than the veneration of images and symbols. It would even be alien to the spirit of the Bible to assert that the world is a symbol of God, and yet there is something in the world that the Bible does regard as a symbol of God. It is not a temple or a tree, it is not a statue or a star. The one symbol of God is man, every man. God himself created man in His image. . . . reverence for God is shown in our reverence for man. The fear you must feel offending or hurting the human being must be as ultimate as your fear of God . . . [36]

Contrast this biblical agada with the following definition of man frequently quoted in Germany prior to the Nazi era:

The human body contains a sufficient amount of fat to make seven cakes of soap; enough iron to make a medium size nail; a sufficient amount of phosphorous to equip two thousand matchheads; enough sulphur to rid one's self of one's fleas.[37]

To dramatize the contrast let us cite a rabbinic agada which asks: "Why did God create a single man [Adam] at the outset of the human story?" The answer: "To teach that he who destroys one life, it is as if he destroyed the whole world, and he who saves one life, it is as if he saved the entire world."[38]

Is it simply coincidental that the cremation of millions of innocent human beings was an instrument of national policy in Nazi Germany? And that the victim Hitler most passionately singled out was the Jew? The enemies we have made are themselves a clue to the meaning of our Jewish existence. Our very vulnerability is a sign of a world whose redemptive promise has not yet been fulfilled. The precariousness of our existence testifies to a view of life, a value stance, which man (and the Jew himself) still honors in the breach. The sanctity of human life and the elemental moral restraints embodied in the Decalogue which drew Hitler's sneers ought make us more willing than ever to take pride in our enemies and in our Jewish vocation. We remain history's charter-bearers of a vision which the world needs desperately, but is reluctant to embrace.

The People Israel Lives: Survival a Sign of Divine Purpose

I stood with my children at the kibbutz of the Warsaw Ghetto fighters and walked through the museum of Nazi horrors. Near the kibbutz one may see the remains of an aqueduct built by the Romans, and further to the south, along the coast, is Caesarea, with its Roman-built amphitheater and statuary. In Caesarea Rabbi Akiba died a martyr's death during the Hadrianic persecutions. Here we were, Jewish descendants of Akiba, standing on the soil of Israel reborn. To visit a Jewish state forged in the furnaces of Auschwitz, or even to stand as Jews today at Berchtesgaden, is a spine-tingling defiance of all the chroniclers of our people's demise. Indeed, the word *Israel* appears outside the Bible for the first time in an inscription attributed to the ancient Egyptian ruler Merneptah. The inscription reads: "Israel is desolate, its seed is no more."[39]

If our vulnerability is a reminder that we are bearers of a vision not yet fulfilled, then our survival is also a sign that He who commissioned us to make known His name and His will for man remains in some sense the Guardian of Israel.

I write this chapter in the season of Chanukah. Chanukah is observed in commemoration of events which occurred in the year 165 B.C.E. A band of Jews, under the leadership of the sons of Mattathias, was able to defeat Antiochus, the Syrian tyrant, and proclaim a Jewish commonwealth. Those were the years just prior to the full ascendancy of Roman power. In the pages of agada (First Book of Maccabees) the victory is perceived as a sign of divine power and grace.

> And all the people fell on their faces and blessed heaven which had prospered them, and they celebrated the rededication of the altar for eight days and offered burnt offerings with joy and offered a sacrifice of deliverance and praise.[40]

Centuries later the rabbinic agadist told the story of a cruse of oil which was found by the Maccabees in the Temple desecrated by Antiochus. The oil seemed adequate to rekindle the Temple lamp for but a day. Wonder of wonders, it burned eight days, and that, says the Talmud, is the origin of the Chanukah festival and the miracle we celebrate by kindling our lamps for eight days.[41]

The halacha for kindling the Chanukah Menorah is based on two diverse agadot: in one, the *miracle* is the *Maccabean victory;* in the other, it is the *cruse of oil* that lasted beyond all expectations. Perhaps the two may be reconciled if, in the perspective of thirty centuries of Jewish history, we who stand as Jews in Israel reborn, or who recite the Shema at Hitler's Alpine retreat, can declare that the great wonder, the sign of our transcendent meaning as a people, is that we are still here to tell the story of our past and to share it with our children. Vulnerability and survival remain twin keys to the significance of our Jewish being.

Indeed the rabbis ask: Why do we kindle the Menorah? Does God need the light? They answer: We kindle the light to signify that God's presence still abides amidst the people Israel. We kindle the light to proclaim to the world that we are still here, and that the task for which we were called into being has not yet been fulfilled.[42]

We are Children of Israel

One agada remains, however, the deepest clue to our vocation as Jews. We are children of Israel. How was Jacob's name changed from Jacob to Israel?

> And Jacob was left alone, and there wrestled a man with him until the breaking of the day, and when he saw he prevailed not against him, he touched the hollow of his [Jacob's] thigh . . . and he said: "Let me go, for the day breaketh." And he [Jacob] said: "I will not let you go except you bless me." And he said unto him: "What is your name?" And he said: "Jacob." And he said: "Your name shall be called no more Jacob, but Israel, for you have wrestled with God and with men and have prevailed."[43]

The commentators debate whether this is to be considered a physical event in Jacob's life or a dream—a prefigurement of Jewish destiny. Choosing the latter, let us acknowledge that the children of Israel have been wrestling with God and man for thousands of years.

Wrestling with God? The Jews' testimony in behalf of God's creative and redemptive power has not come easily. Many were the times when our own experience as a people seemed to mock the faith we bear. Even on occasions when we could not accept our suffering as judgment, we have struggled to reaffirm our basic trust in life's transcendent meaning. When we could not accept our pain as divine justice, we have perceived it as the price of bearing God's promise in an unredeemed world. If oppression has strained our faith, our wondrous survival has provided ever anew an intimation that our Redeemer lives. The tales of the agadists, from Abraham to Elie Wiesel, reflect an unquenchable "passion for meaning''—the determination ever and again to renew our ground of faith.

In his last published work, Abraham Joshua Heschel offered still another illustration of the Jew who wrestles with God but will not let Him go.

A friend of mine, Mr. Sh.z. Shragai went to Poland as a representative of a Jewish agency in the late 1940's, when Poland still entertained good relations with the State of Israel. His visit was an official mission concerning the immigration of Jewish survivors of Nazi extermination camps. After finishing his work in Warsaw, he left for Paris and as a very important person was given a whole compartment on the train. It was crowded with passengers.

Outside he noticed an emaciated, poorly clad Jew who could not find a seat on the train. He invited him to join him in his compartment. It was comfortable, clean, pleasant and the poor fellow came in with his bundle, put it on the rack over the seat and sat down.

My friend tried to engage him in conversation, but he would not talk. When evening came, my friend, an observant Jew, recited the evening prayer, while the other fellow did not say a word of prayer. The following morning my friend took out his prayer shawl and phylacteries and said his prayer. The other fellow looked so wretched and somber, would not say a word and did not pray. Finally when the day was almost over they started a conversation. The fellow said: "I am never going to pray anymore because of what happened to us in Auschwitz . . . how could I pray? That is why I did not pray all day."

The following morning—it was a long trip from Warsaw to Paris—my friend noticed that the fellow suddenly opened his bundle, took out his shawl and phylacteries, and started to pray. He asked him afterward, "what made you change your mind?" The fellow said: "it suddenly dawned upon me to think how lonely God must be. Look with whom He is left. I felt sorry for Him."[44]

This twentieth-century descendant of Israel remains a struggling Jew who contends with God but does not abandon Him. He argues while he prays, he doubts as he serves, and his very demand of his Creator reveals a primordial trust yearning for confirmation.

In the twentieth century, as in the first, a Jew is not permitted to rest with the verdict that life is absurd. A Jew must continually wrestle with God to reclaim his birthright to meaning. To do otherwise is, as Emil Fackenheim reminds us, "to grant Hitler posthumous victories."

Israel was destined to struggle not only with God but with *man*. Somewhere I have heard this capsule account of that struggle: In the days of the early church the Jew was told, "You cannot live among us as a Jew," and they tried to convert us; the medieval ruler said, "You cannot live among us," and they exiled us; the Nazis said, "You cannot live," and they tried to exterminate us.

Ever more clearly does it appear that in denying the Jew his elemental dignity, the nations have imperiled their own human birthright. The Nazi Holocaust brought the people Israel to the brink of annihilation and Western man to the brink of total dehumanization.

There is an agada in which a beleaguered rabbi, distraught by the travail of Jewish existence, uttered this prayer: "O Lord, if You will not send the Messiah to us, at least send him to the goyim [the other peoples]." Obliquely this prayer affirms that the redemption of the Jew and the redemption of his neighbor are inextricably intertwined. The Nazis desecrated the divine image in man when they cremated millions of our people and other peoples. Conversely, the surest sign that human dignity has been confirmed in the world will be the day when the Jew need no longer struggle for his rights as a child of God.

I stood with my children in the State of Israel reborn, a Jewish commonwealth which emerged in the aftermath of the Holocaust. What a chilling exhibit of Jewish survival! But for all its glory, Israel has not transcended the precariousness of Jewish history. Its sovereign Jewish majority abides in a tiny kingdom surrounded by a hundred million people whose rulers have not yet, as of this writing, convincingly demonstrated their acceptance of her right to exist as a nation. My children saw many, many Israeli soldiers in the course of our travels. The goal to which we point remains ahead of us. The struggle which defines our place in God's world has not ended. The struggle of the Jew is, in essence, the struggle of man to bear witness to and fulfill the promise of creation, the meaning of life.

"Your name shall not be called Jacob, but Israel, for you have contended with God and man, (and will find it necessary to do so again), but you have prevailed (and you will prevail) . . ."

IV · Two Faiths in Conflict

*I know that meaninglessness is just as much a
matter of belief as meaning. The caravan of
the intellectuals would have you think that
someone has discovered meaninglessness out there
beyond us in the desert—in the infinities of
space—and brought it home like a phoenix'
egg to prove the world is void. Nothing could be
more childish. Meaninglessness, like meaning,
is a conclusion in the mind, a reading, an
interpretation.*
(Archibald MacLeish, "The Premise of Meaning")

DEVASTATING IT WAS, but the Nazi Holocaust has not been the
only major obstacle to faith for the modern Jew. Nor is it an event
totally unrelated to earlier crises in the life of our people. For its
generation, the destruction of the Temple in 70 C.E. was every bit
as faith-shattering.

To that debacle we must add the destruction of Spanish
Jewry, the massacres during the Crusades, the Black Death
pogroms, the Chmielnicki slaughter in the seventeenth century,
and the Russian pogroms of the nineteenth century. Eliezer
Berkovits asks an appropriate rhetorical question: "Did the Jews
massacred in the Rhinelands in the 11th and 12th centuries have
less reason to ask where God was while those horrors descended
upon them than the Jews at Auschwitz and Treblinka? Was the
problem of faith in a personal God less serious during the Black
Death than it is today because then only half of the half-million
Jews in Europe perished and not six million as in our days?"[1]

The modern Jew is not the first to discover a crisis of faith, nor does the Holocaust render his trauma unique. Why then have we found it so much more difficult than our forefathers to assert confidence in the God of history?

We live in an age whose tastemakers have elevated the concept of life's absurdity to a major premise. Although the Holocaust has pulverized Jewish consciousness with singular force, the corrosiveness of the "modern temper" has impinged on western men and women of all traditions during the last several hundred years. Modern man faces a crisis of self-understanding which theologian Sam Keen has described thus:

> . . . traditional man . . . accepted his life and environment as a meaningful gift which filled him with admiration and gratitude and responded actively by creating a community in harmony with patterns, meaning and value which he believed were homogenized into the cosmos. By contrast modern man increasingly experiences himself in anxiety as the sole value-creating force in what is still called the universe, but what for many has become a chaotic multiverse, devoid of intrinsic meaning.[2]

In the present chapter we shall briefly examine the challenge posed by modernity to the faith mirrored in agada. I shall argue that those who have summarily rejected the God of the covenant have done so not in the name of a compelling objective truth but in the name of a rival faith. Moreover, it is possible to appropriate the new treasures of nuclear science and technology without forsaking or denying the sacred dimension in human experience.

There is, of course, a personal aspect to this discussion. My training at a theological seminary was preceded by college-level secular education. If I chose to become a "defender of the faith," I did so only after wrestling with intellectual currents which have assaulted the world of agada. The contemporary rabbi confronts the agada's version of creation in Genesis after grappling with Darwin's theory of human evolution. He speaks to God's role in the liberation of Hebrew slaves after some exposure to modern physics. He argues for the perpetuation and distinctive vocation of a particular people after being immersed in the waters of cultural relativism. He is called to lead his people in prayer to a

God whom Freud reduced to a projection of man's father fantasies.

The Bible tells a striking agada concerning the prophet Elijah. This champion of the God of Israel is pitted against the prophets of the Canaanite fertility god, Baal. Who will win the contest for the people's loyalty, Baal or Yahweh? Apparently the children of Israel were in one of their restive moods. Elijah felt pressed to demonstrate the superiority of his God. In the presence of the people he challenges the prophets of Baal to a test. The demonstration takes place on Mount Carmel. A bullock is placed on the altar. Elijah dares the prophets of Baal to invoke their god's power and consume the bullock without flame. The Baal prophets try unsuccessfully to accomplish this feat. The bullock remains unconsumed. Then Elijah petitions Yahweh to display *His* power. Elijah's bullock is consumed without flame. The people Israel are impressed and are persuaded, at least for the moment, to acknowledge that "The Lord, He is God."[3]

Quite obviously, such "experimental proofs" of divine power could not be confidently staged by prophet or priest with predictable success. Were such impressive demonstrations possible, we would not read so often of Israel's lack of faith in God's power and love. God provided ample leverage for human doubt even in biblical times. The prophet Isaiah was forced to speak of God's "hiddenness," and much earlier Moses was told that the very meaning of Yahweh denotes a God who is not subject to human control: "I am as I am. I shall be as I choose to be . . ." God cannot be made to appear on human demand. He eludes man's experimental designs.

Moreover, even the moment of divine self-disclosure may be unobtrusive and ambiguous. Elijah himself experienced the more subtle and subjective component in divine revelation. When the prophet was forced to flee from King Ahab, he hid in the mountains. There God was revealed to him not in an earthquake or in a fire or in the wind, but in a "voice of gentle stillness" which the contemporary folk singers Simon and Garfunkel call "The Sounds of Silence." One man's sound of silence may be another's silence without sound, or simply an empty void.

What a world of difference between the predictable flameless consumption of a bullock on an altar and a voice of gentle stillness. From biblical times to our own, the believer has had to live with both kinds of signs and to endure those periods when he must believe in the absence of a sign. There are times when faith must be nurtured by memory, past experience, and hope in the promise of the future. While there are times when the prayers of the believer are wondrously answered, there are times when he too must ask: "Why hast Thou forsaken me?" Every believer has experienced divine hiddenness.

Faith has always required a great measure of trust in the presence of mystery. Even the biblical believer was required to endure the embarrassment and anguish of a God who will not predictably appear upon demand. This divine elusiveness has itself spawned crises of confidence and lent a perpetual fascination to rival faiths. In the time of Elijah the God of Israel competed with Baal. In modern times the God of the agada has confronted even more attractive rivals.

The cults of modern man have reserved a special place of reverence for the goddess of science and technology. The rituals of prayer and sacrifice have yielded primacy to the rituals of scientific method. This ritual is based on the faith that what is true and trustworthy in our world should at some point be reducible to an experimental design. Following certain procedures we ought to be able to predict certain consequences, thereby enabling us to distinguish between what we call truth and untruth.

Zealously performed by a scientific priesthood, this experimental ritual has, in the course of two hundred years, and most dramatically in the past five decades, yielded a dazzling panoply of predictable power. The goddess of technology has enabled man to produce effects far more scintillating than the flameless consumption of a bullock on an altar.

Ancient man looked up at the sky and admired a flock of birds. We look up at the sky and are jolted by the sonic boom of a jet flying faster than the speed of sound. Ancient man saw the distant moon as a divinely imposed, inaccessible frontier, a measure of man's creatureliness in God's world. By grace of technology modern man rockets to the lunar sphere almost at will. The modern age has yielded a mushroom cloud which may inspire as much or more fear and trembling than a volcanic eruption. The latter was traditionally regarded as an ''act of God,'' the former is the fruit of man's worship at the altar of technology.

Responding to man's unremitting petition, technology has prepared him to unleash his most dazzling display: to recreate man himself according to human design. Thus the director of an institute on ''human genetics'' tells audiences that it is not too early to begin thinking in whose image we shall wish to ''re-create'' man.

Faith in science and technology has captivated the heart of modern man. The Jew is very much a man of his time. What has been the corrosive impact of our covenant with science and technology on the world of agada? Let us examine, in turn, the testimony of the modern temper, which appears at least on the surface to undermine the agada's concept of God as Creator, Giver of Torah, and Redeemer.

The Modern Temper of Unbelief

The language of Jewish faith speaks of man as a purposeful creation of God. Genesis tells the story of man, the pinnacle of creation, brought forth for special relation with the root of his being. The world in which he occupies a unique place is not a meaningless maze or an accident but a gift from an ultimate source of power and love. God cares for His creatures. The Creator has invested the world and man with purpose and value. ''And God saw . . . that it was good.'' [4]

Modern critical thought has spun a different story of the ''origin of the human species.'' The most significant part of Darwin's hypothesis was not the assertion that man's emergence took longer than six days or that man's kinship with ''lower creatures'' was closer than he might wish to acknowledge. Most crucial by far was Darwin's assertion that man's evolution reveals no transcendent power-purpose, but is simply the by-product of random mutations and natural selection. Nature, far from being the scene of an unfolding divine creativity, is the arena of blind chance and a brutal struggle for survival which determines which species shall live and which shall become extinct. Darwin once exclaimed: "What a book a devil's chaplain might write on the clumsy, wasteful, blundering and horribly cruel works of nature."[5]

What then became of the traditional relation between God and man? "Modern" thinking has yielded the hypothesis that man, far from being God's creation, is in fact God's creator. Man was not formed in the image of God. God was formed in the image of man. Trapped in a world not of his making, confronted by so many forces beyond his control, ancient man imagined as real what was in truth an illusion. He imagined that he had been thrust into a realm suffused with meaning when in fact his "origin, his growth, his hopes and fears, his loves and his beliefs are but the outcome of an accidental collocation of atoms . . . destined to extinction." [6]

In 1929 Walter Lippmann wrote his widely publicized *A Preface to Morals*. Therein Lippmann asserts that mature man can no longer believe, as did his forebears, that he is part of a purposeful universe. "A man may take you into the open at night and show you the stars but unless he feels the vast indifference of the universe to his own fate and has placed himself in the perspective of a cold, empty illimitable space he has not looked maturely on the heavens."[7]

Where shall man, stripped of the illusion that he is a creature of God, find his strength and comfort? His only consolation lies in the power which technology has granted him over the physical conditions of his life and in the power of human love. This latter theme is poignantly expressed in Archibald Mac-Leish's play *J.B.* At the end of the drama J.B. (a modern Job) and his wife, Sarah, assess man's ultimate source of comfort.

> J.B.: It's too dark to see.
> *Sarah turns, pulls his head down between her hands and kisses him.*
> SARAH: Then blow on the coal of the heart, my darling.
> J.B.: The coal of the heart . . .

SARAH: It's all the light now.
         Blow on the coal of the heart.
         The candles in the churches are out.
         The lights have gone out in the sky.
         Blow on the coal of the heart
         And we'll see by and by . . . [8]

Thus have the canons of modernity divested man of his agadic splendor. Man is deemed no longer the child of God, stamped in His image, but the plaything of blind chance. Man's universe is not a home, but an absurd maze. His capacity to love is not the reflection of a divine love, but a desperate, fragile gesture—a blowing on the coals of the heart in a world of darkness. Such is the cult of modernity's challenge to the agada in the first chapter of Genesis.

Let us now examine how the modern temper has challenged the second tenet of the agada. The covenant faith also affirmed that God is the Giver of Torah. Biblical agada tells the story of the people Israel standing at Sinai and receiving a way of life. Man the creature of God is accountable to Him for the quality of his life. Man finds meaning (his vocation and task) by doing God's will, by sharing with his Creator the fulfillment of creation's promise. Love for one's fellow man is not simply "a blowing on the coals of the heart" but the response to a divine command—man's way of acknowledging his common creaturehood under God.

God has revealed His way through certain men (prophets) and preeminently through a certain people (Israel). The divine will is recorded in sacred writings, which, though they require human interpretation, derive their ultimate authority from God. That which is described as right, as binding, as obligatory, derives its compelling power from the belief that it is God's will.

Thus the agada of worship summons a Jew to declare: "Our Fathers put their trust in Thee and Thou didst teach them the law of life. Be gracious also unto us that we may understand and fulfill the teachings of Thy word. Enlighten our eyes in Thy law that we may cling unto Thy commandments . . . . Praised be Thou, O God, who in Thy love has called Thy people Israel to serve Thee"[9]

The modern critical temper has attacked this faith by denying, first of all, that so-called sacred texts are in any way the word of God. Scientifically oriented scholarship, dating back to the time of Spinoza, has identified different literary styles, even contradictory concepts, which suggest that the Torah was the work of many men over many centuries. This act of scholarship presumably robbed the Torah of at least one source of sanctity. If men in different ages wrote or edited the text, is it not simply the product of the human imagination?

Of course one may accept the human element in the formation of a Torah scroll, and still insist that the authors were inspired by and sought to discover the will of God. The most crucial tenet of the agada was not that God "wrote" the Torah scroll (the Bible itself credits Moses with massive stenographic responsibilities) or even that the Torah was given at one time, but rather that God is the Giver of Torah. Whatever the medium—whether through one or many minds, in one century or many—God is the ultimate source of the truth by which we ought to live. We discover the good and the right. We do not create truth or value. God, not man, is the ultimate measure of all things. We are accountable to God for the quality of our lives.

It is modernity's challenge to *this* assumption which constitutes its most significant rejection of God as Giver of Torah. Some have argued that man is the sole creator of Torah. He spins it out of his psyche. He does not respond to a transcendent source of value. No divine will demands that "you shall not oppress the stranger." All such moral limits or obligations are acts of human self-restraint or matters of human taste.

Among the most eloquent champions of this view was the German philosopher Friedrich Nietzsche. In his drama *Thus Spake Zarathustra* Nietzsche proclaims the death of God as Giver of Torah.

> How He raged at us, this wrath snorter because we understood Him badly, but why did He not speak more clearly? And if the fault lay in our ears why did He give us ears that hear Him badly? . . . Away with such a God. Better to have no God. Better to set up destiny on one's own account. Better to be a fool. Better to be God oneself! [10]

Nietzsche invited man to liberate himself from bondage to an illusory yoke. Let him no longer subdue his passion to gain some heavenly reward. Let him disdain that self-abnegation which benefited only his oppressors. Let man boldly assert his "will to power" and become his own lawgiver, his own master, his own God.

Agada declared that man was most truly free when he committed himself to the service of God. The rabbis compared the Hebrew words *chārut* ("freedom") and *chărut* ("that which is inscribed"). They concluded: The Hebrews experienced freedom (*chārut*) only after they had stood at Sinai and received the tablets of divine law (*chărut*). [11] Jean-Paul Sartre, the French atheistic existentialist, has directly challenged this assertion. The mark of true freedom, he argues, is the absence of any transcendent power to whom man is accountable. "If I have done away with God the Father some one is needed to invent values. . . . life has no meaning a priori . . . it is up to you to give it a meaning, and value is nothing else than in this meaning which you choose." [12]

Sigmund Freud, the great explorer of man's mind, also denied that the Torah was in any sense the gift of a transcendent moral will. The world of agada, with its affirmation of a divine lawgiver, had its origin, Freud claimed, not in an ancient encounter but in an ancient crime. Freud constructs his own agada. He tells the story of primitive sons who resented the authority of the fathers and aspired to preempt their place and possess their women. When any son threatened the father's dominion he was murdered, until the sons, banding together, finally killed the father and usurped his role.

The story does not end here. During the father's life the sons were bound to him by ambivalent feelings—great admiration and hero worship mingled with fear and hatred. Murder removed the father from the external world, but his apparition continued to stalk the sons' unconscious minds, sowing seeds of unbearable guilt and anxiety. How could man deal with this crisis? He projected the father upon the world, acknowledged him as God, and appeased him with a variety of acts. [13]

In a later work Freud applied his agada specifically to the

origin of Judaism. Moses had imposed restraints on the Israelites. (Unlike Nietzsche, Freud emphasized that such restraint on man's "will to power" was the price of civilization. He felt that no society can endure which does not hold man's aggressive impulses in check.) But the people resented Moses' authority and murdered him. The norms of Torah, says Freud, were a "guilt offering"—a way in which the people dealt with their guilt and their need so to order life that such murder would not reoccur. [14]

Nietzsche, Freud, and Sartre each speak for a modern mind which denies the reality of a world affirmed in the language of Jewish faith. Life, they said, is not the gift of a purposeful Creator nor is man accountable to a transcendent source of value. Rather man is a cosmic orphan thrust into a universe with no meaning save that which man himself creates.

How has the modern temper eroded the third pillar of Jewish faith? The world of agada has declared that He who is Creator and Torah-giver is also active in nature and history to fulfill His purposes. This faith in God as an ultimate source of power and love may also be found in Exodus. Hebrew slaves were set free. Their liberation was an act of divine redemption. Thus we pray: "From Egypt thou didst redeem us, O Lord our God, from the house of bondmen thou didst deliver us. . . . Wherefore . . . Moses and the children of Israel sang a song unto thee with great joy saying, all of them, 'Who is like unto thee, O Lord, among the mighty? Who is like unto thee, glorious in holiness, revered in praises, doing marvels?' "[15]

What has happened to this faith under the impact of "modernity"? We need only return to the joke about the Jewish schoolboy who came home and told his father a modern version of the exodus. This version speaks only of Israelite engineers building a bridge over the Sea of Reeds, crossing it, and blowing it up in order to confound their Egyptian pursuers. Rational man, it is argued, may attribute his victory over adversity to his own superior technology or some fortuitous circumstance. He has no basis for celebrating or trusting in the redemptive power of God. He has no transcendent source of hope. He has no "invisible means of support." He ought not thank God for his deliverance nor challenge God in periods of anguish. Man is alone in the universe. He emerged under no divine auspices, is accountable to no divine authority, and may trust in no divine power.

This may rightly be described as the formal *faith* of many modern persons who profess to be "nonreligious." The contemporary Western Jew has been much influenced by this view of life, which directly challenges the world of agada.

The Conflict Between Covenant Faith and Modern Unbelief

The premise of intrinsic meaninglessness remains, however, as much a matter of faith as the premise of meaning. Such intellectual giants of our age as Darwin, Marx, and Freud have made immense contributions to human understanding. Religious believers and unbelievers are extraordinarily in their debt. But their disavowal of the biblical framework of meaning is a matter of personal faith, not scientific necessity. The issues which divide the believer from the nonbeliever are not resolvable by experiment or clinical test. Let us define these issues sharply.

1. There is, first, the significance of religious language, of God-talk or agada. The nonbeliever insists that such language is a human creation, based on elements in man's ordinary experience, and that it tells us nothing about a reality beyond man (i.e., God). Freud contends that man's reference to God as the Father reveals *only* man's inner psychic world and man's relation to the authority figures in his personal life.

Freud once wrote that the divine father of the agada "really [was] the father clothed in the grandeur in which he once appeared to a small child. The religious man's picture of the creation of the universe is the same as the picture of his own creation."[16]

To this the believer will respond: Language is a human tool by which we seek, however imperfectly, to express the texture of our experience. Science itself uses human language to describe a reality which is beyond man's direct vision or personal experience. Science is also a man-made symbol system. Einstein's formula $E=mc^2$ may be described as a projection of Einstein's mind. Its mathematical symbolism is a human creation, but presumably the formula points to a truth about the universe itself. Similarly the words of agada are a human creation, but they may point to truths concerning man's relationship to an ultimate power in the universe.

In our everyday life we draw on words from one realm of experience to illumine another. Thus I may describe to a friend the trauma of traveling on a commuter railway car during rush hour with the phrase "We were sardines in a can." Hopefully some light has been shed on that ordeal, without my friend concluding that I have exchanged my human estate for that of a fish. The similarities between the two kinds of experiences are helpful. The differences need not be spelled out. The use of simile or metaphor is man's way of illuminating and communicating his life experience.

Similarly a person may compare his relationship with God to a person's relation to his father. This does not necessarily imply that the former is simply a projection of the latter. For the believer the similarities may be helpful; the differences self-evident. God is no more literally a father than I am a sardine. What we are confronted with is both the power and the limit of all human language, in science as in religion.

2. The issue of language involves more basic questions. Does agada point to a transcendent reality or is such a reality simply a figment of man's imagination? Ultimately what divides the believer and the unbeliever is not the interpretation of the language which we use, but the interpretation of our life. Emil Fackenheim states the matter well. "Believer and unbeliever inhabit the same . . . world, but for the believer a divine presence is manifest, however obscurely and intermittently, in and through the world. The unbeliever . . . recognizes the feeling of such a presence in the believer and on occasion may even share it, but he denies an actual divine presence."[17]

The ancient psalmist (and his contemporary soul mate) may look up at the star-filled sky and proclaim: "The heavens declare the glory of God, and the firmament showeth his handiwork." H. G. Wells sardonically quipped that the heavenly panoply appears to him like wallpaper in a railway waiting room. Who is right?

Both the psalmist and Wells saw the same physical heavens. Their *interpretations* of that experience radically differed. The choice between the two perspectives is itself an act of faith. H. G. Wells's experience was informed by a different world-view than the psalmist's.

3. One of the psychological arguments modernity has unleashed against the world of agada concerns the matter of "wish fulfillment." The believer is accused of not being strong or mature enough to face the inherent absurdity of an uncaring cosmos. Therefore he fantasies that the world is responsive to his inner needs and deepest wishes. He feels the need for a meaningful world, and so he imagines or conjures that world into existence.

Such "psychological reductionism" is a two-edged sword. One could as easily argue that Arthur Schopenhauer (1788–1860), that great apostle of atheism, proclaimed the meaninglessness of life in response to the dismally pathetic experiences of his own life story. His grandmother was insane, his father discovered his wife to be unfaithful and committed suicide, his mother became a champion of free love. Schopenhauer and his mother vehemently despised each other. He never saw his mother during the last decades of his life. Schopenhauer so distrusted his fellow man that he would not allow a barber to shave him, and he slept at night with a loaded revolver beside his bed. Conclusion: no wonder Schopenhauer was an atheist!

Surely our capacity to feel life's transcendent meaning may be seriously affected by what psychiatrist Eric Erikson has called "the basic trust," nurtured or weakened in early family relationships. But such an analysis may help us to understand only why some persons more easily affirm life's meaning than others. It does not respond to the question: Is there a God worthy of our ultimate trust?

Such psychologizing does not settle the basic issue: has man's millennial fascination by the power and presence beyond the surface of life been simply a defensive reaction to his own fear and powerlessness or a response to a genuine reality? Does man seek God because he is weak or because God is seeking man?

That man needs God is not indisputable grounds for concluding that God is or is not real. A child who cries for a parent may need reassurance. That need as such tells us nothing about whether the parent is present and able to respond. All efforts to resolve the issue of God by appeal to psychological arguments are ultimately fruitless.

The unbeliever will say: You believe because you need to believe. The believer may respond: You disbelieve because you need to disbelieve. The unbeliever may say: You believe because you are weak. The believer may respond: I believe because I need God and have experienced and will experience intimations of His power and love.

4. The most crucial issue involves the test of truth. The unbeliever may say: Only that is worthy of belief which can be tested by experimental design. Since God's reality cannot be established or denied by a decisive experiment, you exclude God from the conventional test of truth.

Actually, the distinction between science and religion in this regard has been overdrawn. In the history of science, theorizing (hypothesis, conceptual scheme) often transcends and is not fully reducible to the experiments by which the theory is presumably tested. When, for example, Pascal sought to test his idea that the earth was surrounded by a sea of air which exerted pressure, he suggested observing the height of a column of mercury measured upon the ground and atop a high peak. All that was directly observed was the different heights of a column of mercury. The grand theory (that the earth was surrounded by a sea of air) was not tested directly. Many assumptions were required to link the test to the larger theory.

Similarly, nuclear physics today assumes the existence of a particle called the neutrino. There are no experimental tests to prove or disprove the existence of this particle. Its existence is required, however, if one is to uphold the basic principle of the conservation of mass and energy. Thus the physicist must choose between postulating the existence of a particle for which there is no direct experimental evidence or assuming that, under certain circumstances, the principle of the conservation of mass and energy does not hold. This is surely a far cry from the popular image of science proving all its assumptions by a clear-cut experimental design.

Correspondingly there is more of an interplay between theory (faith-belief) and experience in the world of agada than is sometimes recognized. Let us cite several examples. When the Jerusalem Temple was destroyed in 586 B.C.E. and thousands of Judeans were exiled to Babylon, many believed that Yahweh could only be worshipped within the borders of Israel and perhaps only in Jerusalem. Jeremiah reasoned: If God is sovereign over all the peoples, then surely He may be worshipped in Babylon as well. Jeremiah sent a letter to the exiles instructing them to affirm their covenant with Yahweh in the midst of their exile. Faced with the new experience of exile, the people were led to reformulate their understanding of the boundaries of God's accessibility. Consequently the concept of a universal God was more fully developed through a combination of Jeremiah's faith and the experience of the people in Babylon.

A still more poignant example of faith's responsiveness to new experience is provided by agada's most difficult question: If God is just and loving, why is there so much innocent suffering? When experience (innocent suffering) contradicted faith (a loving and just God), the biblical and rabbinic agadist developed new ideas to reconcile them: perhaps God is testing us, perhaps it is our task to help God fulfill the promise of creation; the future (messianic time) will vindicate our faith in God's power and love, and so forth. We shall discuss this function of religious theory (agada) further in Chapter VI. The point is simply that a conflict between faith and experience is a problem for religion precisely because in religion as well as science the testimony of experience is not totally disregarded.

Moreover, while agada was essentially an interpretation of human experience, its interpretation was not simply an isolated individual event, but an ongoing process within the community of the faithful. Each interpretation was checked against the cumulative experience and faith of past generations. Thus did tradition serve as a potential corrective to the danger of bizarre or irrational claims and assertions.

In sum: science rests on more than reliance on a test of experience alone, and agada is more than an exercise in "pure faith." Having said this, we must still acknowledge the burden of the unbeliever's challenge. Ultimately the scientist will recognize the need for an experiment of some kind to distinguish between a stronger and a weaker theory, whereas the religious believer is more likely to maintain his faith in God's power and love even though there is no unequivocal test which can be devised to verify his faith. It is far easier to disbelieve in God than in the law of gravity.

To this challenge the believer can only respond that the God of agada is God precisely because He cannot be imprisoned in man's experimental designs. A God who would permit such manipulation would be more Terach's idol than Moses' Yahweh (I am as I am). The believer may yearn for the kind of demonstration which Elijah performed with the bullocks on Mount Carmel, but he is more often compelled to settle for the subtle and mysterious ambiguity of the "voice of gentle stillness."

Ultimately the issue is even more sharply drawn. The believer denies that the mode of perceiving and testing truth affirmed by science provides an adequate net for all human experience or all reality. He denies that all that can be known or is worth knowing must be capable of being seen or measured, or tested, in a controlled experiment. Were the poets and sages in the prescientific era denied all grasp of truth? Can the scientist claim truth's only legitimate franchise in the contemporary world? Fortunately, many of the world's great scientists would themselves be the first to reject such a claim.

"These and These Are God's Revelation to Man"

Must one in fact choose between a respect for scientific rationalism and religious faith? Some of the most fertile minds in science and religion have sought ways of saying that "these and these are the modes in which God's truth is revealed to man." One of the most important attempts to affirm the world of science and the world of agada has come to us from the late Martin Buber, who may well be regarded as the twentieth century's most significant Jewish thinker. Buber identified two attitudes or postures by which man can and does relate to the world. He referred to these as *I-Thou* and *I-It*.[18] *I-Thou* relations are characterized by immediacy, presentness, subjectivity, spontaneity, unpredictability, uniqueness. In *I-Thou* relations that which confronts a person is not a passive object, but an active subject to be confirmed in otherness. By contrast *I-It* relations are characterized by detachment, impersonalism, analysis, objectivity, and the search for an ordered, predictable structure of experience.

Buber believed that both approaches to reality are part of every human life. Both are legitimate ways of encountering reality. Neither without the other is a sufficient basis for living in the world. Moreover, it is possible to relate to the same person, or the same natural phenomenon, or the same art form in both ways on alternate occasions.

A tree in my backyard may be viewed as an obstacle to a good view of the mountains, as a valuable protector of my privacy, as a shelter from the heat of the sun, as a potential source of kindling wood. In all such instances my encounter with the tree is an *I-It* occasion. The tree appears principally as an object whose value is contingent upon its capacity to help or hurt me. Conceivably, however, there are occasions when the tree appears in irreducible otherness, as a wondrous manifestation of God's creative glory. The tree's leafy, gnarled splendor meets me as a sign of the majesty and grandeur of life. On such an occasion *I-Thou* is the character of the encounter. Alfred North Whitehead alluded to the different ways in which we encounter nature in his classic quip: "When you understand all about the sun and all about the atmosphere, and all about the rotation of the earth, you may still miss the radiance of the sunset."[19]

A similar contrast may be suggested with regard to the arts. During a music appreciation class, a Brahms violin concerto may be analyzed by the instructor. This study reduces the composition to an object. The instructor may help me to focus on the major theme, the structure, the relation of this composition to Brahms's other works, and the place of this piece in the history of classical music. Such is an *I-It* occasion. When, however, I respond to the music in a concert hall with the fullness of my being, the music is no longer primarily an object for study, but a subject, a presence addressing and fully engaging me, and evoking a spontaneous response. On this occasion I have returned to the realm of *I-Thou*.

The contrast between these two postures is especially apparent in the human sphere. The obstetrician delivering a baby requires the detachment and objectivity associated with *I-It*. He coolly manipulates that bouncing bit of new life out of the mother's body into the world. At best he is a skillful technician and the delivery is routine. But the same man, if he is the father of that child (and especially if the child is his first), may be overcome by fear, wonder, gratitude, love. He is incapable of cool detachment. This new life is his son or daughter. The child's first cry pierces his soul, and he responds not as obstetrician but as father. Here is an instance of the difference between *I-It* and *I-Thou*. Because the two roles are in tension, most obstetricians will not deliver their own children.

The dominant posture of the laboratory is *I-It*. When man perceives the world as object, he produces the fruits of modern science. The scientific method seeks not only to objectify the moon and the human cell, but man himself. The social sciences (anthropology, sociology, psychology) are the by-product of such an approach to human reality. The greatest achievement of *I-It* in the modern world is human science. The greatest achievement of *I-Thou* in every age is human love and, as we shall see, the love relationship between man and God.

When our relationship to persons is governed, consciously or unconsciously, by such considerations as what I will gain from the bond and how I can bend him (her) to my purposes, we are in the realm of *I-It*. When the bond between two persons reveals a confirmation of each other's unconditional value and dignity—a desire to respond to each other's needs, a true opening of each to the other (with all the risk of being hurt which such opening entails), then we are in the realm of *I-Thou*.

It may well be argued that the scientific enterprise is not

totally devoid of the *I-Thou* dimension. Thus, for example, the scientist's quest for truth is grounded in a basic trust in the majestic and mysterious orderliness of the universe. Neither is a love relationship devoid of *I-It* dimensions. There is room in a mature courtship for such questions as: Does he (she) really demonstrate a responsiveness to my needs? Nevertheless it is fair to say that man as researcher lives dominantly in the realm of *I-It*, and that man as lover is encompassed by *I-Thou*. Both postures are part of an authentic life. Buber writes: "without *it* man cannot live. But he who lived with *it* alone is not a man."[20]

From his understanding of man's two postures in the world, Buber approaches the question of religion. Everything in man's world may be transformed into an *It*—a tree, a Brahms violin concerto, a person; each of these transformations of a *Thou* to an *It* may reveal one dimension of them, but there is, says Buber, one reality that does not yield to man's attempt at possession, objectification, analysis, or manipulation. That reality is God, the *Eternal Thou*.

All attempts to speak about God or prove God's existence are inherently limited. Indeed all agada, all God-talk, is at best a pointer toward a transcendent reality who eludes man's categories. God is the *Thou* who may not be reduced to an *It*. This is Buber's way of saying that the real God demands to be encountered, or trusted, even in His hiddenness. He may not be captured in an experimental design nor made to appear upon demand. *The language of agada is the language in which man speaks of his relationship to the Eternal Thou.*

If God may not be possessed, how may man encounter Him? Buber would deny that God is encountered by turning away from the world of ordinary experience. Rather, in every *Thou* man potentially glimpses the *Eternal Thou*. Thus in my encounters with a tree as *Thou*, I may receive a sign of the world as God's creative gift and discern the presence of the Giver. When I respond to a human need in love, I may discern Him who has called me into being that I might sanctify His world through love. To hear what is expected of me, I need not turn away from the everyday world in mystical contemplation. Rather, "each concrete hour allotted to the person . . . is speech for the man who is attentive . . . but the sounds of which the speech consists . . . are the events of the personal everyday life."[21]

While God may not be made to appear upon demand, the *Eternal Thou* is accessible to us through the finite *Thou*s of our life. He who cultivates the power to address and respond to the world with the fullness of his being may discern at times that his life is lived in the presence of an *Eternal Thou*. He who listens for that which is expected of him in each concrete hour of existence will discover that his life is a "summons and a sending."

As already indicated, the scientist is by no means a stranger to the world of *I-Thou*. First of all, the scientist as person encounters the *I-Thou* dimension in his relationship to others in his life and conceivably in his relationship to a particular religious tradition. Contrary to some popular misconceptions, a scientist may be a deeply religious man. But even in the pursuit of his quest for scientific knowledge, the *I-Thou* dimension may be present. Great moments of scientific discovery are accompanied by a sense of awe and wonder at the majestic order and the all-encompassing mystery of the universe.

Dr. Charles H. Townes, a distinguished physicist, has written that "most of the important scientific discoveries . . . are much more closely akin to revelation."

> The term itself is generally not used for scientific discovery since we are in the habit of reserving revelation for the religious realm. In scientific circles one speaks of intuition, accidental discovery, or says simply that "he had a wonderful idea." If we compare how great scientific ideas arrive, they look remarkably like religious revelation viewed in a non-mystical way. . . . Such ideas much more often come during off moments than while confronting data. A striking and well known example is the discovery of the benzine ring by Kekule, who while musing at his fireside was led to the idea by the vision of a snakelike molecule taking its tail in its mouth. We cannot yet describe the human process which leads to the creation of an important and substantially new scientific insight, but it is clear that the great scientific discoveries, the real leaps, do not usually come from the so-called "scientific method" but rather

more as did Kekule's—with perhaps less picturesque imagery but by revelations which are just as real.[22]

Einstein himself suggests (though he did not use the term) that a scientist may experience the *I-Thou* dimension in the very depth of his quest for illumination: " . . . anyone who has seriously studied science is filled with the conviction that a spirit tremendously superior to the human spirit manifests itself in the law abidingness of the world before whom we with our simple powers must humbly stand back."[23]

If scientific language may sometimes be associated with *I-Thou* experience, agada (religious language) may sometimes be associated with an *I-It* experience. At those moments when a reader of the Bible, or a rabbinic story, seeks to understand how this passage compares with another, or when it was written and by whom, at such moments the student of agada is functioning on the level of *I-It*. The agada has become an object for study. By contrast, at those moments when the agada leads one to experience or express his personal relationship to God, as in an act of prayer, then the words point toward the *I-Thou* dimension of life.

When I analyze parts of the Passover Haggadah to determine its major themes, strucuture, or purpose, I am in the realm of *I-It*. When I speak the words of the Haggadah to affirm my relationship to those events, and become, through the rituals of Passover, a participant in the drama of redemption—then the words are a bridge between me and my people and the God of the covenant, and it is truly "as if I went out of Egypt anew."

In short, while the language of science is most naturally associated with a detached, impersonal objective relation to the world *(I-It),* and agada is most naturally paired with the religious dimension of life *(I-Thou),* the distinction may be overdrawn. A person inhabits the realm of *I-It* when he looks at a rainbow and describes it as a "phenomenon produced by the refraction of the sun's rays on raindrops." Such a person may enter the depths of *I-Thou* when he sees the same rainbow and perceives it (as did the biblical agadist) as a sign of the relation between heaven and earth, between God and man.

God said: "This is the sign of the covenant that I set before Me and you and every living creature with you for all ages to come. I have set My bow in the clouds, and it shall serve as a sign of the covenant between Me and the earth."[24]

Whether he be scientist or theologian, a person inhabits the realm of *I-It* when he asks: "How can you believe in the existence of a living God when there is so much innocent suffering in the world?" The same person enters the realm of *I-Thou* when, faced with the experience of suffering, he cries out in anguish and in hope: "How long, O Lord, wilt Thou continually forget me? How long wilt Thou hide Thy face from me? How long am I to lay cares upon myself and trouble in my heart daily. Look upon me and answer me, O Lord, my God . . ."[25]

A Faith for Us

Guided by a new awareness of reality's multiple dimensions, we may discover that the perspective of science need not compel us to surrender a deeper quest for life's meaning. Let us now reexamine the complementarity of the scientific and religious orientations to reality.

We begin with God as Creator. Science is concerned with the processes by which one form of matter changes into another, or the process by which inanimate reality evolved into human form. Religion focuses on these processes as the manifestation of divine power and love. Science seeks to discover and harness the laws of nature. Religion is drawn to the Source of all life and the Orderer of Nature.

When Major Alfred Worden returned from his *Apollo 15* mission to the moon, he described his experience while orbiting the lunar sphere in his command module. Major Worden spoke as a scientist: "We were in this big metal vessel . . . built by man . . . an essential oasis in space. . . . there is no noise aboard, no sound . . . none of the usual vibrations of flight because there are no engines pushing you, only the laws of nature, (orbital mechanics) taking you around and around on this smooth voyage about the moon." The major spoke also of "the apparent evidence of a great deal more volcanic activity in the moon's past."[26]

Major Worden's observations constitute an *I-It* report on his orbital flight. He used elaborate scientific equipment to increase our knowledge of the moon.

Were there other sensitivities unleashed during the major's orbital flight around the moon? If he had been moved to a posture of prayer, he might have borrowed the words of the biblical agadist who once declared:

> O Lord, our Lord, how glorious is Thy name in all the earth. . . . When I behold Thy heavens, the work of Thy fingers, the moon and the stars which Thou hast established, what is man that Thou art mindful of him? . . . Yet Thou hast made him but little lower than the angels and hast crowned him with glory and honor. Thou hast made him to have dominion over the works of Thy hands. . . . O Lord, our Lord, how glorious is Thy name in all the earth.[27]

The *I-It* perspective enables the James Wordens to build a space capsule and orbit the moon, explore its surface, assess its age, and confirm man's power and puniness. The *I-Thou* perspective enables one to perceive himself as part of the vast, purposeful creation in which he has been given significant power and responsibility.

I-It empowers man to analyze the development of complex from simple forms in the evolutionary process. *I-Thou* inspires man to perceive the grand evolutionary drama as the ultimate working-out of the divine purpose. *I-It* empowers man to probe the dynamics of the human brain, the heart, or DNA (the molecule of heredity). *I-Thou* evokes man's appreciative wonder in the presence of Him who "renews daily the work of creation." *I-It* enables man to acquire and use his technological knowledge and power. *I-Thou* permits him to receive that knowledge and power as a divine gift, and to praise the Giver.

* * *

What now of God the Giver of Torah? In the domain of *I-It* a Torah text is a human document for analysis. One may compare its contents with other codes of law. A student may discern, for example, that some legislation appears to favor those classes in society which had much to do with its promulgation. Thus the Bible's legislation provides generous remuneration for the priestly class, reflecting man's tendency in all ages to regard as sacred that which is to his self-interest. The student may also explore ways in which the code needs to be reformed if it is to fulfill its own lofty intent. All such explorations are legitimate enterprises in the domain of *I-It*. The Torah is a document for analysis and reappraisal.

But he who studies Torah with the eye of faith and asks from the depth of his soul: "What does God require of me? How can I fulfill my covenant?"—he may discern in and through its words a divine "summons and sending." Buber writes:

> My own belief in revelation . . . does not mean that I believe that finished statements about God were handed down from Heaven to earth, but rather it means that the human substance is melted by the spiritual fire which visits it and there now breaks forth from it a word, a statement which is human in its meaning and form and yet witnesses to Him who stimulated (inspired) it and to His will. We are revealed to ourselves and cannot express it otherwise than as something revealed.[28]

In the perspective of *I-It* the commandment "love your neighbor as yourself, I am the Lord" appears as a useful antidote to human egocentricity, a survival mechanism for the social order. In the perspective of *I-Thou* those same words may address me as a personal commandment and demand a personal response. I accept responsibility for an order of being which I may confirm or betray by my actions. I must affirm the sacredness of every human personality, not because it is good for society or because I wish my neighbor to do the same, but because I am accountable to an *Eternal Thou*.

Most significantly, the ultimate values by which I feel obliged to live are not the products of my creative imagination, but the gift of a commanding and loving presence.

One can believe in and accept a meaning or value, one can set it as a guiding light over one's life if one has discovered it, not if one has invented it. It can be for me an illuminating meaning, a direction giving value only if it has been revealed to me in my meeting with Being, not if I have freely chosen it for myself from among the existing possibilities . . .[29]

* * *

What of the third affirmation of agada—that God acts in human life to fulfill His purposes? As historians deal with the political, economic, and psychological factors contributing to a sequence of events, a historian who stood at the Red Sea would reconstruct that event in terms of a strong tide and the vulnerability of the Egyptian rulers. Such is the perspective of *I-It*.

The perspective of *I-Thou* views history as a dialogue between God and man. God acts in history to fulfill His purposes. In this perspective one encounters miracles. What is a miracle?

Let a religious scientist offer a definition: " . . . miracle may be defined informally as an event in which God is sensed to be present and working out His purposes of love and redemption in an especially wonderful, mysterious and convincing way. . . . according to this conception whether or not such an event can be explained scientifically has nothing whatever to do with the question of whether it is a genuine miracle or not."[30]

A miracle is an event which inspires man's awe and is perceived as a manifestation of God's redemptive power and love. Buber adopts this view of miracle in his interpretation of the crossing of the Red Sea. Let us follow his account.

We do not know where the pursuers caught up with the fugitives. . . . wherever it may have happened there begins a natural process or a series of natural processes (whether a combination of tides, with unusual winds . . . or the effect of distant volcanic phenomena or the movements of the sea) which, together with a daring advance on the part of the Israelites and a destruction of the Egyptians, whose heavy war chariots are caught in the sand or the swamp, leads to the saving of one and the downfall of the other.[31]

What then is the miracle? Buber concludes:

> the real miracle means that in the astonishing experience of the
> event, the current system of causes and effect becomes, as it were,
> transparent and permits a glimpse of the sphere in which a sole
> power not restricted by any other is at work. To live with the
> miracle means to recognize this power on every given occasion as
> the affecting one.[32]

Miracles are perceived in the realm of *I-Thou*. They are
events which evoke man's awe, mediate deliverance from evil,
and are received as a sign of God's power and love.

We already noted that a scientifically trained man can share
this sense of miracle. Let physicist Schilling testify again:

> We are no longer inclined to deny the reality of the unexpected
> bursting forth, of glowing health where incurable illness seemed to
> prevail; the revival of the seemingly completely crushed spirit; the
> compelling eruption of utter goodness or beauty or sensitivity out of
> the seemingly unmitigated evil . . . the redemptive transformation
> of even hatred and love. Indubitably these are realities and realities
> that do not occur every day, but when they do happen and are
> sensed as extraordinary manifestations of the power and purposes
> of the ultimate and the transformation of situations for good, then
> the need arises for the concept of the miraculous.[33]

Some of the miracle stories of the Bible may be compared to
good theater. The action and dialogue of a two-hour stage play are
not literally what we would see and hear in an average two-hour
segment of everyday life. The coincidences are unusual, the
characterizations exaggerated, the dialogue sharpened, the plot-
line streamlined. A two-hour play is not the equivalent of any two
hours of life. Nevertheless such drama at its best reveals some
essential truth of life. If we open ourselves to the dramatic
experience, we leave the theater with heightened sensitivity and
enlightenment. We say: "This is life."

A good miracle story—like good theater—telescopes and
refocuses our experience in a dramatic way in order to illumine

our lives. God's power and grace are actually present in the "normal" events of life (the birth of a child, the redemptive power of true love, the marvels of the normal heartbeat, the glory of a sunset). But we often take for granted or totally ignore the everyday manifestations of God's redemptive presence. It is the melodramatic event (the hair-raising escape from slavery, the unexpected recovery of a chronically sick infant) which inspires the word *miraculous*. A miracle story is agadic drama. It is the biblical storyteller's way of heightening our awareness of God's great gifts in our everyday life. A miracle is an event which inspires awe, involves deliverance from some evil, and is perceived as a gift of God. Miracles occur in the realm of *I-Thou*.

Conclusion

In this chapter we have attempted to explore the impact of modern thought on the world of agada. The conflict between belief and unbelief in our time has been described variously as a battle between science and religion, between reality and illusion, or between reason and unreason. In truth the conflict, if there be one, pits those who affirm an infinite source of power and love at the heart of life's mystery against those who deny it. It is a battle between those who reduce all man's images of God to a psychological phenomenon and those who believe with Buber that great images of God fashioned by mankind "are born out of real encounters with divine power and glory."

Modernity has precipitated a conflict of faiths. There are those who believe that the only truth man can respectfully proclaim is that which derives from his immersion in the world of *It*, with its experiments, analyses, and "objectivity." And there are those who insist that the world appears to man not only as *It* but as *Thou*. The language of agada bears witness to man's encounter with the *Eternal Thou*. It is the language in which we speak of our life as covenant with God.

We have come a long way in fulfilling the Bible's promise of dominion. From our modern standpoint, our prescientific ancestors sought mastery through prayer or priestly blessing over that which we now know is better revealed to and controlled by the mind of the scientifically trained technician. Our concern for weather conditions leads us more to the meteorological station than to the synagogue or church. If I am ill I am less concerned about my physician's praying habits than his mastery of the discipline of modern medicine. If I must make a choice, I would prefer my doctor to be a great diagnostician rather than a religiously sensitive person.

On the other hand, my healing may be considerably enhanced if he is both. The full realization of man's human potential requires that he be a citizen of two interdependent realms—the world of *It* and the world of *Thou*. Modern man has learned that God rules the world through ordered and intelligible structures of nature and that man's dominion requires him to understand and accommodate to these structures. But man can ill afford to be fascinated by the gift and forget the giver. *I-It* empowers him better to negotiate with life's physical perils. *I-Thou* alone can endow his life with the gift of meaning.

The danger of modernity is that man remains at this juncture technologically nouveau riche. So mesmerized is he by the solid and trivial, the noble and terrifying fruits of modern science, that he has often depreciated or even attempted to deny the reality of the world's *Thou* dimension. Yet those who predict that man will become increasingly "postreligious" as the new century dawns might well consider that man, for all his preoccupation with the world of *It,* remains more essentially related to the realm of *Thou*. Loren Eiseley eloquently cautions man not to forget this basis of his humanity.

> It is not sufficient any longer to listen at the end of a wire to the rustling of galaxies; it is not enough even to examine the great coil of DNA in which is coded the very alphabet of life. These are our extended perceptions but beyond lies the great darkness of the ultimate Dreamer who dreamed the light and the galaxies. . . . Let us remember the self-fabricator who came across an Ice Age to look into the mirrors and magic of science. Surely he did not come to see himself or his wild visage only. He came because he was at heart a listener and a searcher for some transcendent realm beyond him-

self. This he has worshipped by many names even in the dismal caves of his beginning.[34]

Many men today may find it awkward to speak the language of agada. Formal worship is difficult for some, and stories of God's relationship to man may be embarrassing. But in his life, if not in his words, modern man continues to reflect intimations of transcendence. That is the theme to which we now turn.

V · Where Then Is God?
Signs of Sacredness in a Secular Age

God says to Israel: would that they
forsook me and observed my commandments,
for in so doing they will come to know me.
(Jerusalem Talmud)

I HAVE NEVER FORGOTTEN those dark angry eyes and the sunken cheeks, or the bitter grunt in response to my first greeting from the door of the hospital room: "How are things today?" Almost the moment I uttered those words, they seemed unconscionably inane. But then how does one greet a tall, once handsome man in the prime of life, who is suffering the physical indignities and the emotional anguish of terminal cancer?

In succeeding days I entered the room simply with a "Shalom" and strangely felt more at ease in his presence. His flashes of anger and ill-disguised envy were eclipsed by gestures of unmistakable gratitude for my regular visits.

My hospitalized friend was a psychiatrist, a dereligionized ethnic Jew who felt that the world of agada was a beautiful but arcane system of self-deception, a way of sweetening the real story of man's cosmic fate. "I wish I could believe it," he sighed. "It would come in handy, especially now."

During one visit my friend seemed unusually mellow. He turned to me and in a halting, confessional tone, said what he had never told anyone else, not even his wife or children. "Ever since I was a child, I recited some prayers each morning and night. I have never stopped doing so."

94

How did my friend regard this "archaic gesture"? Was it a childish fixation he was unable to outgrow? Was it an embarrassing skeleton in his emotional closet? Did this blemish deny him the accolade of full maturity?

Or was it something he cherished but could not integrate into his world of psychiatric reductionism—a precious intimation of a primordial faith which violated the secular canons of his vocational life? I did not press the issue, nor did he elaborate. Thereafter he appeared to me as a kind of spiritual marrano. Overtly he professed a particular brand of secular modernism: the trinity of id, ego, super-ego had supplanted the agada's world of God, Torah, and Israel. Freud was his rebbe, but secretly he continued his ties to that broader, deeper framework of meaning. Each morning before listening to his patients he talked to God.

My friend succumbed several months later. At the funeral I kept his secret. I did not accuse him of having been an underground believer or even a man captivated by an irrepressible longing for the bonds of faith.

The phenomenon of "underground" prayer continued to intrigue me. How many others, devotees of a nonreligious world-view, live secretly in the world of agada, and why the cover-up?

I have encountered other instances of secret or suppressed religious gestures. A college student heard me speak of the religious view of life as a "sense that musical, artistic, intellectual talents, like life itself, are ultimately a divine gift." After the worship service, the young man told me: "I like what you said. In a way I feel it, but can't bring myself to proclaim it."

Why should young people in a synagogue feel embarrassed to express prayerful sentiments yet enter a religious-camp situation and respond with spontaneous affirmations of faith? It may be because the synagogue is a fragmented island of institutionalized piety in a world from which most God-talk has been exorcised, whereas the camp establishes a total religious community in which such sentiments are actively reinforced.

In the Middle Ages a villager had to mobilize great personal courage to affirm a nonreligious world-view. He was swimming against the cultural stream. In certain parts of our society, the professing believer must still manifest the courage of nonconformity. Specifically, a psychiatrist who professes the halacha and agada of Freud without denying the traditional covenant of faith may be perceived by some colleagues as breaking unwritten canons of professional orthodoxy.

The secular bias of modern culture has much to do with the decline of formal religious affirmation, but we may remain more religious than we feel comfortable professing. Conversely, if a resurgence of public interest in religion or a greater openness to religious sentiments is present on campus today, at least one factor is that the campus culture itself has become more encouraging and more supportive of such feelings and interests.

Whether or not we use the traditional language of Jewish God-talk, do our words, gestures, acts, reveal "signals of transcendence"?[1]

Does the God who is Creator, Giver of Torah, and Redeemer find a place in our lives if not in our formal declarations? Do the marks of religious faith (gratitude, wonder, accountability, hope) continue to invade our so-called secular existence?

Intimations of God the Creator

Let us examine the traditional agada in which God's creative power is proclaimed. The first chapter of Genesis speaks of unformed chaos prior to God's creative word: "In the beginning God created the heaven and the earth. Now the earth was unformed and void, and darkness was upon the face of the waters."[2] Man does not appear until the sixth day. The rabbinic agadists ask: Why did God not create man at once? Many replies were given. Two concern us at the moment. Man was not created at once, says the agada, lest he assume that he was a partner with God in the very formation of the world. Alternately: he was created last so that if man grows haughty, he may be reminded that even the gnats preceded him in the creative scheme.[3]

Clearly the affirmation of God as Creator implies the *creaturehood* of man. To be human is to be conscious of an order of being which precedes us; to be aware of a limiting reality over and against us. In the first as in the twentieth century, to be a person is to live with a sense of dependence upon a power or powers beyond the directly perceptible or controllable world, whether such a limiting reality be called fate, destiny, or God.

One of the most obvious ways by which man acknowledges an ultimate limiting reality over against him is the gesture of swearing. We swear in situations of high frustration when we feel thwarted or threatened by an impinging and constraining power. Interestingly enough, such acknowledgment often is a form of God-talk and is present even among those who profess not to believe in God. Many a doctrinaire atheist will be heard to use expressions like "God damn it." The use of such language is itself unwitting testimony to a transcendent power before whom (which) we live our lives.

But surely the heart of the faith that God is our *Creator* is linked not only with *threat* but with *fulfillment,* not only with *denial* but with *grace.* Nathan Scott phrases the issue well. "To affirm God's existence . . . is . . . to declare as a matter of radical faith, that Being is steadfast, reliable, gracious and deserves our trust. To say that God 'exists' is, in short, to say the Wholly Other, the uncreated Rock of reality is for us, not against us."[4] Such indeed is the declaration of the Genesis agada. A world is ordered by God's word, "and behold it was good."

To what extent does the sense of an ordered, supportive cosmos inform the consciousness of modern man? There are intimations thereof even in man's conception of the message of science. We conceive the world as governed by dependable regularities. We speak of the "laws of nature." We count on the predictable properties of water, we plan our lives according to the seasons, we build our high-rise giants and our space capsules according to the laws of physics. Professor John Hayward reminds us that the very concept of law implies the "drama of a governing agency promulgating its decrees."[5]

Even our concept of evolution implies a cosmic judgment and purpose. All entities in the evolutionary scale must satisfy certain conditions to be deemed worthy of survival. And the dynamic thrust of the entire enterprise is toward the development of more complex forms of life. Moreover, the theory of evolution retains the sense that man is a distinctly higher form of being, the culmination of a millennial process.

Our activity in the world reveals some faith in the goodness of creation. We act as if the world is pregnant with promise. *Our very quest for understanding, whether pursued in the cancer laboratory or on a psychoanalytical couch, is a gesture of faith that man can unlock a secret which will fulfill the inherent value of creation.* The passion of research is fed by the faith that we are not simply teased through a labyrinth that leads nowhere but can, by the application of intelligence, discover illumination and healing. Are not the search for a cancer cure and the probing of the human psyche assertions of trust in the order of the created world?

We assume that the world to be explored within our psyche or the starry heavens is cosmos not chaos. Moreover, we act on the assumption that there is some congruence between our minds and the "mind" of the universe. As seekers of knowledge we betray a primordial trust that a "supreme intelligence" has fashioned an intelligible universe.

In a sense the supportive structures of life—the laws of nature—are so dependable that we are prone to take them for granted. Max Planck, the great theoretical physicist, once observed that the reason we adults no longer wonder is not because we have solved the riddles of life, but because we have grown so accustomed to the laws governing our world picture. And yet, Planck concluded, the question of why these particular laws hold and are operative is just as worthy of our awe and wonder.

There are occasions when that which we normally take for granted is called into question. At such moments we confront anew the mystery of being. We ask: Why anything? In later life the great analytic philosopher Ludwig Wittgenstein spoke of occasions when "I have to wonder at the existence of the world, I am then inclined to use such phrases as 'how extraordinary that anything should exist.' "[6]

Children commonly ask: Which came first, the chicken or the egg? Or: Who created God? Such questions are a child's way of encountering the mystery of Being itself. Periodically we too are pressed to the boundary question: how come there is anything? To ask such questions is already to acknowledge in some way the presence of an ultimate creative power in the universe, a Source of being.

*   *   *

We may ask the questions, but do we experience intimations of God's creative presence? The author of Genesis appears to have been overcome by God's creative majesty. The author of our prayerbook sensed man's abiding dependence on one "who in His goodness renews daily the work of creation." But what of those among us who stand outside the precincts of formal faith? Are there experiences in the life of "secular man" which may parallel those of the traditional believer?

The late Abraham Maslow of Brandeis University studied "peak experiences." His first recorded observations were based on personal interviews with 80 "subjects" and written responses by 190 college students to the following instructions:

> I would like you to think of the most wonderful experience or experiences of your life; happiest moments, ecstatic moments, moments of rapture, perhaps from being in love, or from listening to music, or suddenly being hit by a book or a painting, or from some great creative moment. First list these and then try to tell me how you feel in such acute moments,—how you feel differently from the way you feel at other times; how you are at the moment, a different person in some ways . . . (With other subjects the question asked rather about the ways in which the world looked different.)[7]

Dr. Maslow found an initial resistance even among those who later admitted to having such experiences. They seemed to fear that in the climate of scientific rationalism which still pervaded our campuses fifteen years ago, they might be stigmatized as unsophisticated squares, or, worse yet, abnormal personalities. But once resistance in the interviewee was overcome, a large number reported what in Maslow's terms were basically religious experiences.

These "peak experiences" may be associated with great moments of love (a mother fondling a newborn infant), moments of aesthetic appreciation (observing the spray of the sea on the rocks at dawn or dusk), moments of peak creativity (some meaningful and difficult task, adequately performed), or great moments of insight and discovery.

In the wake of such experiences persons may report feeling wonder, awe, reverence, humility, surrender, and even worship. They recall feeling that they are the recipients of gifts, owe for what they have been given, and are under obligation to repay by acts of goodness. Under these experiences the whole universe is perceived as a meaningful and integrated whole, "and one feels that he has a place in it, that he belongs in it."

When Dr. Maslow asked his subjects how different the world looked at such times, they replied that love and justice and all the values which we call religious appear to be part of the very structure of the world. The world is not just there; it is essentially good.

Commenting on this latter dimension Maslow says:

> If for the sake of argument we accept the thesis that in peak experience the nature of reality itself may be seen more clearly, and its essence penetrated more profoundly, then this is almost like saying what so many philosophers and theologians have affirmed; the whole of being when seen at its best, and from an olympian point of view, is only neutral or good and that evil or pain or threat is only a partial phenomenon, a product of seeing it from . . . too low a point of view. (Of course this is not a denial of evil or pain or death, but rather a reconciliation with it, an understanding of its necessity.)[8]

Maslow further contrasts ordinary cognition and peak experience. The first is highly volitional and therefore demanding, prearranged and preconceived. In the peak experience, the will does not interfere, it is held in abeyance. It receives and does not demand. We cannot command the peak experience! It happens to us. (This is reminiscent of Buber's distinction between *I-It* and *I-Thou*.).

If such testimony be believed, we have not lost our power to perceive the goodness of creation even though we may not always formally acknowledge the Giver. That inner fulfillment, that sense of wholeness, rightness, and well-being which must have inspired the agadists of old, is still felt—and not only by children, formal believers, and poets—but by each of us at least at some moments in our lives.

Although the "peak experiences" may not be commanded or programmed, are there life events which seem especially to trigger them? Can they be shared—public events? The event of birth is a natural evoker of the peak experience. Now that hospitals are encouraging the father to be present at the moment of birth, the emotional and spiritual impact on both parents will undoubtedly be heightened. While most religious celebrations of the gift of life occur considerably later than the emergence of the child from the womb, that moment when mother and attending father touch the infant for the first time may well be a peak experience. One woman in my congregation suggested that we need a liturgical expression (agada) to embody our feeling of awe and gratitude, closer to the moment of birth. Her point is that even if no formal liturgy celebrates the moment of birth, its potential as a peak experience is considerable.

What of the social dimensions of the peak experience? Several weeks before writing this chapter I spent some time at a youth camp. The high point of that interlude was the celebration of the Sabbath. The camp was transformed into a singing, dancing community, celebrating the gift of life and the precious joy of fellowship. The normal work schedule was suspended. We lived by Sabbath time. The festive attire, the special food, the worship in an outdoor chapel, all played a role. Unquestionably the participants were "turned on." Without exception they admitted to feeling a communion with each other and a special at-homeness in the world. We seemed attuned to the vital frequencies of a mysterious, wonderful universe.[9]

The Feast of the Sabbath brought under its spell a goodly number who would deny being especially "religious." Reflecting on that event, and our reactions to it, I recall the words of Harvey

Cox: "Religious language including the word God will make sense again only when the lost experiences to which such words point become a felt part of the human reality. If God returns we may have to meet him first in the dance before we can find him in the doctrine."[10]

Intimations of God: Giver of Torah

The rabbinic agadists ask: Why did God create man on the sixth day and not before? Two additional answers now concern us. The matter, said the rabbis, is comparable to a king who intends to invite an honored guest to a banquet at the palace. First the king sets the palace in order and provides all the elements for a festive banquet, then he invites his guest to enter. So, say the rabbis, at the time of creation, God set the world in order and then invited his honored guest to enjoy the glory of creation.[11]

Another answer: God created man on the sixth day so that as soon as he appeared he could immediately manifest his accountability to God by fulfilling a divine commandment—by observing the Sabbath.[12]

These agadists remain faithful to the story of Genesis. Man is the climax of the creative process. He has a unique place in the order of being, a special dignity and honor. That is his gift from God. To be a person is to be conscious of divine gifts and to be able to celebrate them in a special way. The Sabbath is given to us, not the beasts, though we are ordered to provide for their rest also.

To be human is also to be accountable to God for the quality of one's life. In other words, God the Creator is also God the Giver of Torah. The Sabbath is at once both a gift and a command. Through the Sabbath man both celebrates his gifts and acknowledges his responsibility to God.

Similarly the Genesis agada proclaims man's dignity under God as both gift and command. Early in the pages of Genesis, man's special kinship with his Creator is imprinted on the human soul ("In the image of God created He man"). But long before the giving of the Torah at Sinai, Noah is reminded: "Whosoever sheddeth a man's blood, his blood shall be shed by man, for in the image of God did God create man." [13]

The gift of dignity is also a command to respect the dignity of all God's creatures. The rabbinic agadists elaborate upon this theme. "Why did God create a single man to begin with rather than a whole universe of men?" Answer: to teach the sacredness of each person. "He who saves a single person, it is as if he saved an entire world, and he who destroys a single soul, it is as if he destroyed an entire world." [14] *God the Creator is God the Giver of Torah. He who forms man in His image, commands that the inviolable dignity of each man be confirmed by others.*

In the world of agada man acknowledges God as the source of grace and as the source of commandments. The ultimate commandment is linked to the supreme creative gift: life itself. Though modern man may not always formally celebrate the grace of God, he does, as we have seen, experience (with awe, reverence, humility, and gratitude) the goodness of creation. *Does a person who is unable formally to acknowledge a "divine commander or giver of Torah" also speak and act as if he were accountable to some transcendent reality for the quality of his life?*

At some point in the confirmation year, I will confront my class with this problem: As you leave this building you see a blind man, holding a tin cup. The cup is half-full of coins and dollar bills. You may easily dip into the cup, snatch a few bills, and escape without detection. In fact, let us assume that no one will witness your act. No one will ever question you about it. Let us further assume that there are some things at the corner drugstore you would like to buy and would now be able to purchase. Should you perform such an act? The response of the class is (thank God) a predictable no.

RABBI:	Why not? (I take the role of the devil's advocate.)
STUDENT:	You wouldn't want it done to you, Rabbi.
RABBI:	It's not being done to me, I am doing it to him.
STUDENT:	He's helpless, you are taking advantage of his blindness, Rabbi.

RABBI:	Why shouldn't I? If he were big and able to see, I wouldn't be able to steal from him. Here's my chance.
STUDENT:	Suppose everyone did it, Rabbi.
RABBI:	I'm not concerned about what everyone would do. I am doing it. Why shouldn't I?
STUDENT:	Something teaches us it is wrong, Rabbi.
RABBI:	Suppose your parents and the majority of citizens in the city voted that it is right to steal from a blind man. Would you think it is right?
STUDENT:	No, it would still be wrong, Rabbi.
RABBI:	Okay, why?
STUDENT:	My conscience would bother me . . .

The dialogue continues in some such form. Students are surprised by the depth of their feeling and frustrated by their inability to support such "gut reactions" with unassailable arguments. Each why leads to a new reason and a new question.

These students find themselves wrestling with the root of our obligation to another person, with the ultimate premise of our moral imagination. Few if any of the students say simply: "God commands us." (If they did, this chapter would have no point.) But they are manifesting a faith in the inviolable sanctity of a human being, in the inalienable dignity of another person. The attachment of absolute value to a person is not simply derivable from the physical or social sciences. We live under the commandment to respect the image of God in every man, though we may not speak of it as a commandment or speak of man as created in God's image.

In his book *The Moralist*, Allen Wheelis strived to explain man's consciousness that certain acts are absolutely wrong, irrespective of any attempt by other persons or even the state to condone them.

We can't prove it, but we know in our hearts that some things are wrong in a way that no legislation could ever make right. . . . We know, even if the legitimate murder of Jews in Nazi Germany had, by virtue of the triumph of German armies . . . been supported by the enactments of similar laws and the instigation of similar procedures in all countries of the world, that all these laws would still be unjust, that no consensus of lawmakers could ever make them right. [15]

But why is it wrong? Wheelis contends that an earlier generation might have referred the issue back to God. This option, says Wheelis, is not open to modern secular man. And yet when the author describes the root of man's moral consciousness, he argues that man is the discoverer, not the creator, of right and wrong, and he characterizes man's moral sensitivity in terms which appear suspiciously religious.

> We are more than we can know, so we cannot be guided by rules that conform only to that part of ourselves which we can understand and communicate. We are what we do, but we are more than we intend. . . . As rules of the game cannot be part of the play, so rules of life must be beyond our living. The knowledge of good and evil is something we must seek to find, not aspire to determine. [16]

Linked to the sense of moral responsibility is our capacity for guilt. It is fashionable to discredit guilt as part of the overkill aresenal of Jewish mother (à la *Portnoy's Complaint*) or to pooh-pooh it as a neurotic symptom. Nevertheless guilt remains the badge of our humanity. Like other human capacities, including intellect and sexuality, guilt may be distorted. An entire profession is devoted to healing the wounds of irrational guilt. But surely we need to distinguish between neurotic guilt feelings and existential guilt, even as we must distinguish between lust and love, or casuistry and rational analysis. Neurologically the same nerve endings may be engaged, but the phenomena are not identical.

Existential guilt assails us not because our mother was like Portnoy's or because of the repressed traumas of our childhood, but because "each man stands in an objective relationship to others; the totality of this relationship constitutes his life . . . it is his share in the human order of being . . . for which he bears responsibility." [17]

Existential guilt arises from failure to fulfill our responsibility. Our guilt reflects that sense of being held to account which is the mark of our humanity. Such is the guilt described by the agadist in Genesis after Cain kills Abel. God calls to him: "Where is your brother Abel?" He replies: "Am I my brother's keeper?" But he hears God calling him to responsibility. "Your brother's blood is crying to me from the ground." [18]

Man's capacity for existential guilt is reflected in much of general literature. Joseph Conrad's great sea story *Lord Jim* tells of a sailor who abandons a sinking ship for a raft without informing the other passengers of their imminent doom. After all, he rationalizes, there weren't enought lifeboats for everyone anyway. Jim is later obsessed by a sense of moral failure, and Conrad builds a great novel by taking the issue of Jim's guilt seriously—"as if the obscure truths involved were momentous enough to affect mankind's conception of itself." [19]

A modern novel by a gifted Israeli writer focuses on a Jewish clown who is haunted by the memory of his past. This Jew clowned for the Nazi commander of a concentration camp and for the doomed inmates in order to save his own life, while his family was taken to the gas chambers. His rationale: they would have been taken anyway, I spared them from realizing their true fate by lightening their minds. But the memory assaults him and drives him mad. He cannot absolve himself from responsibility. [20]

In his drama *After the Fall,* Arthur Miller contends that no one can stand before the chimneys of a Nazi extermination camp and feel totally clean. To acknowledge our own capacity for evil and to stand accountable for our sins is the mark of our humanity. The destructiveness manifest in my personal human relationships and the evil wrought at Auschwitz are ultimately cut of the same human cloth. To symbolize the link, the characters in the drama play out their own personal selfishness and exploitation of each other against the backdrop of a wall from a concentration camp coiled with an ugly tangle of barbed wire.[21]

Intimations of God the Giver of Torah may be discerned not only as we explore the major premise of our moral reasoning, or confront the reality of existential guilt, but by focusing on our sense of life as sacred vocation. We yearn to discover and fulfill that which is intended for us, that which will permit us to call our life blessed. The heroes of Saul Bellow's novels bear articulate witness to this "longing for sacredness."

Henderson, the fifty-five-year-old Connecticut Yankee, lives on a farm with wife and children. He is blessed with freedom, affluence, high social status, yet he confesses: ". . . there was a disturbance in my heart, a voice that spoke there and said, *I want, I want, I want!* It happened every afternoon, and when I tried to suppress it, it got even stronger."[22]

Henderson is a picaresque hero, a man of gentle madness whose yearning leads him to Africa. There he adopts the role of a Rain King. He returns from his extended escapade with a greater capacity to love. Bellow will not permit us to dismiss his hero as a cranky neurotic. He who cries "I want, I want" also explains: "Oh greatness . . . I don't mean pride or throwing your weight around. But the universe itself being put into us, it calls out for scope. The eternal is bonded onto us, it calls out for its share." [23]

The biblical *where art thou?* also overtakes another Bellow character. Moses Herzog is a middle-aged academician who stands on the very brink of total disintegration. The earlier promise of high academic achievement has faded. He is nursing the wounds of a disastrous second marriage and has lost custody of his children. Yet somehow Herzog succumbs neither to madness nor despair. "Evidently I continue to believe in God. Though never admitting it . . . . My behavior implies that there is a barrier against which I have been pressing from the first." [24]

Elsewhere Herzog confesses the credo of the believing agnostic. In the spirit of Henderson he exclaims: ". . . we owe a human life to this waking spell of existence, regardless of the void. After all, we have no positive knowledge of that void."[25]

This same sense of accountability, of living under the terms of a contract, is most explicit in Bellow's later novel *Mr. Sammler's Planet.* Toward the end of the work, Sammler, an elderly survivor of the Holocaust, stands by the corpse of his nephew benefactor and prays:

Remember, God, the soul of Elya Gruner . . . . At his best . . . He was aware that he must meet, and he did meet . . . the terms of his contract, the terms which, in his inmost heart, each man knows as I know mine, for that is the truth of it—that we all know, God, that we all know, we know, we know, we know, we know.[26]

The sense of ultimate responsibility for the quality of one's life, which in agada stands unequivocally rooted in the commanding presence of God, continues to haunt the literary imagination and the consciousness of so-called postreligious man. Bellow's heroes are generally more religious than they feel comfortable professing. Their affirmations are hedged with escape clauses. But their words, gestures, deeds reveal that they live under the pressures of a contract—or shall we say a covenant?

In effect, Mr. Sammler has recited his own version of the traditional Jewish prayer (agada) El-male-rachamim, which is part of the liturgy of the funeral service.

In the conversations I have had with families between the death of their beloved and the time of the funeral, the mourners speak to me as if there is a transcendent standard by which the quality of their beloved's life must be judged. They seek, sometimes with a strained earnestness, to proclaim that the life of their beloved was good. The bracket of death starkly compels our awareness that life is a contract, the terms of which "each man knows as I know mine." At its best the eulogy is an agada proclaiming that within his mortal limits a particular human being now deceased "did meet . . . the terms of his contract."

Next to the ritual of mourning, no event so effectively evokes and helps express this awareness of a life contract as the High Holy Day service, that autumnal convergence upon the synagogue by many who are conspicuously absent during the rest of the year. Why this lingering deference to the sanctities of Jewish life?

Many reasons have been advanced for the full house on the High Holy Days, but the most cogent is not expressed often enough. Vast numbers of Jews come to synagogue on those days because the liturgical theme (the agada) of that season responds to the deepest sensibilities of even so-called nonreligious Jews. We are a year older. Another chapter in our book of life has been completed. We do not deny that something is expected of us, or that at least in some ways we have failed to fulfill our responsibility.

The liturgy proclaims: "Our God and God of our Fathers, let our prayers come before Thee. Turn not away from our supplication, for we are not so presumptuous and stiff-necked as to say before Thee that we are holy, righteous and have not sinned. But verily, we have sinned, we have sinned, we have transgressed, we have done perversely." [27]

We need confirmation that we are worthy despite our flaws, and that new opportunities will be granted us to more adequately meet the terms of our contract.

In the preceding paragraphs we have attempted to identify traces of transcendence, intimations of belief in a "Giver of Torah" even among those who may not formally acknowledge the God of our Fathers. Such transcendence appears as we wrestle with the ultimate ground of our moral judgments and passions, in existential guilt, in our sense of life as sacred vocation so aptly revealed by the literary imagination, and in our response to the consecration of the New Year or the limiting reality of death.

Intimations of a Particular Covenant

These intimations of God's commanding presence impinge upon persons of all faiths and of "no faith." Traditionally, however, there is a particular convenant between God and Israel. God's convenant with Adam and Noah is followed by his covenant with Abraham. The convenant of Abraham yields special obligations. The Torah contains demands which are incumbent upon sons and daughters of the convenant only. What intimations of God's commanding presence touch us directly as Jews? Are there specifically Jewish imperatives which function as commandments of the Torah and have a transcendent claim upon even the formally nonreligious Jew?

First of all, the Jewish community, it may be argued, has resisted the implications of its own crisis of faith at Auschwitz.

Jews have been assaulted with special virulence by the value-defying atrocities of the twentieth century. No group had more reason to conclude that good is simply what the powerful define as such. After all, many a Nazi, as far as we know, was able to attach moral significance to the annihilation of the Jewish people. How natural for us Jewish survivors of the Holocaust to deny that there is a Giver of Torah—a transcendent source of value.

By and large, however, Jews have failed to rally around synagogues which are based on the assumption that "God is dead." Such humanistic synagogues have appeared, but they have not proliferated. Why not? Eugene Borowitz suggests that for all our despair over the silence of God at Auschwitz, Jews have not been prepared to conclude that there is "no standard of value at the heart of things, and seeing around them the growing evil effects of a value-free view of things, American Jews began to realize that there are some things they stand for and believe in."[28]

Our inability to rally around the "godless" synagogue is in part a visceral awareness of the link between genuine values and a transcendent source of good and evil.

So much for the particular Jewish intimations of a Giver of Torah in a post-Holocaust world. Are there any specific imperatives which press their compelling claim upon us and function as particular commandments in our lives? In the introductory chapter I tried to suggest that even secular Jews need to feel that history yields obligations; hence there is a continuing resonance among our people for the commandment "know ye the heart of a stranger, for you were strangers in the land of Egypt." That this commandment remains functionally operative is attested by the philanthropic thrust of the Jewish community in America and by the special uneasiness with which Israelis played the role of conqueror in the occupied Arab territories of 1967. Morris Bober, Bernard Malamud's Jewish grocer in *The Assistant,* is not far off the mark when he encapsules the Torah in the words: "for everybody should be the best, not only for you and me." The rabbi eulogized Morris Bober with the words: " . . . he was true to the spirit of our life—to want for others that which he wants also for himself."[29]

Most fundamental of all is the continuing resonance of the

commandment to survive as Jews. The acceptance of the burden of the covenant is described by the rabbis in contrasting agadot. One rabbinic agada portrays Israel as hesitant to accept the Torah at Sinai. Presumably our fathers intuited that the Jewish vocation could be hazardous, whereupon God suspends the mountain over their heads and exclaims:"Either you be My people or here will be your burial place."[30] Another agada depicts God offering the Torah to many people. Each refused. Only Israel replied: "All which the Lord has spoken we shall do and we shall hearken."[31]

Peoplehood remains the primary aspect of Jewish self-consciousness in the modern world. It imposes a claim upon even the nonreligious Jew which functions as mitzvah—as commandment. It presses upon him when he is "proud to be a Jew" and when he does not wish to stand up and be counted as a son of the covenant.

This commitment to remain a Jew and to see that his children transmit the identity to their children betokens a primordial claim which he is not free to reject and may not wish to reject. Israel's covenant-boundness may be alternately perceived as a burden and a privilege.

What evidence exists for the Jew's covenant-boundness? Analyst Ernest van den Haag suggests that a Jew finds it more difficult to casually shed his identity than a Christian his Christianity. He characterizes the "Jewish mystique" thus:

> Jews may call themselves humanists, or atheists, socialists, or communists; they may indifferently or passionately repudiate any reason whatsoever for remaining Jews; they may even dislike Jewishness and feel it—to use an apt metaphor—as a cross they have to bear. They may deny its existence in scientific terms . . . [but] They won't give up being Jewish even when they consciously try to, when they change names, intermarry, and do everything they can to deny Jewishness. Yet they remain aware of it, and though repudiating it, they cling to it; they may repress it, but do act it out symptomatically. . . . Unconscious or not, at least some part of every Jew does not want to give up its Jewishness.[32]

One may, of course, grant that most kinsmen feel a covenant-boundness, but interpret this phenomenon as a "negative identity,'' a defensive response to the residual barriers by which the non-Jewish world still invites us to keep our distance. Such a view has been argued most consistently by Jean-Paul Sartre. The non-Jewish world, says Sartre, essentially defines the Jew. Covenant-boundness is nothing more than a direct response to anti-Semitism. The Gentile world still perceives us as Jews. Therefore we are forced to accept our fate and make the best of it.[33]

But such a view is by no means the only option. There are many who can identify with Israel's fervent acceptance of the covenant—who feel that we remain custodians of a precious truth, though many would be hard pressed to delineate it and readily admit to being less than the most faithful witnesses thereof. Still they say and feel: ''I am proud to be a Jew.''

The classical agadist also acknowledged a relation between *seenah* (the world's hostility) and *Sinai* (the Jews' covenant commitment). Israel anticipated that carrying the burden of the covenant in an unredeemed world would not be easy, that the very presence of hostility was and is proof that the burden and the privilege (the mission of Israel) have not yet been discharged.

The day to which the Jew bears charter hope has indeed not yet dawned. On the day when being Jewish no longer exposes one to special hazards anywhere in the world, on that day the covenant may lose its primordial claim. Then the Jew may no longer be commanded to survive as a Jew, for on that day ''the Lord shall be one and His name one.''

Until then, even the Jew who does not profess to believe in God, the Giver of Torah, still *hears the commandment* to be a Jew and to transmit the burden-privilege to his children. In this perspective Emil Fackenheim has explored and understood the remarkable renaissance of commitment to Jewish survival after Auschwitz.

> Jews throughout the world—rich and poor, learned and ignorant, believer and unbeliever—were already responding to Auschwitz, and in some measure have been doing so all along. Faced with the radical threat of extinction, they were stubbornly defying it,

committing themselves, if to nothing more, to the survival of themselves and their children as Jews. . . . In the age of Auschwitz it is in itself a monumental act of faithfulness . . . [34]

Traditional agada enumerates six hundred and thirteen commandments deriving from the "Giver of Torah." Fackenheim suggests that post-Auschwitz Jews live under the six hundred and fourteenth commandment: "Jews are not permitted to hand Hitler posthumous victories."[35]

I have tried to suggest that intimations of traditional covenant faith, the sense of living with the terms of a contract, have not eluded the consciousness of even the "secular" Jew. He may not easily speak of a "Giver of Torah," and he may distinguish between his personhood and his Jewishness, but in both roles he continues to feel a "summons and sending."

Such intimations of transcendence are exquisitely expressed by the anthropologist Loren Eiseley.

Most animals understand their roles but man by comparison seems troubled by a message that it is often said he cannot quite remember or has gotten wrong. Implied in this is our feeling that life demands an answer from us. That an essential part of man is his struggle to remember the meaning of the message with which he has been entrusted. That we are in fact message carriers. We are not what we seem. We have had a further instruction.[36]

Intimations of God: The Redeemer

The God who appears in the pages of agada not only creates and commands. He also helps, redeems, saves. Biblical agada speaks of God the Creator preeminently in the first pages of Genesis and of God the Giver of Torah most dramatically in the twentieth chapter of Exodus, when Moses ascends the mountain and returns with the tablets of the law. God the *Redeemer* is manifestly celebrated somewhat earlier in Exodus when the slaves are liberated from Egyptian bondage. Following their redemption, the Hebrews exclaimed: "Who is like unto Thee, O Lord . . . doing wonders. . . . The Lord shall reign forever and ever."[37] Pursuing the theme of this chapter to its logical conclusion, we now ask: Where in the consciousness of modern "nonreligious" man do we find traces of trust in a Redemptive Presence?

Curiously enough, our very speech preserves such intimations. Even as swearing (God damn it) reflects a lingering sense of a transcendent limiting reality, so the exclamation "thank God" preserves the sense of a transcendent saving power impinging upon us. The self-conscious agnostic will be careful to say "thank goodness" in response to a redemptive experience, but many a confirmed agnostic has been heard to proclaim "thank God" when reflecting upon a threat from which he was liberated or a crisis that was favorably resolved. Thus do our idiomatic expressions reveal what our deliberate professions may deny.

The experience of grace (redemption) frequently invades our life as a surprise—an event hoped for but not fully anticipated: the high fever subsides and we are told the crisis is over; impending failure is reversed by a stunning success; the fear of total rejection is dissipated by an act of bountiful forgiveness or love; a devastating defeat is unexpectedly followed by new opportunities for fulfillment. Whether we respond to such happenings with a prayer of thanksgiving, a spontaneous exclamation of "thank God" (thank goodness), or simply a sigh of relief, such occasions nurture our visceral trust in the redemptive promise of life.

Intimations of faith in redemption may be found in the moral imagination of children. A child requires that a story have a "happy ending." He needs to confirm the triumph of the good and the just over the demon and the oppressors. Children demand reassurance that life is trustworthy, that there is an order of existence which may not be violated with impunity, and that our nobler impulses can find fertile soil upon the earth.

Though the loss of innocence overtakes us and we discover that good guys may finish last, nevertheless, as adults, we also feel pressed to celebrate a moral order in the world. Many a professing cynic will still instruct his children to cherish integrity and compassion. He who may sardonically recount the triumph of ruthless businessmen in the marketplace, or recite a dirge over a corrupt society, will still flinch from the logical conclusion. He is not prepared to counsel his children: "Be a bastard and you won't get hurt."

We cannot bring ourselves to offer such cynicism as final counsel because, on some level, we believe that goodness is at the heart of life's meaning, that the sanctity of man finds ultimate reinforcement in the soul of the universe.

Such belief is a perpetual struggle, hardly reinforced consistently by the events of our lives. At times we echo the lament of the talmudic skeptic that "there is no justice and no righteous judge," or find no trouble understanding the cry of the psalmist, "O Lord, why hast Thou forsaken me?" But the psalmist's last word is a reaffirmation of a hope: "All the ends of the earth shall remember and turn unto the Lord . . . for the kingdom is the Lord's and He is the Ruler over the nations."[38] We may be less overtly theological, but we too continue to celebrate a redemptive power, a nourishing goodness at work in the universe.

We continue to prefer happy endings to the stories of life and leave the cinema unreconciled to "realistic" dramas which deny us emotional closure. It may be argued that this penchant for a cinematic triumph of justice is wish-fulfilling fantasy, but it may also be taken as intimation of a spiritual order revealed to the deepest levels of our being.

Popular culture seems, at the moment, less hospitable to our need for spiritual reassurance. The classical Western more directly paralleled the form of traditional agada: John Wayne's encounter with the cattle rustlers, his initial setbacks, and his ultimate victory (ending with a triumphal gallop toward the sunset) permitted us to feel the threat of evil, even as we symbolically reaffirmed the reality of a moral order.

The current cinematic vogue sneers at the John Wayne or Gary Cooper syndrome. It has become fashionable for the outlaws to gallop triumphally toward the sunset.

This new cinema may reflect in part man's age-old ambivalence toward authority. (We all fantasy a successful pursuit of the illicit, a defiance of moral sanctions.) Often, however, such outlaw-heroes qualify for our sympathy because they possess some redeeming personal virtues and because the official guardians of the city are considerably more venal than they. If so, such cinema obliquely makes it own moral statement: the triumph of good may not always be simply identified with the victory of the authorities. Indeed, part of our current political crisis in America is the dearth of credible heroes in the establishments of the land.

Nevertheless the need for moral heroes persists, and it reflects, I submit, more than a wish-fulfilling jag, but an intuition about an order of life. Such an order may be affirmed on terms less flamboyant and more sophisticated than the old Westerns. Indeed one variant of the new cinema offers a hero considerably more vulnerable to pain and defeat than the bullet-dodging John Wayne who, nonetheless, projects great moral authority.

Consider the portrait of Sam ''The Lion'' in *The Last Picture Show*. He is not an invincible warrior on a handsome steed, but the aging, weather-beaten proprietor of several small business establishments (including a bankrupt movie theater) in Anarene, Texas. Anarene is becoming a ghost town. The surrounding oil wells have dried up, and Sam's business prospects have drastically shriveled. He has tasted defeat not only in the marketplace but in the world of romance. The great love of his life did not prosper. Life bruises him. Sickness and death stalk him.

But Sam is profiled against the bleak, gray backdrop of Anarene as a man of deep moral strength. His integrity is unassailable. He lives his life as if there is an order which ought not be violated. And we, the audience, like some of the younger protagonists in the film, are invited to identify with his testimony. The conventional hallmarks of cinematic triumph are denied him. (He does not get the girl, and he dies before ripe old age.) But his imposing moral presence binds us to a spiritual order of truth and value which, through him, we are drawn to acknowledge and affirm.

I have tried to suggest that we adults no less than our children continue to respond to stories which confirm the reality of a moral order in the universe. The cinema and the TV situation drama are par excellence the agada of secular man.

For further intimations thereof we may explore the personal and public sector of our lives. Each of us feels the need to think well of himself, to justify his acts in moral terms. Even the most dereligionized persons may retain a lingering trace of the faith that we live in a universe in which we are more likely to prevail if we deserve to prevail.

Nations also reflect the need to justify their policy in moral terms. This is as true of us as of our adversaries. Each seeks, through its official spokesmen, to label the other aggressor. Why this need for national self-justification? Why not simply assert one's nation's right to all the power it can attain? Why must national policy be defended in moral terms?

Such self-justification attests a lingering sense that if we are right, we deserve to have our cause triumph and are more likely to see our claims vindicated. Though historical experience may often strain the credibility of faith in a moral universe, and the actual conduct of men and nations often belies it, *we continue to search for historical signs of a moral order, for evidence that the power that commands us to be accountable does in fact call all persons and nations to account.*

In our liturgy we Jews continue to proclaim this faith. During the High Holy Days especially we acknowledge the morality of history, i.e., the kingship of God. In the midst of reigning injustice we pray that "the dominion of arrogance shall pass away from the earth."[39] Our sense of history as an arena of judgment has been secularized, but its religious roots stand revealed to the discerning eye. Consider the humanistic liberal who makes a fervent plea for black liberation on grounds of pragmatism: either we give blacks a stake in our society or we spawn violent anger which will engulf us in a web of destruction. Such formulations of enlightened self-interest, though formally devoid of theological terminology, bear striking resemblance to the words of the prophet-agadist Isaiah, who warned the people of his day: if you want peace, rest, tranquility for yourselves, then "give rest to the weary."[40]

Similarly the Marxist vision of a proletarian triumph and the emergence of the classless society is a secularized messianism. In effect, the Marxist preaches that there is a transcendent power in history assuring the defeat of those who oppress their neighbors. I am not at the moment judging the adequacy of the Marxist and capitalist claims but contending that each appeals to man's abiding sense of a moral order in life.

A lingering faith in God as the Judge of Nations has much to do with the current malaise in America today. The protracted Vietnam War, which despite our power denied us a convincing semblance of victory, has nurtured the growing suspicion (even the passionate conviction) that we did not win because we did not deserve to win.

Such a view occasionally invaded the editorial pages of our secular newspapers. Witness, for example, the words of James Reston of the *New York Times*.

> . . . what happens in the world over the longer perspectives of history is not really decided by military or economic power alone. The United States has more military or economic power than any other nation on earth, and this has been true for more than a quarter of a century, but its military power did not work in Vietnam. . . . It has not really proved that power alone determines the destiny of the human family, or that nations anymore than individuals are immune to the moral judgments of history. . . . there is a moral judgment of history on nations as well as individuals and this is the point that the man of power seems to miss, even after all the failures of power in Vietnam and elsewhere.[41]

Many of James Reston's readers, far more emancipated from the world of religious faith than he, believed that the Vietnam War chastened a great nation which abused its power.

At this writing the United States has but recently emerged from the Watergate scandal. Above the din of partisan politics hovered the strong conviction that the White House reaped the whirlwind for inexcusable negligence and a ruthless arrogance. Many persons formally emancipated from the claims of biblical faith perceived a note of retributive judgment in the spectacle of a President, elected by a landslide, suddenly compelled to resign or face impeachment. Even the "secular" American has not lost his capacity to discern the signs of a moral order in history.

A nation and its leaders not only find their fortunes interpreted in moral terms, but feel pressed to judge the present level of achievement even at its best in terms of still higher standards. As Robert Bellah has observed, "every society is itself forced to appeal to some higher jurisdiction, to justify itself not entirely on its actual performance, but through its commitment to unrealized goals or values . . ."[42] There are always persons whose lot needs to be ameliorated, whose dignity must be enhanced lest we be found wanting and are judged accordingly.

The implication is unmistakable: if we strive toward still higher goals, we shall find ourselves blessed with success and well-being. The world is hospitable to our redemptive vision. Even in a secular age the biblical notion of nations weighed in the balance by the God of history remains very much with us.

Israel's Rebirth as Sign of Grace

The world of agada did not regard history's verdict as unambiguous. There were those who viewed the destruction of the Temple in 70 C.E. as a "punishment for our sins," and there were others who saw Israel's suffering as the price of serving God in a world which does not yet acknowledge His kingship.

At times history offered a dramatic vindication of a just God's redemptive power. At other times the "dominion of arrogance" sorely tested one's faith in God the Redeemer (e.g., the exile from Spain). In each and every case, the testimony of history was to be taken seriously. It could not be ignored. One was moved to declare either "Yea, my Redeemer liveth" or "Why hast Thou forsaken me?" Each declaration, in its own way, presumed a prior faith in a God who appears in the events of history as man's Judge and Redeemer.

The Jew has been schooled (through agada) to search for signals of transcendence in current events. Jewish faith has been most bitterly strained and most exaltingly confirmed by history. As we noted earlier, no event more virulently strained that faith than the Nazi era. *No event has been of greater redemptive significance to the Jew than the rebirth of Israel.*

After the Holocaust the Jewish people were desperately in need of an earthy, mundane, dramatic sign of redemption. Israel's rebirth was received on some levels, even by secular Jews, as such a sign of grace.

When in 1967 Arab rhetoric and troop movements raised a specter of another Holocaust, Jews all over the world realized, many for the first time, how deeply revelatory Israel's rebirth had been in 1948 and how Israel's survival now became a crucial sign that the Jewish adventure was not absurd. With fear and trembling we asked: "Is our sign of grace to be destroyed so soon?"

The reaction of world Jewry to Israel's victory under trial in 1967—gratitude, relief, awe—betokened a continuing need to find clues of meaning in our history. The significance of June 1967 for world Jewry revealed that even the nonreligious Jew remained captive on some level to faith in God the Redeemer.

A Structure of Meaning

The agada's three characterizations of God (Creator, Giver of Torah, Redeemer) are inextricably intertwined. Together they constitute a *structure of meaning*. God has fashioned a purposeful world (creation). There is a way (Torah) by which we can help to fulfill the promise of creation, and by which our performance is judged. He who creates a world and summons us to fulfill its promise is also active in the world to judge our performance and redeem our hopes.

Is there a structure of meaning in the actual life, if not the formal faith, of "nonreligious" man? Huston Smith compellingly argues that man today, however nonreligious, continues to organize his life in terms of five categories of meaning. The first is *trouble:* "It is the presence of trouble that threatens our primordial sense of meaning." Man usually responds to trouble with a second category of meaning—*hope:* "Those who suffer from bondage and confinement dream of freedom. Those who walk in darkness see in their mind's eye a great light." Hope assumes diverse forms, but all share in common "the prospect of a fulfillment which . . . exceeds the present." Hope takes the form of an unrealized goal which leads us to the third category of meaning: *work*. The spirit of man distinguishes between what is and what ought to be and mobilizes his energies to bridge the gap. Man's vision of possibilities "indentures him to the ceaseless mother-labor of creation, a constant reaching toward an ampler life."

To work effectively man must in some sense trust in the underlying foundations of his existence. He must have ground for believing that the goal is fulfillable. He needs to feel supported by the scheme of things. "Endeavor can . . . succeed only within a matrix that supports and sustains it . . . . to have confidence in life entails confidence in the sea that sustains it. A measure of *trust* is hope's strict correlate."[43]

The work toward a goal always implies on some level a confidence in the built-in (given) promise of life, or in a nurturing power that helps man fulfill that promise. This is so whether or not we actually proclaim with the psalmist: "Establish Thou the work of our hands, yea, the work of our hands, establish Thou it." [44]

In this spirit Buber explained: "An animal's actions are concerned with its future and the future of its young, but only man imagines the future. The beaver's dam is extended in a time realm, but the planted tree is rooted in the world of time and he who plants the first tree is he who will expect the Messiah." [45]

According to Huston Smith, the fifth and final category in terms of which man structures his life is *mystery:* "The awareness that whatever our level of knowledge, there is an immense gap between our actual experience and the total reality of which we are a part." [46] We suffer, hope, work, and trust in the presence of mystery. Neither hope nor trust, nor sense of mystery, need be consciously articulated, but they are man's most common response to trouble and are at once the catalyst and foundation of effective work.

Is such a structure of meaning simply the figment of man's imagination, a useful fiction which he projects on a meaningless universe? Are man's intimations of transcendence merely a useful mechanism which has no relation to the demands, possibilities, and promises of life?

Man *discovers* the great meaning of his life. He may shape but does not create such meaning. "It is neither exclusively subjective nor exclusively objective, but something of each. It emerges as man answers in continuing dialogue the beckonings that come from a world that envelopes us while transcending us and all that we know." [47]

The categories of trouble, hope, work, trust, and mystery are the *form* of man's quest for meaning. Agada provides its Jewish content. Agada is the story of the Jew's quest, struggle, and discovery that life is precious and good. Agada declares: "Our Redeemer liveth!"

A New Agada?

Whether or not secular man feels comfortable with the language of agada, he knows the limiting and redemptive reality which brackets his life. He is the receiver of gifts, is overcome by wonder, gripped by sacred accountability, and remains a prisoner of hope.

Our life, if not always our formal declarations, attests these "signals of transcendence" which agada was designed to evoke and express. If the experiences persist, do we need a new language to evoke, articulate, and interpret them? Does the postmodern Jew require a new agada to match his vision and yearning? To that question we must now turn.

VI · A New Agada?

The Torah speaks in the language of man.
(Babylonian Talmud)

THE BULGING ENVELOPE contained a Xeroxed copy of an article from *Playboy*. The sender was a confirmand of several years vintage. An accompanying letter suggested that the enclosed might be helpful the next time I discussed the creation of the world with the Confirmation class.

The brief illustrated article was titled "The Creation: A Mirthfully Mephistophelean Rescripting of How It All Began," by J. B. Handelsman. Each day of the original biblical agada is "rescripted" with an accompanying illustration. Sample:

> It occurred to God that although there was plenty of light, it seemed to come from nowhere in particular. Philosophically as well as scientifically it made no sense. Therefore God made the sun, throwing away the failures that were too hot or the wrong color. You can still see them, and they are called stars. He also made the moon and threw it away and you can still see that too. And the evening and the morning were the fourth day.[1]

The *Playboy* agada ends with God facing the consequences of man's free will.

> And the man and the woman played free will against God. They took chances, bought property, were fruitful and multiplied, went to jail, worshipped titles, turned to salt, mortgaged the railroads, mortgaged the air and the food supply. God asked Lucifer to take over and went back to solitaire, and the evening and the morning were everyday.[2]

123

Such a playfully irreverent revision of the Genesis agada serves as a useful point of departure for this chapter's theme. Many readers may concede the authenticity of the religious dimension but question the adequacy of the *symbols* used to embody, evoke, and express it. Does the old symbolism need a radical overhauling? Has the traditional agada lost its power to move us? Do we require a new language to "update" the intuition of meaning which, as we discovered in the last chapter, still plays a role in our lives?

Handelsman's God-talk is calculatingly "tongue in cheek" by contrast to the original Genesis story. But let no one conclude that whimsy and humor have no place in biblical agada. Quite the contrary. (Witness, for example, the story of Balaam's talking ass.) Rabbinic agada also eloquently attests a dry (and not so dry) sense of humor. We encounter the story in which God consults with the angels before creating man. To an angel they counsel against going through with it. They warn the Holy One, Blessed be He, that He is in for trouble. God ignores the angelic counsel and stubbornly persists with His creative plan. Alas, when the early generation begins to "play free will against God," the angels irresistibly exclaim: "We told you so!" Nevertheless, God commits Himself to bear with His creation, hoping that His confidence will ultimately be vindicated.[3]

Even more whimsical is an agada which depicts a confrontation between Rabbi Eliezer and his rabbinic colleagues.

On that day Rabbi Eliezer brought forward every imaginable argument [to support his case], but they did not accept them. Said he to them: "If the halacha agrees with me, let this carob tree prove it." Thereupon the carob tree was torn a hundred cubits out of its place—others affirm four hundred cubits. "No proof can be brought from a carob tree," they retorted. Again he said to them: "If the halacha agrees with me, let the stream of water prove it." Whereupon the stream of water flowed backwards. "No proof can be brought from a stream of water," they rejoined. Again he urged: "If the halacha agrees with me, let the walls of the schoolhouse prove it." Whereupon the walls inclined to fall. But Rabbi Joshua rebuked them [the walls of the schoolhouse], saying: "When scholars are engaged in a halachic dispute, what right have you to interfere?'' Hence they did not fall in honor of Rabbi Joshua, nor did they resume the upright position in honor of Rabbi Eliezer, and they are still standing thus inclined. Again he said to them: ''If the halacha agrees with me, let there be proof from heaven.'' Whereupon a heavenly voice cried out: ''Why do you dispute with Rabbi Eliezer, seeing that in all matters the halacha agrees with him?'' But Rabbi Joshua rose and exclaimed: ''It is not in heaven.'' ''What did he mean by this?'' said Rabbi Jeremiah. ''That the Torah had already been given at Mount Sinai. We pay no attention to a heavenly voice . . .'' Rabbi Nathan met Elijah and asked him: ''What did the Holy One, Blessed be He, do in that hour?'' ''He laughed [with joy] and replied saying: 'My sons have defeated me, my sons have defeated me.' ''[4]

The humorous tone of such agada must not obscure its earnest intent. Many a serious theological truth is declared in agadic jest. Note that the agada in *Playboy* pictures a God who has created the game and now leaves man to play it. He may be ''alive and well'' but is not getting involved. The talmudic agada (Rabbi Eliezer and the Voice from Heaven) suggests that God's creative plan provides for a great deal of human initiative. God is like a father who relishes his son's self-reliance and even takes defiance as a sign of the very independence he has tried to instill in the lad!

All versions of the Genesis story, whether from the Talmud or *Playboy,* remind us that agada is a work of literary art, a story fashioned by man. The ''original'' biblical story of creation is itself a burst of inspired poetry from an anonymous writer whose words were immortalized beyond his wildest dreams.

That our religious symbolism (God-talk) is necessarily human poetry does not impair its capacity to evoke and point to the transcendent reality before whom we live. By the same token, Einstein's formula $E = mc^2$ is a man-made symbol illuminating our understanding of a world outside the human mind.

* * *

Be it scientific or religious, all symbolism is fallible. From time to time we may need to alter our ways of speaking about God or the world because we have altered our ways of experiencing or thinking about them. This is certainly true in the realm of science. It may also be true in religion.

On occasion we may grope for a better way of *expressing* a time-hallowed belief. For example, our ancestors declared that God has compassion for man. The ancient agadist pictured God "weeping" over the destruction of Jerusalem and in some sense feeling the bondage of Israel and Egypt ("you and I went out of Egypt"). Do we need new ways of expressing God's presence and concern for us in the current traumas of life?

At the same time Jewish agada resisted the Christian image of God so loving man that He became embodied (incarnated) in human form. Speaking within a Christian context, an imaginative activist minister opened a meeting with the words: "O God who lives in tenements, goes to segregated schools, is beaten in precincts, is unemployed, help us to know You. . . . O God who is cold in slums in winter, whose playmates are rats, from four-legged ones who live with you to two-legged ones who imprison you, help us to touch You."

A contemporary Jewish agadist would be uncomfortable with such bold incarnational imagery. Yet we too may search for a more contemporary image than that of a God who weeps for the destruction of the Temple and shares in some measure the exile and oppression of His people. Can the Jews speak of God accompanying His children to the crematoria at Auschwitz?

All such new agada would be essentially an *idiomatic* revision—a new way of expressing an old truth. But some revision may be *theological,* a way of expressing a different understanding of God's relation to Israel and the world. Thus those who have called on Jews to stop speaking of the "chosen people" have in effect called for a new perception of God's relation to the peoples of the world.

We return to the central question before us. Does the modern Jew require a new language to respond to his contemporary religious needs? I shall contend that in many respects the traditional agada has not lost its power to speak to us, for us, and through us. Some idiomatic and theological revisions may be required and will be proposed on the following pages. At the same time, a number of suggested revisions do, upon careful examination, reinforce the power and truth of the "original" agada.

In this chapter we shall focus on four issues: (1) the personal imagery for God in agada (anthropomorphism); (2) the agada's way of dealing with the conflict between faith and experience; (3) the agada's understanding of God's relationship to the Jewish people; and (4) the agada's image of messianic fulfillment.

The Agada Is Anthropomorphic

One of the most common assumptions I encounter as a rabbi is that anthropomorphism (the image of God as person) cannot be reconciled with a mature, sophisticated understanding of life. "Surely, Rabbi, you don't believe that God is a superperson somewhere out there, do you?" How perplexed my interrogators become when I declare that the personal God-talk of Agada is less inadequate to me than any of the modern reconceptualizations.

The case for revision has been championed, among others, by Mordecai Kaplan, the founder of Reconstructionism, and has been most forcefully expressed by Rabbi Roland Gittelsohn, one of Kaplan's ablest disciples. Here is a sample of Gittelsohn's argument.

> . . . earlier man found it necessary to personify the forces he felt about him in the universe. He could understand the storm only as a cosmic temper tantrum, differing merely in degree from his own occasionally wrathful behavior. We have progressed far beyond that point as far as stories are concerned but still think too literally in terms of a cosmic person. . . . the purpose or order we perceive in nature, the exciting though sometimes excruciating development from protozoa to man . . . all this we should now be able to conceive as energy or power, or force, or intelligence rather than person.[5]

For many "modernists" an anthropomorphic God is primitive, childish, immature. On the other hand, for many believers, myself included, the image of God as energy or force diminishes the grandeur and intimacy of faith.

Religious language seeks to describe that mysterious Other which ultimately brackets our life and does so in terms drawn from ordinary human experience. The biblical agadist already understood the inadequacy of all his imagery. In Exodus God responds to Moses' inquiry concerning His name with the words: "I shall be as I shall be."[6]

Man's consciousness of God is a sign of his unique place in creation. Man's inability to find adequate words for his religious experience is a sign of man's finitude. But speak he must, and a way of speaking must be chosen. The agada speaks of God *as if* He were a person. In so doing, the rabbis remind us, "the Torah speaks in the language of man." This is the best way in which mortal man may, from his limited perspective, speak of the infinite God.

The medieval philosophers were embarrassed by the personal imagery for God. They felt such talk compromised divine purity and transcendence. Thus Maimonides painstakingly sought to translate the anthropormorphic assertions of rabbinic and biblical agada into abstract conceptual language. Generally Maimonides and his followers sought to deny any direct relation between the attributes of God and the characteristics of man. Maimonides was especially discomfited by any suggestion that God was corporeal or talked or lived in the sense usually attributed to man.

When we speak of God as merciful, claimed Maimonides, we are describing not God's essence—which we cannot know—but only what we infer from our human experience of God's world. The closer we seek to penetrate to the essence of God, the more we must rely on "negative attributes." To say God is One is to affirm that God is not to be compared to other beings. He is unique. To say that God lives is to affirm that God is to be distinguished from inanimate matter. To say that God is incorporeal is to distinguish Him from the material things or creatures, and so forth.

Revolting against the abstractness and remoteness of the God of the philosophers, the mystical movement (Kabbalah) took considerably more liberties than traditional agada in humanizing God. At some points the Kabbalists added a sexual and even an evil component to their image of the deity, the very mythological elements which the Hebrew Bible rejected in the pagan world.

The problem of God-talk is, as Gershom Scholem so well expressed it, how to speak of God in ways which *"preserve the purity of the concept of God without loss of His living reality."*[7] I feel this tension in my own experience. I sense the power of referring to God as one "who goes to segregated schools . . . whose playmates are rats." But I prefer that such overpersonalization be used sparingly. In such talk God is overly created in the image of man. On the other hand in depths of anguish I find it difficult to conceive of myself communing with an "energy or power or force."

The ancient rabbis observed this same tension. On the one hand they used bold, intimate imagery to describe God's kinship with man: God weeps over the destruction of Jerusalem, God prays, God permits himself to be defeated by His creatures, and so on. But the rabbinic tradition also maintains that the tetragrammaton (probably Yahweh, commonly mispronounced Jehovah), the primary name for God, was not to be uttered except by the high priest in the Holy of Holies on Yom Kippur. To this day the tetragrammaton, when it appears in print, is not sounded literally, but is represented by the word *Adonai* (Lord). Thus did rabbinic Judaism maintain the tension between intimacy and distance, between claiming to know Him so well and acknowledging God's ineffable mystery.

I prefer the classical agada's approach to the problem of anthropomorphism: use reasonably bold imagery and remind yourself from time to time that God transcends all our images.

Anthropomorphic imagery seems to express best both the *unique kinship* between man and God and the *distinction* between the finite and the infinite. Some traditional agada pictures God as the supreme exemplar, man's ultimate model. The Bible itself illustrates this view. In the poetry of Genesis we read: "And God said: 'Let us make man in our image, after our likeness and let them have dominion . . . over all the earth.' . . . So God created man in His own image, in the image of God created He him, male and female created He them."[8]

The human community reflects, in larger measure than any

other part of the world, some qualities perceived as attributes of the Ultimate One in the universe. Specifically the poet alludes to power. In power—"dominion over nature"—man finds a special kinship with God. Biblical agada also speaks of God as a moral model. "And the Lord spoke unto Moses, saying: 'Speak unto the children of Israel and say unto them, You shall be holy for I, the Lord your God, am holy.' "[9] A rabbinic agadist elaborates: "You shall be holy . . . O be like Him—as He is gracious and merciful, so be thou gracious and merciful."[10]

Man is uniquely capable of discovering values—of asking not only what he can do but whether he ought to do it. Man is uniquely a captive of moral passion which empowers him to dream and work for a world transformed by justice and love into the divine kingdom. The agada pictures man and God capable of sharing a spiritual vision, a sense of life's final goal.

As I was writing this section, my oldest daughter handed me a clipped-out newspaper excerpt of Dr. Spock's book (*Raising Children in a Difficult Time*). This particular segment dealt with the question of telling children about God. Spock considers the problem for parents who are humanists or agnostics—those who believe in certain virtues (love, justice, truth) but are not prepared to declare that such values have their origin in a reality beyond man or that such a spiritual reality can be described in personal terms.

When confronted by a younger child (preteenager), Spock advises, parents should "take into account the child's desire for something definite. If I believed in spiritual values and could accept the idea of God as the symbol of man's aspirations, I'd tell my child, yes, I believe in God. My reservations can wait several years until the child is ready for greater subtleties."[11]

For myself the age of "greater subtlety" would elicit this explanation: we do speak of God as if He were a magnified person. We are using the best available poetic symbol. We are declaring that man's creative power, intelligence, consciousness, freedom, moral passion, are gifts from the ultimate reality in the universe. In our human experience we associate these qualities with persons rather than forces. Such anthropomorphic language provides the best way of imagining and speaking of the qualities which are linked to the highest rungs of the evolutionary scale. The age of subtlety does not require us to abandon speaking of God *as if* He were a person. It requires a sensitivity to the symbolic quality of all human language, especially that language by which we seek to express our relatedness to the transcendent mystery of life.

* * *

At its best agada's anthropomorphism also alludes to those characteristics which *distinguish* man and God. Man's life, says the psalmist, is like a dream, whereas "a thousands years in Thy sight are but as yesterday when it is past and as a watch in the night."[12]

Man as we know him is *essentially limited,* not only by his mortality, but in the comprehensiveness of his capacity to love. Deep concern is linked to our consciousness of an individual and our power to interact with such a person. We are essentially conscious of and able to interact with only a few persons on this planet. By contrast, God is imaged as Father of all, conscious of and concerned with the life of every creature.

In rejecting the personal language of agada, Rabbi Roland Gittelsohn rejects also this image of a God who is conscious of me as an individual. He argues: "I do not expect the President of the United States or even the Governor of my Commonwealth to be aware of my location, or conduct at any given moment. . . . if I am not important enough for the Governor of Massachusetts to keep track of my comings and goings, why should I require or expect such personalized attention of the governing power of the universe?"[13]

I would argue that anthropomorphic language best enables us to suggest not only kinship but *distinctness* from the infinite. Man's consciousness and love *are* limited by man's place in space and time. God is that personal presence who both transcends our individual lives and is capable of confirming our significance and worth as persons. Such imagery can be used to suggest ways in which man is distinguished from God. The God I affirm *is* conscious of my individual existence. What is not possible for the President of the United States or the governor of a commonwealth is possible for God.

One of the basic distinctions between man and God concerns the reality of an evil impulse. Man, so claims the dominant strand of the agada, is capable of pursuing evil, whereas God does not possess an evil impulse. Even in the presence of those events which challenge man's trust, the Jew has been taught to declare that "the Lord is righteous in all His ways, and holy in all His works . . ."[14] This distinction raises, of course, the problem which we turn to in the next section. If God is infinite power and goodness, why is there evil in this world? For the present, the point we make is that *personalizing the ultimate reality of the universe is the best way to point to both the kinship and the distinction between man and God.*

*   *   *

A second reason for preferring anthropomorphic imagery is that the relationship (covenant) between man and God finds its richest analogue in the relationship between persons. In moments of spiritual illumination we feel addressed and obligated, a claim is placed upon us, we are accountable, we are judged. That which can exercise such a claim, or evoke a faithful response, may best be imagined as a personlike reality.

The religious experience of being blessed, forgiven, loved in spite of failure is also best associated with personal relationships. Moreover the fundamental religious experience of being both held accountable and accepted in our brokenness—the central Jewish affirmation that a creative tension between justice and love is at the heart of human existence—that concept too is best described in personal terms.

The agada portrays a God who "shuttles" between the throne of justice and the throne of unconditional love. A contemporary agadist might describe the role conflict of God as that of an employer who has taken his son into the business. On one level the son must be judged by the contribution he makes to the goal of the enterprise, but he is, after all, tied to the employer as son to father. The tension we feel between being judged for *what we do* and loved for *who we are* is best lifted to cosmic proportions through the anthropomorphic image of a relationship (a covenant) between man and God.

Even the struggle for trust in the relationship may best be described as "man's quarrel with God." The arguments between man and God, richly etched in biblical and rabbinic agada, offer the best possible image for the crisis which man faces in his struggle to affirm the meaning of life.

One of the symbolic ways in which man proclaims his relationship to the highest is prayer. In prayer man speaks to God. Speech is the symbol of a bond between man and the infinite reality which brackets his life. In Judaism man speaks directly to God. Prayer loses its evocative power if we address an *It* rather than a *Thou*. We harness energies. We speak to and are addressed by persons. Significantly, even those who self-consciously reject the notion of personalizing God are inclined to retain the use of the *Thou* imagery in prayer.

We have been trying to suggest that at the very core of the religious experience in Judaism is a perceived bond between the finite and the infinite. Man is a creature capable of entering into a covenant with the ultimate reality in the universe. The characteristics of such a relationship as perceived by man—demand, forgiveness, quarrels, fidelity, betrayal—are best symbolized by the image of a personal God.

* * *

What is finally at stake in the use of anthropomorphic imagery is the *value* attributed to the highest reality. Man can be uplifted and inspired only by that which is at least equal to or transcends the significance attributed to his own level of being. In this regard Frederick Plotkin writes:

The idea of personality is, as it were, the window through which we look out upon the limitless beyond; it is the smoked glass through which alone we can behold the sun. . . . it is preferable to expand the idea of personality rather than to contract our idea of God. To think or to speak of the infinite in abstract and impersonal terms is unconsciously to liken him to forces lower, poorer and less full of vitality than ourselves, such as the electric current, or the life principle, or a tree. To say that God is "personal but something more" is to say that the creative principle must be higher than the highest, richer than the richest, more full of life than the most alive of all things it has produced.[15]

Our choice is between two inadequate modes of speech. His glory transcends all our images, yet if we feel impelled to speak, we need words. Liturgical agada acknowledges this paradox. The call to worship ("Praise ye the Lord who is to be Praised") is followed by a whispered declaration from Nehemiah 9:5 ("His name is exalted above all praises and blessings"). This in turn is followed by a public declaration ("Praised be the Lord who is ultimately praised forever and ever"). Professor Steven Schwarzschild's comment on this sequence is instructive:

This is an extraordinary and paradoxical declaration: on the one hand, the worshipper proclaims that God is so great, as it were, no praise can do justice to Him. The logical conclusion to be drawn from such a recognition would be to refrain from trying to praise Him. But, on the other hand, the worshipper immediately proceeds to do that which he has just stated to be impossible: he praises Him.[16]

The problem of symbolizing God has attained new dimensions in an era of women's liberation. Note the sweatshirt bearing the slogan "God is Good, She will Provide." I vividly recall a student in my college class disputing the adequacy of the male symbolism for God. Is this not a relic of the sexist, male-dominated age? she declared. If God is both infinite power and tender love, why not use male and female symbolism?

There are two choices here. Retain the traditional symbolism, but take ever greater pains to deny its literalness or adequacy, or reconceptualize God in male-female terms and risk the taint of paganism—which was the strategy of some Kabbalah. I prefer the first option, but the feminist concern highlights the critical issue. In speaking of God we must choose the lesser of several inadequate modes of speech. No one has convinced me that an alternative to the classical agada's personal God is any more adequate. Significantly, even those who argue that God is more like energy than person still prefer the words "Praised be Thou" to the words "Praised be It."

Agada and the Problem of Evil

We have already noted that agada is the language in which Jews struggled to reaffirm the gift of meaning even in the presence of life's apparent absurdity. The problem: how reconcile faith in a personal God of love and justice, who cares for all men and is the ultimate power in the universe, with an eleven-year-old girl's death from hepatitis, or a child's cremation in the ovens of Dachau? If He is, as classical agada maintains, the ruling spirit, then evil as well as good must be linked to Him.

The classical agada confronted such crises of faith in the Book of Job, the story of Rabbi Meir's two sons, and the vast literature devoted to understanding the destruction of the Temple and the subsequent conversion of Jerusalem into a pagan city.

We have seen that the agada attempted to confirm faith in a variety of ways: God's servants may suffer, but in time their trust will be vindicated (the messianic hope); the righteous suffer in this world, but will be rewarded in the world to come; we cannot understand His ways, but must trust in Him as a faithful son trusts his father, and so on.

Amid all the possibilities of dealing with the problem, two were unequivocally rejected. The agada wrestled with God for the gift of meaning, but refused to concede that life is devoid of meaning. Secondly, the ancient rabbis could not conclude that there are two divine powers in the world—a power of good and a power of evil—as did Zoroastrianism. While this "solution" would have divested God of all implication in evil, such an answer would have also divested God of that infinite power on which the believing Jew relied for the fulfillment of his noblest dreams. This solution sustains God's goodness, but diminishes His grandeur. It would also destroy the heart of monotheism—the unitary vision of life.

And so, despite the difficulty, the agadist declared that God is the Ultimate Reality before whom man lives his life. Our forebears sustained faith in God's infinite goodness and power. They chose to struggle with the problem of evil rather than dissolve it by crimping divine power or by assigning evil to another deity. Hence the daily liturgy proclaims God as "Creator of light and darkness, Maker of peace, Creator of all."

There are believers in our time who claim we need a new agada to resolve the crisis of faith. How, they argue, can man believe in an infinite source of power and love who permits Auschwitz or is implicated in the death of an eleven-year-old child from hepatitis?

One alternative is offered by Mordecai Kaplan. Let us, he says, speak of God only in relation to the gracious phenomena of life. God is "the sum of the animating, organizing forces and relationships which are forever making a cosmos out of chaos. This is what we understand of God as the creative life of the universe."[17] God is to be associated only with the peak experiences of our lives, but has no relation to evil. "Evil is chaos still uninvaded by the creative energy [of God], sheer chance unconquered by will and intelligence."[18]

Kaplan's faith in God undergirds his confidence that the universe "responds to man's creative powers," and that reality is so constituted as to endure and guarantee the realization in man of that which is of greatest value to him. "Whatever ought to be can be, even though it is not at present in existence."[19]

I find two objections to this new agada. First, it dispenses with personal imagery (discussed in the previous section), and second, Kaplan's God is not capable of being the ground of my faith in the ultimate fulfillment of the cosmic adventure. What of those forces "uninvaded by the creative energy [of God]"? Are they of the same potency? Do we have here an intimation of Persian dualism, of a cosmic battle between two divine powers, and if so, what is the basis of my faith that the good will prevail? Who or what is the ultimate ground of the universe, the reality which transcends both order and chaos? By seeking to solve the problem of evil too easily, Kaplan causes the dimensions of God to shrivel. His God is not able to respond to man's deepest metaphysical question: How come there is anything at all?

Another response to the problem of evil is offered by the late Henry Slonimsky. A beloved dean of the Hebrew Union College, Dr. Slonimsky focused on those traditional sources which accentuated God's dependence on man for the realization of his creative plan. Thus one agada takes Psalm 123 ("Unto Thee I lift up mine eyes, O Thou who sittest in the heavens") and renders it as follows: "If it were not for me (if I did not lift up mine eyes), Thou, O God, wouldst not be sitting in the heavens."[20]

On the scaffold of such agada Slonimsky builds the image of a personal but essentially limited God. "God in the full meaning of the term seems to stand for the end, not the beginning. On that day He shall be one and His name shall be one. He must be made one, and man is the agent in whose hands it is left to make or mar that supreme integration."[21]

Slonimsky's agada tells the story of a God who is Himself in the process of becoming. Man, in a very real sense, bears the total responsibility of bringing God into full being. Thus the evil in the world is that which man must overcome so that God's full realization may occur. The relation between God and man is a relation of "give and take or reciprocal enrichment, resulting in the slow change and growth not merely of man but God."[22]

Slonimsky's revised agada is appealing. He retains the personal imagery and takes seriously the implications of man's responsibility as a covenant partner. But I am troubled by the image of a "developing God" and by an agada which speaks of a covenant in which it is difficult to decide who is the senior (the more powerful) partner, God or man. Classical agada was dialectical. It regarded man's power as real but not ultimate. Thus man is summoned to work as if all depended on him and to pray as if all depended on God. By contrast Slonimsky's God, like Kaplan's, is not grand enough to be the ultimate ground of my hope. In this theology, man and God appear limited by a transcendent reality (evil) that is *essentially* bigger than both of them.

Groping for a New Agada

Can we reformulate an agada, rooted in the traditional monotheistic claim of God's infinite power and love, yet more adequate perhaps to the demands of our own struggle for meaning in the contemporary world?

The traditional agada offers a key in its notion of divine self-limitation. *Whereas man is by nature a limited being (with death as the most ineluctable mark of his finitude), God's limits are "self-imposed" in order to fulfill divinely appointed purposes.*

The concept of divine self-limitation is illustrated by a talmudic text which asks: "Why are Ezra's generation of Jewish leaders called 'men of the great assembly'?" What feat earned them this distinction? The agada responds that they restored the "old glory to the divine crown." Moses had referred to God as "the great God, the mighty and awesome." But Jeremiah, mindful of the prosperity of the wicked, could not affirm God's awesomeness. Daniel, conscious of the captivity of God's children, could no longer speak of God as mighty, but Ezra and his assembly restored God's glory by explaining that God's patience with errant man is itself a supreme sign of divine power.

> That indeed is his mightiness, that he subdues his inclination and grants long suffering to the wicked, and that in itself is proof of His awesomeness. Were it not for the fear of Him, how could one people [Israel] survive among the nations?[23]

Professor Eliezer Berkovits, a distinguished Orthodox Jewish theologian, elaborates upon this agada. Were God to give the wicked their just deserts the world could not stand. God's patience with the wicked, though it inflicts tragic suffering on their victims, is the price of the world's endurance. God's "self-restraint" in the presence of wickedness is a sign of God's overarching purpose: that the sinner return rather than be snuffed out, that man endure and be ennobled rather than destroyed. Yet even within the limits of divine self-restraint, God's power and awesomeness are attested by the wondrous survival of the people Israel.

Berkovits adds:

> Suffering of the guiltless is the indirect result of the decree of creation. The thought finds its moving expression in the awesome liturgy of the ten martyrs which is recited on the Day of Atonement. The very angels in heaven cried out bitterly: "Is this then the Torah and this its reward?" Whereupon a heavenly voice was heard: "If I hear another sound, I shall turn the world back to water and my throne's footstool (i.e. the earth) to total *tohuvavohu* (a formless void)."[24]

Thus does Berkovits retell the classical agada. Undeserved suffering is the price which God and man pay for the drama of creation and history.

A variant of this image of divine self-limitation is found in an agada spawned by Isaac Luria, the kabbalistic mystic of the sixteenth century. Let us turn for a moment to 1492. The year Columbus discovered America was the fateful year when Jews were expelled from Spain. Centuries of dazzling creativity and prosperity came to a dismal end. Spanish Jewry had fallen. Its most affluent members became wandering beggars. How would the people's faith in the God of history survive this catastrophe? The most important theological response came from a little town overlooking the Sea of Galilee.

To this day, if you visit the quaint, picturesque city of Safed, you can enter the synagogue where Isaac Luria prayed, meditated, and agonized over the fate of his people. What follows is a simplified capsule of Luria's agada.

Before God created the world all was God and God was all. To make room for a world, God withdrew unto Himself. This act of divine contraction or self-limitation (known as *tsim-tsum*) created space for a world. The drama of creation was alternately an act of divine power (grace) or divine self-limitation. God poured His spirit upon the world. The frame (the vessels) of the created universe could not contain His effulgent splendor. There was a cracking, a breaking (*shevirah*). Thus, from its inception, the world was flawed. Ever since creation, the world has been in need of repair (*tikkun*) or redemption.

The exile of the Jew is both a manifestation of cosmic disharmony and an opportunity for its repair. The Jewish people is assigned a special role in gathering up the scattered sparks of the divine spirit and fulfilling the intended goal of creation. Note that evil becomes not simply the wages of human sin, but part of the price which God must pay in order to fulfill His purpose in the creation of the world. This agada was the language in which Luria struggled to reconcile his faith in God's infinite power and goodness with the tragic dimension of human life. [25]

In my own struggles with the problem of evil, I have recast traditional agada with an assist from Isaac Luria. As a creature of the twentieth century, I have experienced both the *power* and the *silence* of God. And by appreciating His power, I have been better able to deal with His silence. Where do I find signs of a God "who renews daily the work of creation"? In my very existence this instant. Every breath and heartbeat points to the Giver of life. The drama of evolution, that tortuous trek from amoeba to man, discloses for me the glory of God. So does the marvel of growth and maturation, exemplified in a sapling or a little girl. I have been blessed with peak experiences.

Each time I search for understanding of the universe, through verbal inquiry, reading, or silent ruminations before a crackling fire, I act on the faith that there is order, pattern, and meaning, I pay witting or silent homage to an Infinite Creative Spirit.

God's gifts are manifold. He offers a world governed by dependable laws. The dependable structure of the universe is part of the blessing of creation. It renders science possible. It permits us to plan for the future. We can predict when the tides will ebb or the sun will rise. We may consume a liquid with the properties of water, confident that it will quench our thirst, not burn our gullet. We may count on the law of gravity and the principles of aerodynamics to catapult us across continents, even to the moon.

But God's gifts bear a price. God's manifestation of creative power is in itself also an act of divine self-limitation. Although I may be the most pious saint, if I jump into a ten-foot tank and cannot swim, the dependable properties of water will threaten, perhaps even terminate, my mortal years on earth. Similarly, the pressure systems of our weather develop according to the structure of meteorological law. Given certain conditions these pressure systems will produce tornadoes which God may not directly will or fully control. *I experience God's power in nature, and I also experience that divine self-limitation which is the price we pay for a lawful universe.*

With classical agada I too affirm that God acts in history. I experience God's power-purpose in the survival of my people. That power is symbolized by the Arch of Titus, which overlooks the Roman Forum. It was erected to commemorate the utter defeat of Judea by the Roman legions under Titus, and on it was carved a striking relief portraying the triumphal processional of the Roman victors bearing booty from the Temple in Jerusalem. Today, almost two thousand years later, the people of Israel lives, and the Third Jewish Commonwealth stands reborn on the site of ancient Judea.

When I seek for a sign of God in history, I am drawn irresistibly to the black man's quest for dignity. Here is a twentieth-century scenario for the ancient Haggadah. The God of history summons the Pharaoh within us to "Let My people go."

But He who is active in history is also at times hidden from history. He who liberated my people from Egyptian bondage hid His face at Auschwitz. Such "hiddenness" is a manifestation of divine self-limitation. History implies a dialogue between God and man. That dialogue requires some sharing of divine power. Man must be free to serve or betray the divine summons. *Freedom includes the power to defy the will of God.* Man is a creature who may say no to his Creator. Hitler is the demonic fruit of human freedom. *History is the scene of both divine power and divine self-limitation.*

In André Schwarz-Bart's novel *The Last of the Just,* Ernie, the hero, speaks with the doctor, a fellow inmate in the concentration camp. Each of them ponders that most terrifying question: If

God is good, why is an Auschwitz possible? The doctor replies: "When I was a gentleman, one of my friends used to tease me by asking if God, in His omnipotence, could create a stone so heavy that He couldn't lift it. Which is my position? I believe in God and I believe in the stone . . ."[26]

In nature and history we experience both God's power and God's silence. We experience the wondrous gift of life and the tragic curse of untimely death; the unyielding demand to free the oppressed and the ashes of the oppressed who were not freed. *Where does God's power end and His self-limitation commence? The drawing of that line is the mystery of divine providence.* Our prayers of petition are grounded in the hope that the line will be drawn in our favor. But, alas, our prayers are not always answered. We may ask: Why did God not save or heal me? Our hopes may be dashed when we experience the anguish of a man of faith.

A second unspoken question is part of our argument with God: Is creation worth the price? Granted that God does not directly will tornadoes or cancer or Auschwitz, He creates a world in which they are possible. Granted that the blessing of freedom may yield a Hitler, that a world of dependable physical law may yield a tornado, *is creation worth its price?*

The biblical agadists responded affirmatively. "Behold, God saw all that He had made and found it very good." The rabbinic agadists answers: "Yes, a man is called upon to praise God for the evil as well as the good." [27] Creation is worth its price. To confirm our faith, we too must say yes. We must assert our confidence that there is a "plus at the heart of the mystery." But there are moments in all of our lives when we are not certain. These are the difficult times in our quest for meaning.

Some believe that if modern man is to recover his faith in life's meaning, God may not be regarded as personal or as the Ultimate Source of Being (Creator of good and evil), but only as the "power that makes for salvation." Such a god is *essentially* limited, rather than *self-limited,* by his purposes. For some this radical revision of agada may enhance the capacity to affirm the meaning of life. For myself I prefer a view which strives to reconcile the infinite power and love of God with the reality of evil in a world He creates, sustains, and redeems.

Schubert Ogden has compellingly argued that religious experience, at its primary level, is an awareness of ourselves as part of an encompassing whole and the confidence that life so experienced is worth living. [28] The experience of evil challenges this primal faith. Agada is the variety of stories by which Jews seek to reaffirm that life is worth living..

The agadic framework of Judaism is exceedingly open. Different stories were told by rabbis during the major crises of Jewish life. (We dwelt at length on this in Chapter III.) The choice of agada was dictated by the situation and the temperament of the storyteller. All such stories, whether told by the ancient rabbis, by Mordecai Kaplan, Henry Slonimsky, Eliezer Berkovits, or you and me—attest both our struggle for and our confirmation of life's meaning. All are ways of retelling the agada of Genesis, "and behold God saw all that He had made, and it was good." All agada is a way of affirming that life is a precious gift, not a dirty trick—and that at the heart of the mystery, there is meaning.

God's Covenant with Israel

Agada is not only the words by which a Jew affirms life's meaning but the language in which he proclaims his share in Israel's covenant with God and in the particular destiny of the Jewish people. Through agada the Jew stands ever anew at Sinai (Praised be Thou, O Lord, Giver of the Torah) and continually role-plays his liberation from Egyptian bondage. Agada is the language of Jewish particularity—the words and stories by which a Jew symbolized his Jewish identity.

Characteristic is the agada which provides the script for the Jewish wedding ceremony. That liturgical agada celebrates the love of two Jews and invokes God's help as they seek to establish a "home amidst the people Israel worthy of praise." Such was the agada which celebrated the union of that boy from Iowa and the Jewish girl from Chicago.

There are many young people, however, who find such covenant-boundness, such commitment to establish a Jewish home, tribalistic and intolerably confining. They are not content to enter the universal community as a Jewish couple and find unacceptable any particularist claims which might qualify their universal loyalty. For them a new agada must govern the marriage vows.

The model wedding for two potential mates so inclined is a civil ceremony. They meet in the presence of a judge, neither as Jews nor as Christians, but as lovers and friends. Such a ceremony may be more than a civil contract. It may symbolize the transcendence implicit in the mystery of human love. I attended such a ceremony recently at a university chapel. The bride was Jewish, the groom of Protestant-Catholic background. A judge presided, but a friend of the couple led them in the recitation of a liturgy they had written for the occasion.

The ceremony began with a poem by e. e. cummings ("Love is more thicker than forget—more thinner than recall"); it ended with an Apache Indian poem ("now you will feel no rain—for each of you will be sheltered to the other"). And these were the vows: "We promise to be open to the ways of our love. We promise to be of this love more careful than of everything else. We shall respond truthfully and honestly to the needs and obligations that this union brings. We promise to understand, to discover, to create, to build for, accept, to share together the mystery that is life."

The ceremony included a commitment not only to "deepen their relationship" to each other, but to "understand more easily all others in the human community, to this end then must be a pledge each to the other and from them to that community."

The overtones of this ceremony were clearly religious: a sense of life and love as a mysterious and wonderful gift, a sense of ultimate accountability for the quality of their relationship to each other and other men, and a throbbing hope in the promise of the future.

Conspicuously absent was any commitment to a particular tradition, Jewish, Protestant, or Catholic. There was no promise to establish a Jewish home, no indication or affirmation in this event that each of these two persons had a share in a particular community of fate and faith.

This couple believed that all boundaries, all ideas, all commitments which in any way separate us from our neighbors, have outlived their usefulness. Let Abraham become simply Adam. This so-called higher wisdom is not new to us as Jews. It appears to tempt us in every age. Neither is it so wise. In its Latin root, the word *wisdom* signifies that which we can literally taste. Wisdom clings to earth. The wise person takes seriously who he is in his concrete particularity. He respects the tastes, the symbols, the stories, yes the agada, of his own past and wants to transmit them to his children.

The truth is that while Abraham must remember he is also Adam, Abraham must remain Abraham. There is no easy resolution of the tension between the particular and the universal. The wisest of persons strive to live with this tension creatively. Agada is unequivocally committed to Jewish particularism.

Let us consider now the larger issue. *May we expect a contemporary generation of Jews to accept the notion of a particular people, singled out by God for a special role in the divine scheme?*

Some, like Mordecai Kaplan, retain the value of Jewish particularism but have called for the elimination of the concept of a "chosen people" as racialistic and presumptuous. *Do we need a new agada which will reject the notion of chosenness?*

Agada is a people's interpretation of its history. Our history attests that in antiquity a group came into being who affirmed the sovereignty of a single, universal, imageless, creative-moral God, unencumbered by mythological counterparts, the ruler of fate, nature, history. This God (Yahweh) demanded exclusive loyalty from His worshippers, and His will was intended to govern every sphere of life. So much is "history of religion," but how did the covenant between this people and their God come into being? Why *this* people?

The agada itself seeks to understand the mystery of Jewish particularity. It links the covenant to an act of Israel's choosing.

God offered the Torah to many other peoples. They were not prepared to accept it. Then He offered it to Israel, and this people responded: "All which the Lord has spoken we shall do and we shall hearken."[29]

Subsequent interpreters from Judah Halevi to Kaufmann Kohler have also sought to rationalize the relationship between God and Israel. Halevi posited a biogenetic endowment which enabled this people to receive God's revelation.[30] Many centuries later the Reform theologian Kaufmann Kohler would speak of "hereditary virtues and tendencies of mind and spirit which equip Israel for His calling."[31]

But traditional agada also retains the notion of divine initiative. If in a sense Israel chose God, it is no less true that God chose Israel. Rabbinic agada preserves this nonrational dimension in the covenant.

> We would not know whether God chose Israel for His treasure or whether Israel chose the Holy One, Blessed be He; the answer is taught in the following: "And the Lord your God chose you." And whence do we know that the Holy One, Blessed be He, chose Jacob? As it is said: "Not like these is the portion of Jacob, for He is the creator of all things, and Israel is the tribe of His inheritance . . ." [Jeremiah 10:16].[32]

Can this agadic view of Jewish particularism be sustained? In my own judgment, yes and no. *We need to distinguish between the mystery of election (being singled out by God for a particular vocation) and the concept of special love.*

All attempts to fully rationalize the history of the Jewish people are doomed to failure. Why did this particular people come to believe in the God of the covenant? Why did this people come to represent a unique view of God and God's relation to man? Such answers as "ripe historical conditions" or "biogenetic endowments" or "creative genius" or "chance" are no more compelling or illuminating than the answer of agada. I am prepared to understand this people's uniqueness in the agadic terms of divine initiative (revelation) and the mystery of divine grace. *God singled this people out and the people responded.*

The agada's image of a people singled out for special covenant with God challenges us in every age to contend with our fate
and faith as Jews. We noted earlier that our historical *vulnerability has itself been a mark of our particularity*. The Jew has paid a
price for his covenant. Remember the rabbinic play on the words
seenah (hostility) and *Sinai*. Freud once quipped that the greatest
evidence of Jewish chosenness is the reality of anti-Semitism.
Hitler's singling out of the Jew has already been discussed in this
regard.

In the twentieth century we have also learned that nothing so
thoroughly discredits a seemingly idealistic cause as its resort to
Jew-hatred. The hypocrisy of the Soviet march toward a sup-
posedly classless society was unmasked by Stalin's fatal flaw. He
proved even more prone than the Czars before him to employ
anti-Semitism in the service of his ambitions. At the present
moment the openness of the Soviet system, its readiness to
accommodate diversity, is being radically tested. Of all the ethnic
and religious groups in that vast nation, the Jews find themselves
singled out as Exhibit A, an acid test of Soviet intentions, a
measuring rod of Russia's move toward or away from a closed
society.

Should the tender plant of American freedom be assaulted by
a repressive right or revolutionary left, there is little doubt that the
Jew will be among the primary victims.

What student of Western civilization can fail to be intrigued
by the Jewish witness to a society's state of moral health. By its
very being the Jewish people judges a society's distance from its
noblest goals, not because the Jew as an individual is better or
worse than his neighbor, but because by his presence the Jew
disturbingly reminds man of goals betrayed, of noble visions not
yet fulfilled.

*   *   *

A second sign of Jewish singularity we identified earlier as the
improbability of our survival. Classical agada itself dramatizes
the wonder of it all. At the very outset, the career of this people
was jeopardized by Abraham's journey to Mount Moriah. Had

Isaac not been spared, the story would have come to an end. In the saga of Jacob and Esau, the destiny of the people is necessarily placed in uncertain human hands. God must choose (as Isaac's successor) between Esau, who valued the birthright so lightly that he was prepared to sell it for some lentil soup, and Jacob, who valued it so much that he was prepared to cheat to acquire it.

The story might well have ended in Egyptian bondage if Pharaoh's chariots had prevailed, or at the foot of Sinai if the dancers around the golden calf had captivated the hearts of the people. The saga of Israel might also have ended in Canaan, through total assimilation, or at the time of the Babylonian exile, when ten of the tribes had already been lost.

History mingles with agada to tell the story of a remarkable survival. If Jewish suffering has sorely tested our faith, Jewish endurance has caused even the skeptic to be overcome with awe. In 1899, before the catastrophic events of our century, Mark Twain observed that "all things are mortal but the Jew. All other forces pass but he remains. What is the secret of his immortality?"[33] The language of Jewish faith still provides the most compelling response to that question. *Our vulnerability (anti-Semitism) and our survival are signs of our chosenness. "You are a people consecrated to the Lord your God. Of all the peoples on earth God chose you . . ."*[34]

Israel is singled out not only to be but to teach—as a "light unto the nations."[35] The son or daughter of the covenant is heir to a message and understanding of the covenant between God and all men which we may often betray by our actions, but which remains nonetheless the primary vision and substance of our vocation. Israel is heir to nothing less than a sustaining answer to the questions: Who is man? What his power and his limits? What his task? What his hope?

We shall examine this message and its contemporary significance for human culture in the next chapter. For the present, let me contend that the agada's image of Israel's *special vocation* continues to provide the basic rationale for the survival of the Jew. We have been entrusted with a message and a task. Our reason for being is not to be measured by the Nobel Prizes we accrue, or the cultural ferment we generate, but by the role we have been given by the Master of the Universe.

There be some who feel comfortable affirming only that Israel chose God. But once we ask why Israel did so, we lapse into a realm of mystery best encompassed by traditional agada: God singled this people out and the people responded.

*   *   *

I believe in the mystery of Israel being singled out for a divine vocation, but I reject the traditional agada's concept of special love as a key to the mystery. I cannot believe that God actively stimulates sibling rivalry. Classical agada did at times embody this concept of greater love. Thus Rabbi Berechia said:

> Heaven and earth were not created save for Israel, as it is said: "In the beginning God created," and the beginning refers to Israel, as it is said: "Israel is holy unto God, first of His choice fruits."[36]

One may mitigate the invidiousness of such statements by remembering the lot of the Jew in the early centuries of the common era. Persecution and the threat of a rapidly expanding church claiming to be the new Israel bruised the Jewish people's ego. The agada's concept of special love was a balm of reassurance whose utility did not dim in subsequent centuries.

Liturgical agada recorded both the anger of the Jew toward his persecutors and his own sense of spiritual superiority. The service for Passover petitioned God to pour his wrath upon the nations who knew Him not. The traditional adoration prayer offers praise to God for not having made the Jews like the other peoples of the world.

Reform liturgy has excised such sentiments, and in addition the early reformers made more explicit the universalistic implications of the traditional agada. Thus: "As Thou hast redeemed Israel and saved him from arms stronger than his own, so mayst Thou redeem all who are oppressed and persecuted. Praised be Thou, O Lord, Redeemer of Israel."[37]

I believe that God singled the people Israel out for a special role in history, *but not out of special love*. Moreover, the mystery of divine grace is also present in the experience of other men. I need not deny that Christian and Jew each has a role in the work of redemption. Even as our histories diverge, however, so the stories we tell about our relation to God differ. Jewish agada finds its Christian equivalent in the God-talk of the New Testament.

Since our religious self-understanding and our histories are different, each may be expected to remain faithful to the truth as it has been given him. Without compromising our distinctiveness, we have reason to acknowledge our common humanity and be zealous for our common dignity as children of God. The mystery of Jewish particularism need not be dissipated by modernity, nor need it be affirmed at the cost of denying God's relation to other people.

I believe that Judaism possesses a greater measure of religious truth than the alternative formulations of God's relation to man. I am not offended when Christians or Muslims make comparable claims for their covenants with God. Fidelity to what has been made known to us is compatible with the humbling realization that all our images bear the mark of our human fallibility. When all has been said, no God-talk can fully encompass God's reality or God's relationship to man.

True to the best we know, we are called upon to remain steadfast in anticipation of the day of the Messiah. One of the signs of the messianic age—when the goal of history is fulfilled—will be the emergence of a "pure language" reconciling men's conflicting images of spiritual truth and bringing them ever closer to each other and to God. Only "on that day the Lord shall be One, and His name One."[38]

Messiah or Messianic Age

Agada focuses on the contrast between reality and the ideal, between what prevails and what ought to prevail and will prevail someday in a world governed by God. Whether we turn to biblical agada—especially the prophets—or talmudic literature, or the traditional prayerbook, we confront the hope for the day when God's plan will be fulfilled.

This hope has been called the belief in the coming of the Messiah, or the messianic expectation. The term *mashiach* refers to one who has been anointed by God and whose act or presence will bring about, or at least signify, the dawn of a new age.

In the world of classical agada, the emphasis was placed at times on a personal Messiah, a descendant of the household of David who would be God's agent. In Isaiah we read:

> A shoot will spring from the stem of Jesse, and a sprout from his roots will bear fruit. And the spirit of the Lord will rest upon him. . . . Righteousness will be the girdle around his loins, and faithfulness the girdle around his waist.[39]

Elsewhere the emphasis is placed on the time ôf fulfillment rather than on a particular individual as its principal hero or agent. God is the central figure in the drama of redemption. Thus we read in Ezekiel:

> As I live . . . with a strong hand and an outstretched arm and with fury poured out will I be King over you, and with a strong hand and outstretched arm . . . will I bring you out of the peoples and gather you from the lands over which you are scattered . . . [40]

The messianic hope focuses on the people Israel. They will no longer be oppressed, but restored to their land. They will now be faithful to the lord—more faithful than their ancestors. But the hope also embraces other peoples. For all men will acknowledge the sovereignty of God, and peace and justice will prevail in the affairs of nations.

Many questions may arise out of our contemporary consciousness. Is the personal Messiah a viable symbol for redemption, or should we depersonalize the hope? How can messianism come to terms with a new Jewish state, with Israel restored as a center of Jewish sovereignty? Do we need new images of history's spiritual goal?

Let us consider first the preferred symbolism for redemption.

We know that tradition offers two conceptions. The classical liturgy embodies both in the Amida prayer:

> And to Jerusalem, thy city, return in mercy, and dwell therein as thou hast spoken; rebuild it soon in our days as an everlasting building, and speedily set up therein the throne of David. Blessed art thou, O lord, who rebuildst Jerusalem. [41]

The Reform movement discarded the belief in a personal Messiah from the House of David. Such an image was linked to the restoration of the Jewish people to Zion. It was this concept of restoration which, in part, made the personal Messiah unacceptable.

In addition a personal Messiah has seemed to affront the sensibility of man's rational temperament. How can we expect a single man, a mortal no less, and related to the dynasty of David, to appear on the scene in our time and proclaim God's kindgom. Besides, monarchy has become a political anachronism in the modern world.

On the other hand, one may argue that the retention of the personal Messiah is desirable. It dramatizes the hope in a form which has gripped the heart of our people for centuries. We need not take the image literally any more than we do when we speak of God as "*King* of the Universe," or as "our Father." It may be valuable to retain the personal image because of the characteristics of the redeemed society. Love, justice, and peace are most vividly imaginable in terms of a human model—a righteous ruler. Besides, redemption is most concretely mediated through the impact of other persons on our lives.

A contemporary liberal theologian has forcefully argued for restoring the agada of the personal Messiah. Dr. Steven S. Schwarzschild contends that the Reform movement's repudiation of that image in favor of a messianic age has, in effect, reduced a belief in God's redemptive power to nothing more than man's progressive march toward Utopia. The concept of a personal redeemer, he claims, revives the notion that man alone *cannot* bring about the kingdom. Man's efforts are relevant, but God must send the Messiah. Living in an age where man's arrogant moral pretensions have been shattered, we need an image of hope, he suggests, which accentuates man's reliance on the power and love of God. [42]

Rabbi Schwarzschild properly chides liberal Judaism for tending to reduce messianism to humanistic political utopianism. Nowhere does the agada regard the kingdom of God as man's progressive evolution toward the good society. Agada celebrates man's power but also duly acknowledges his limits. It is possible, however, to safeguard the irreducible divine role in messianism without retaining the symbol of a personal Messiah. After all, as we have seen, one strand of the biblical-rabbinic tradition did just that.

Having weighed the two images, I prefer the tradition's impersonal symbol of redemption. I prefer to speak of the messianic age rather than of a personal Messiah because histori-cally the greatest danger of idolatry has come from false indi-vidual claims to that title. This century has especially dramatized the peril of the personality cult, of the secular Messiah. Though the biblical and rabbinic Messiah was not regarded as divine, how strong is the tendency for mankind to offer, and authoritarian figures to demand, that worship which ought to be reserved only for God. For these reasons I prefer the traditional imagery which does not assign any particular mortal being a central symbolic role.

Whether we choose to retain the personal image or to focus on an age rather than a man may be as much a matter of temperament as anything else. Having expressed my preference, I feel no urge to press for one or another symbolic mode. Both are grounded in our heritage; both are intellectually defensible.

* * *

A more central issue is this: Do we need an agada which divorces the messianic hope from the concept of the gathering of all exiles and the restoration of Jewish sovereignty in Israel? The Reform movement answered that question with a resounding affirmation

in 1885, when a group of rabbis, meeting in Pittsburgh, proclaimed: "We consider ourselves no longer a nation but a
religious community and therefore expect neither a return to
Palestine nore sacrificial worship under the administration of the
Sons of Aaron . . ." [43] Instead Reform Judaism envisaged an age
where Jews could dwell securely in their respective habitats all
over the world. In 1885 it seemed that age was dawning, but by the
1930s the rise of Hitler had compelled a reassessment of Reform's
anti-Zionism. The Columbus Platform declared: "In the rehabili-
tation of Palestine, we behold the promise of renewed life for
many of our brethren. We affirm the obligation of all Jewry to aid
in its upbuilding as a Jewish homeland by endeavoring to make it
not only a haven of refuge for the oppressed but also a center of
Jewish culture and spiritual life." [44]

Then came World War II, the revelation of attempted Nazi
genocide and the rebirth of Israel out of the ashes of the
Holocaust. During the last decade the Reform movement has
reversed even more dramatically the anti-Zionism of its
nineteenth-century past. For a number of years now the anniversary of Israel's rebirth has been celebrated as part of the service
in the Reform synagogue. We gratefully acknowledge Israel as a
sign of grace in a terrible century, a ground for renewed hope in
our covenant with God.

But what relation can Israel have to the traditional messianic
hope? Surely no one is claiming that Israel is the messianic
kingdom. Not even Orthodox Jews believe the time has come to
rebuild the ancient Temple. What can it mean to pray "next year
in Jerusalem"? Many Jews who care to move there may do so, yet
most choose to live outside the boundaries of a sovereign Jewish
state.

An appropriate answer is suggested by the new Reform
liturgy, *A New Passover Haggadah*. In this Haggadah (or shall we
say agada) the phrase "next year in Jerusalem" is restored. Let us
examine the text and context.

LEADER: Peace!
GROUP: Peace for us, for everyone!

LEADER: For all people, this our hope.

GROUP: Next year Jerusalem, next year may all be free. (Next year in Jerusalem is ever the hope of our people. Still we affirm that all people will rejoice together in the Zion of love and peace.)[45]

What is the significance of this new agada? It restores the traditional phrase and creatively refashions its meaning in the light of a new historical reality. Israel is reborn, but the Messiah or the messianic age has not yet come. Next year in Jerusalem always meant more than simply a physical return of Jews to a place in the Middle East. The place evokes a vision of the ultimate dream of a world in which men acknowledge their kinship with God. The Jerusalem meant here is more than the concept of Jewish statehood. It is not so much a place as a condition, a way of life yet to be bestowed upon all God's children.

In this sense all persons, including Jews who now live in the city of Jerusalem, are exiled from God's kingdom. The world has not yet become a place where God or man can feel completely at home.

The Messiah or messianic age is always a symbol of man's ultimate goal. Such goals cannot be translated into simple, concrete political programs, but depend for their fulfillment on more than human effort alone. Messianism ever beckons man beyond that which appears presently within his grasp.

*   *   *

What images beyond restoration to Zion does the agada employ to symbolize the messianic kingdom? Are these images viable for us? In the world of agada, Elijah the Prophet is to be the herald of the new age. The Elijah ceremony at the Passover Seder table poignantly suggests the futurity of the messianic vision. We open the door. We reserve a place for him, but Elijah has not yet come. What does his name evoke?

Elijah was a prophet who spoke truth to established power,

as when he intervened in Naboth's behalf against the arrogant attempt of King Ahab to expropriate that commoner's property.[46] In premessianic times there is always a tension between power and virtue. Every establishment needs to be challenged by "prophets." Those in authority often possess power without goodness, and the good are often without power. *Messianism is the vision of an establishment in which power and goodness will be united as in the symbol of a righteous ruler.*

Another common experience of man is that he raises questions beyond his powers. At every turn the human quest for certainty is riddled with ambiguity and paradox. The talmudic sages declared that there are certain questions which will only be fully resolved when Elijah comes to herald the age of the Messiah.[46] Thus does the messianic imagery condition man to live with less than final answers to the questions he poses, to blend boldness with humility in the search for truth.

According to the Book of Malachi, when Elijah comes, "he shall turn the heart of the fathers to the children and the heart of the children to their fathers." [47] The tension between the generations is also an abiding reality in human history. The ultimate goal is to show respect without yielding independence, to offer wisdom without domination. Reconciling this tension in a way consistent with the integrity of both generations is more than an issue for the psychoanalyst. It is a messianic hope.

The peace between the generations is, in its larger embodiment, a peace among men and nations. The goal of history is linked to justice, respect, love, freedom, peace, for Israel and for all mankind.

There exists within the framework of traditional agada enough grist for twentieth-century visions. The age of Messiah will be a time when (1) righteousness and power are bound together, (2) the great ambiguities and mysteries of human life will be resolved, and (3) conflicts will yield to a reconciliation grounded in respect for the integrity of all.

All such images of the time to come, if they make a claim for legitimacy, must embody the noblest visions implanted within us, and provide a standard by which we may judge where we are and where we are going. Like the North Star, messianism helps us to steer a course which endows our life with significance and binds the finite to the eternal.

Should we wish to place our own particular impress on the agadic mold of hope, we may surely do so. If I am asked to complete the sentence "the messianic age is the time when . . ." one contemporary image most urgently comes to my lips: it is a time when peoples will truly perceive each other's pains and triumphs as their own. Our present world is marred by insularity and indifference. Messianism is the age of universal empathy. Let me illustrate with two vignettes.

While attending Chaplaincy School I heard a guest lecture from a visiting German pilot who had served with the Luftwaffe in World War II. Following his lecture, the Jewish clergy in the class plied him with questions about his experiences in that war and his self-conscious service of Hitler. During the coffee-break, our supervisor asked me what I thought of the lecture. When I replied that it was difficult for me to listen without thinking about the horrors of Nazism, our supervisor replied: "Oh yes, being Jewish you would feel that way. For me he was just fighting in the war the way I was."

Vignette number two: A number of white clergymen listened to a black activist describe the turning point in his civil rights career. He wrote a date on the blackboard and asked us if we knew what it stood for. In retrospect I don't remember the date (which is itself part of the story). When we pleaded ignorance our black lecturer said: "That was the date those black children died, when the church was bombed in Birmingham. The world went on with its business as usual. But my life would never be the same." Messianism is an age when we shall truly enter "each other's history"—an age of universal empathy.

Another image: messianism is the time when the current relation between majority and minority will be transformed. Majorities will not oppress minorities. Minorities will not feel like strangers in a strange land.

Thus may we embellish the traditional images of the messianic age even as we continue to find in our past a durable and renewable vision of God's goal for man. By its very nature *messianism is the highest reach of man's moral imagination. Its images are goals not reducible to concrete political platforms. It is a vision which dramatizes both man's aspirations and his limitations, the importance of his labor and his reliance on the redemptive power of God.*

Messianism need not conjure up a homogeneous society when all particularity will be dissolved in sterile oneness. Let messianism project an age when majorities and minorities neither dominate nor languish under the oppressive yoke of the other, when a Jewish majority in Israel will feel secure enough to acknowledge the full political and cultural dignity of its Arab minority, and when a Jew living in Diaspora need no longer worry about the specter of anti-Semitism anywhere in the world.

Conclusion

In this chapter we have explored issues which underlie all talk about the need for liturgical reform: does the language in which we symbolize our religious experience need radical revision? Do we need a new agada? We explored four areas in which such revision has often been proposed: symbolization of God as person, the affirmation of God's infinite power and love in a world riddled with evil, the belief in God's particular covenant with Israel, and the messianic hope.

I have contended that, for all its inadequacies, the personal imagery of agada is the least inadequate way of talking about or to God. I have argued for the retention of the agada's image of God's infinite power and love in preference to a variety of alternate concepts which limit God's essential power. By accentuating and embellishing classical agada's concept of divine self-limitation, I find it possible to affirm: "Praised be Thou, O Lord, Creator of Light and Darkness. Praised be Thou, O Lord, Creator of All."

I have insisted on the viability of Israel's chosenness (the particular divine vocation of Israel in the contemporary world), provided such an affirmation does not deny legitimacy to other covenants, or make the claim that Israel is bound to God by special love. The mystery of Israel's election need not imply special love, and the diverse images of God's relation to man may only be fully reconciled at the end of time.

Finally, the traditional agada's image of the messianic time retains its evocative power. New historical realities (Israel's rebirth) only impel us to accentuate those aspects of prophetic and talmudic agada which include but transcend the goal of Jewish sovereignty over Jerusalem. Messianism continues to embody our noblest visions. Such visions illuminate the ultimate goal of the human adventure and affirm both the relevance of man's efforts and man's reliance on the redemptive power and love of God.

In the world of agada, God's convenant with man (Adam) precedes the covenant with Abraham. The symbolic power of agada finds its most crucial test, therefore, in its capacity to interpret the human situation, to tell a compelling story of man's place in the contemporary world. Does agada speak to our situation in a technological age? To that issue we now turn in the next chapter.

VII · Who Is Man?

What are we? . . . What our power?
What our heroism? Yet from the
first Thou didst single out mortal
man and consider him worthy to stand
in Thy presence.
(High Holy Day Prayerbook)

WHEN THE HASIDIC RABBI Schneur Zalman was a prisoner of the Czar, the warden came into his cell one day to tease him: "If your God is so all-knowing, Rabbi, why in the Book of Genesis does he have to ask: 'Adam, where are you?' " Zalman replied: "God spoke not only to Adam but to every man in every generation. God speaks to each of us saying: 'O man, so many days and years of your life have passed. You are now forty-seven years old. The days remaining are numbered. Where are you? How far have you gone with your life?' " When the warden heard the rabbi mention his own age, he flashed a look of understanding and trembled. He had initiated the conversation to tease his prisoner, only to be terribly discomfited by the recognition that the story of Adam was the story of his life.

The warden's question and the rabbi's response establish the theme for the present chapter. Agada enabled the believing Jew to see a dimension of his own subjectivity. It was the story in which each man was revealed to himself. Can the traditional image of man mediate our self-understanding? Does agada still tell the story of our place in the world?

There is a prayer (agada) in the daily liturgy which is also recited on the afternoon of Yom Kippur. It begins with the

confession: "What are we? What is our life? What our righteousness? What our justice? What our virtue? What our power? What
our heroism?" This declaration of human inadequacy concludes:
"yet from the first Thou didst single out mortal man and consider
him worthy to stand in Thy presence."[1]

The great Jewish philosopher Hermann Cohen has reminded
us that this agada proclaims our personhood. Man, finite though
he be, has been appointed to stand before the infinite.

Who is man? Man is a creature capable of imagining and
experiencing a covenant with God. Agada tells the story of such a
covenant and declares this relation between the finite and infinite
to be at the very heart of the mystery and grandeur of the human
adventure. The covenant defines man's place in the world.

But ours is a time of revolutionary change in virtually every
sphere of life. Most notably the triumphs of science and technology have impelled us to reexamine man's place in the universe.
Have we, then, outgrown the image of man revealed and preserved in the heritage of agada?

Man's Dominion Over Nature

Covenant man is endowed with dignity and power. He is given
"dominion over nature." He is partner with God in confirming the
order and meaning of life. He assigns names to the creatures of
earth. According to a rabbinic agada, man names himself Adam
("for I was created out of the ground") and even assigns a name to
God ("Adonai, for you are Lord over all your creatures").[2]

Nevertheless the boundary between God and man is well
defined. Man is aware of his limits: "When I behold the heavens,
the work of Thy fingers, the moon and the stars which Thou has
created, what is man that Thou art mindful of him?"[3] Another
psalmist proclaims: "The earth is the Lord's and the fullness
thereof."[4] And again: "It is He who hath made us and we are
His."[5]

To be sure, man is a tester. He seeks to transcend his physical
limits and dispossess God, but such efforts are met with a
dramatic divine response that reconfirms man's place in the

world. In biblical agada there is the famous Tower of Babel story. A tower is built reaching up into heaven so that "we may make a name for ourselves."[6] God responds to this act of human defiance by scattering the people and confounding their tongues. Presumably it is harder to unite for conspiracy if you do not understand each other's language.

Rabbinic agada contains a classic story of man's failure to acknowledge his human limits. The villain of the tale is Hadrian. Upon returning from his conquests, Hadrian demanded that his courtiers deify him. When they reminded him that he had not captured God's city (Jerusalem) and house (Temple), the king proceeded to ravage the Holy City and exile its people. But when the victorious emperor returned for his deification, he was further challenged by some philosophers. The first sage suggested that one cannot claim to have displaced the king if one is confined to the king's palace. God's palace is heaven and earth. Only by transcending such boundaries might Hadrian claim himself to be God's cosmic successor.

A second philosopher taunts Hadrian with this challenge: "Do me a favor, a vessel with all my belongings is becalmed several miles at sea." Hadrian responds: "I'll send a legion after it." The philosopher retorts: "Why not just activate the winds? If you have no control over the winds, how can you declare yourself God?"[7]

Thus did the agada confirm the limits of man's physical power. But who will deny that we live in a radically different age? Man's mind has devised tools in our own lifetime which stagger the imagination. The biblical agadist looked up at the sky and proclaimed: "The heavens declare the glory of God." Theologian William Hamilton reports taking his son out to the backyard to identify some constellations for a school assignment. The son looked up and asked: "Which are the ones we put up there, Dad?"[8] How speak of physical limits to a creature who can place stars in the sky and walk on the surface of the moon?

The crucial difference between man's situation in the age of agada and ours is this: so much that was once an unchallengeable province of divine power has become an accepted domain of human self-assertion. An update of the Hadrian story would make the philosopher's vessel nuclear powered, and the emperor, by pressing a remote-control switch at Hadrian Control, could command the vessel's return. Indeed, Hadrian's successors have set forth some impressive credentials to support their power ploy. In a technological age, the boundary lines between the power of Caesar (Hadrian) and the power of God have radically shifted. This being the case, can the agada symbolize the power and limits of the human situation on the threshold of the twenty-first century?

In the Book of Isaiah this question seems almost to have been anticipated. We read: "And Thou has said in Thy heart, I will ascend above the heights of the clouds, I will become like unto God." Rabbinic agada identifies the author of that boast as the Babylonian King Nebuchadnezzar. But, says Rabbi Johanan b. Zakkai, his efforts were doomed to failure because the journey to the end of the firmament would take one thousand years whereas the days of man's years are at best fourscore.[9]

The astronomical calculations of Rabbi Johanan are as outdated as the biblical agada's estimate of the age of the earth. He spoke of one thousand years to reach the ends of the heaven, we speak of two billion years at the speed of 186,000 miles per second to approach the nearest star. But although the numbers have changed, the roles of the principals remain unaltered. Even the nearest star is so astronomically distant that it is forever beyond our reach. Ironically, as C. P. Snow reminds us, the space age brings us to the end of man's last physical frontier. Our solar system appears dead, and the "distances to any other systems are so gigantic that it would take the entire history of mankind from paleolithic man to the present day to travel at the speed of Apollo XI the distance to the nearest star."[10]

Spaceman, peering through his telescope, may still ask: "When I behold Thy heavens, the work of Thy fingers, the moon and the stars which Thou hast created, what is man that Thou art mindful of him?"

New dimensions of man's technological prowess are displayed not only in the heavens, but on earth. He is capable of reshaping his terrestrial environment in ways which the ancient sages could not anticipate. Nevertheless, the agada's concept of man's stewardship and accountability will repay an earnest hearing. Long before the invention of the combustion engine or the bulldozer or the atomic bomb, the agada portrayed Adam in the Garden of Eden receiving this divine admonition: "Behold, all which I have created is for your benefit. But beware lest you despoil and destroy my world, for if you do there is no one who will repair it after you."[11]

Significantly, some of the most trenchant updating of that agada has come not from preachers but from men of science. Biologist Garrett Hardin writes:

> We are a terribly clever people, we moderns. We bend nature to our will in countless ways. We move mountains . . . fly at speeds no other organism can achieve and tap the power of the atom. The essentially religious feeling of subserviency to a power greater than ourselves comes hard to us clever people. But by our intelligence we are now beginning to make out the limits to our cleverness. We are experiencing a return to a religious orientation to the world.[12]

*   *   *

The technological revolution has not discredited the agada's view of man's finite dominion and accountability for his stewardship of nature. In one respect, however, the agada needs revision. You will recall the story of the angels remonstrating with God against creating man. God discarded their counsel, proceeded with His creative act, and discovered man's destructiveness; whereupon the angels teased God for failing to heed their advice, but God remained determined to bear with His creatures.

To update this tale I must acknowledge that man is now capable of proving decisively that the angels were right. Man's power to do evil was playful mischief compared to his present capabilities. Man may now destroy his species and undermine the conditions required for human life on our earthly orb. The stakes are much higher now. We have, as someone has observed, moved from the sandlot to the major leagues and may take ourselves out of the ballgame. In that case He whom the agada refers to as "Master of Worlds" would be compelled to start anew.

Thus, whether I peer through a telescope or ponder an ecological manual, I discover that man's awesome power remains paradoxically the confirmation of his finitude, and the terms of the covenant remain intact: "I have set before thee life and death . . . choose life."[13]

Human Nature

As he accepted the Nobel Prize for literature, William Faulkner asked rhetorically: "Will man prevail?" Indeed the key question of our time is not how much dominion man will attain, but how he will use his power. Is he likely to destroy himself and his world, or will he measure up to the requirements of survival? William Faulkner answered his question by offering this tribute to our species:

> I decline to accept the end of man. . . . I believe that man will not merely endure, he will prevail. He is immortal, not because he alone among creatures has an inexhaustible voice but because he has a soul, a spirit capable of compassion, sacrifice and endurance.[14]

Some years earlier, Bertrand Russell offered a more dour assessment of the human species.

> Why . . . this glorification of Man? How about lions and tigers? They destroy fewer animals or human lives than we do and they are much more beautiful than we are. . . . Would not a world of nightingales and larks and deer be better than our human world of cruelty and injustice and war? . . . If I were granted omnipotence and millions of years to experiment in, I should not think Man much to boast about as the final result of all my efforts.[15]

Which image of human nature shall we choose? During the first years of my ministry, a congregant entered my study one day and confessed to feelings of intense personal inadequacy. She explained that Judaism, as she had come to understand it, offered no easy way to "get off the hook" for failing to fulfill divine expectations. While she admired the moral rigor of our tradition, she found the burden of guilt it inspired at times difficult to bear. She had discovered that what she had conceived as Judaism's image of man's spiritual prowess bore only scant resemblance to her "real" self. The conflict between image and reality engendered great personal anguish.

Nevertheless my visitor was convinced that any downgrading of divine expectations would constitute a betrayal of her liberal Jewish birthright. Judaism "believed in man" and summoned us to high attainment. Ours was a tough-minded, ethical faith which gave man no quarter to nurse his wounds of spiritual failure. When I reminded my visitor of the High Holy Day confessional and its liturgical drama of repentance and forgiveness, she dismissed this pageant as an annual concession to Orthodoxy, a sentimental retreat from the sturdy posture of a liberal faith.

This jaundiced view of "the Jewish image of man" is the price of modern apologetics. It was cultivated at a time when nineteenth-century West European culture celebrated the essential perfectability of man. Many a Jewish preacher asserted that since Judaism was not saddled with the albatross of original sin, our view of man was custom-made for the prevailing cultural mind-set. To this day, some untutored Jews will, if pressed, capsule their creed with such statements as "we believe man is good."

The "rediscovery" of human brutality in the twentieth century, and of all places in the very land where a positive image of human perfectability was so zealously nurtured, swung the pendulum to the other extreme. Most recently the popularized ethological views of Konrad Lorenz, Robert Ardrey, and others have provided new ammunition for those who would assail any notion of man's inflated moral possibilities. Thus Richard Rubenstein warns us against a facile idealization of the human animal.

> Assuring men that they are higher than other animals does not lead to insight; it leads to self-deception. If we could recognize the extent

to which we remain predatory animals we might understand that our very nature presents the greatest single obstacle to a peaceful society. Our chance of survival as a species may ultimately depend on our recognition of how profoundly and completely we are tied to our animal inheritance.[16]

Today we may often encounter either an eloquent celebration of man's essential goodness or a passionate disquisition on human brutishness. Neither view does justice to the complexity and richness of our experience. Far more than secular images, with their periodic oscillation between odes to human nobility and dirges on man's ignobility, classical agada embodies and integrates the concrete tensions of the human spirit.

In the twentieth century, we know man to be both noble and brutish, self-serving and loving. Man appears divided against himself, torn by conflicting impulses. He alone dreams exalted dreams, sacrifices for them, and betrays them. He alone consciously seeks both good and evil and is aware of a transcendent standard by which to judge his life. He alone asks for life's meaning. He is both rooted in the animal kingdom and transcends it.

In this section I shall argue that the agada's vision of man's moral power and limits remains illuminating and compelling. It tells the story of our life. The agada presents its image of human nature in two fundamental ways: first, by its characterization of the covenant between man and God; second, by its exploration of that unique creative-destructive energy in man called *yetzer*.

The Covenant

The nature of a relationship testifies to the partners' estimation of each other. In the agada, God's relation with Israel is the model of God's relation to man. What is the fundamental nature of the covenant? Is it essentially a *conditional* partnership, grounded in a generous estimate of man's moral potential and governed by the contingencies of mutual responsibility? Does God say to Israel, in effect: "I shall expect much from you and hold you accountable because you are capable of being a faithful partner."

There is much in agada to sustain a generous estimate of man. Such biblical commands to man as "Justice, justice shall you pursue," "Thou shalt love thy neighbor as thyself," and "You shall be holy as I am holy" are expressed within a framework of lofty possibilities. Moses says to the people in God's name:

> For this commandment which I command Thee this day is not too hard for thee, neither is it far off. It is not in heaven that thou shouldst say: "Who shall go up for us to heaven and bring it unto us and make us to hear it that we may do it?" Neither is it beyond the sea that thou shouldst say: "Who shall go over the sea for us and bring it up to us and make us to hear it that we may do it?" But the word is very near unto thee in thy mouth, and in thy heart that thou mayst do it.[17]

Man is capable of lofty spiritual achievements. Since he has the power to be a faithful partner, God can say to man: "You shall be holy as I am holy." The power to choose fidelity also implies accountability for failure. Thus man under the covenant is subject to judgment for betraying its terms. God pays man the compliment of holding him accountable.

One may ask, of course, how much moral dignity adheres to man if he must be goaded into goodness by promises of reward and threats of punishment. The agada assigns a special merit to those who are faithful out of love for God—"who serve their master like servants who do not expect a reward." Man is capable of rising to a level of moral passion, a readiness to sacrifice out of a love that expects no tangible, measurable, immediate reward. This already implies that the covenant, from the human side, is more than a strictly conditional arrangement: Israel (man) is capable of choosing the lofty goal not only because he seeks reward and fears punishment, but because he is capable of an act of love.

The extra-conditional dimension in the covenant may also be described from the divine side. God judges Israel but also forgives iniquity. He relates to man not only as King but as Father. That God extends mercy is a sign of divine love; that man needs forgiving love is also a sign of man's frailty. Man could not sustain a totally conditional covenant. He needs not only to be held accountable but to be forgiven and loved despite failure. He needs a sense of worth to be sustained not only by what he achieves but by what he is: a beloved child of God.

The nature of the covenant between God and Israel reflects a tension between conditionality and unconditionality, between judgment and forgiveness—between a high sense of man's moral possibility and a sober assessment of human frailty.

The High Holy Day liturgy (agada) beautifully mirrors this image of man. Rosh Hashanah is preeminently a day of judgment. Animals do not stand before God and acknowledge that they are accountable for a standard of life, that they are capable of more than they have achieved. Man does. But Yom Kippur is essentially a day of divine forgiveness. Man pleads: "What are we, what our goodness, what our justice; what can we say before Thee?" And God replies: "Even I blot out thine iniquities for My sake, and thy sins will I remember no more. I have made thy sins to vanish like a cloud and thy transgressions like a mist. Return to Me for I have redeemed Thee. On this day shall you be forgiven and cleansed from all your sins. Before God shall ye be pure."[18]

The agada's image of the covenant mirrors the mysterious complexity of the human creature. It speaks of a conflict between lofty potential and frequent failure which, though logically untidy, is welded together in the poetry of religious symbolism and in the concreteness of life.

Man's Yetzers

If man can be faithful, why does he fail so often? This question brings us to the agada's concept of the *yetzer,* that primary energy which endows man's freedom with dynamic power. At times the agada pictures an inner struggle, a divided self, a war between *yetzer hara* (the evil inclination) and *yetzer tov* (man's good inclination). Man needs help in struggling with his *yetzer.* Rabbi Tanhum prays that the evil *yetzer,* "the yeast in the dough, be subdued."[19] But there can be no leavened bread without yeast! Thus the very energy which uniquely empowers man's monstrous evil is also enlisted in man's noblest achievements. The spiritual goal for man is to "serve God with both *yetzers*."[20] This is the model of integrity—wholeness—and the struggle to attain it is the enduring spiritual challenge of man's life.

Buber's rendering of the relation between the two *yetzers* in an "integrated" person may be helpful.

> This important doctrine cannot be understood as long as good and evil are considered . . . as two diametrically opposite forces or directions. . . . [they are] . . . similar in nature. The evil urge of passion, is *yetzer ra,* that is the power peculiar to man without which he can neither beget or bring forth, but which left to itself remains without direction and leads astray, and the good urge (*yetzer tov*) as pure direction . . . as an unconditional direction . . . toward God. To reunite the two urges implies: to equip the potency of passion with the one direction that renders it capable of great love and of great service. Thus and not otherwise can man become whole.[21]

This unification of the two urges is the dynamic of mature goodness. What is the dynamic of evil? Buber describes two stages. The first is the result of a human being flexing his *yetzer,* testing the manifold possibilities of self-assertion which he is uniquely capable of imagining and acting out. He is a divided self, not yet discovering the one direction which enables him to fulfill the purpose of his life. Think of children at play: they explore, romp, test each other. First there is laughter and suddenly there are tears. Think of bored teenagers (or adults) roaming around looking for things to do. How an innocent caper so easily escalates into a fist fight, or worse! This is the evil of unfocused *yetzer* and results in the aimless dissipation of man's creative energy.

The second stage of evil is an attempt to find unity or wholeness by affirming oneself, not as a junior partner of God in the covenant of life, but as the ultimate reality. "If he affirms himself . . . nothing else must remain worthy of affirmation than just that which is affirmed by him . . ."[22] This second stage of evil is man's conscious exercise of freedom to defy God, to oppose the intended direction of his life. Man can consciously will evil.

The model of the righteous man (*tzaddik*) in the agada is he who has gained dominion over both *yetzers;* he has united them in the service of God. The wicked man (*rasha*) is he who permits his *evil yetzer* to rule over him or he who wills to defy the intended direction of his life. Most people, says the agada, are "in between." They oscillate between the two directions.

Man *knows* that his power may be used to serve or betray the will of God. That is the meaning of the agada in which Adam eats of the Tree of Knowledge of good and evil.[23] Man's unique endowment—*self-conscious power and freedom*—renders him potentially the most noble and brutish creature on earth. Man alone is capable of being God's faithful partner and most dangerous enemy. The temptation to defy God is an everpresent reality. Two models of betrayal among others are featured in agada. The one is sex, the other idolatry.

In our faddishly sensate culture, it has become camp to divest sexuality of moral overtones. For all its celebration of the goodness and beauty of physical love, the agada maintains that sexuality is never morally neutral. In biblical agada human sexuality is identified with the loss of innocence. Adam *knew* he was naked. Sexual awareness is part of man's broader consciousness of his power to serve or flout the purposes of his Creator. Many of the references to the evil inclination in rabbinic literature are sexual, but the rabbinic wedding benedictions also celebrate the gift of physical love. Thus, *sex is a primary manifestation of the energy which in man uniquely becomes a way of sanctifying or profaning the intention of God.*

Despite our culture's attempt to regard sex as play or as alternative to violence (make love, not war), many of the four-letter words expressing hostility have patently sexual overtones. This alone suggests that sex is the manifestation of a broader human power. Sex may be an expression of mutually sanctifying love or a manipulative, hostile ploy.

The most flagrant manifestation of man's abusive power is idolatry—the desire to displace God or destroy God's power. Nebuchadnezzar purportedly proclaims: "I will ascend above the heights of the clouds. I will be like the most high."[24] Such attempted displacement may consist not only of physically challenging the boundaries which confirm man's finitude, but disarming God's presence or authority on earth. Thus King Ahaz decrees the shutting of synagogues and schools in order that study and prayer will cease and God will not permit his presence to dwell on earth. Thus would the domain of God yield by default to the dominion of Ahaz.[25]

The sin of idolatry is, in one form or another, an effort to usurp that ultimate authority which belongs to God. This sin is especially manifest in persons with political power who deny their accountability to God. Indeed, both biblical and rabbinic agada confirm that in premessianic days there is a tension between power and goodness. Even the greatest biblical king was in need of prophetic judgment. David required Nathan. Only in the end of days will that tension be resolved. The Messiah is the one in whom power and goodness will be united.

In our culture as in ancient Judah, politics is an illuminating exhibit of man's struggle for responsible personhood. Most manifestations of totalitarianism in recent history have featured impressive acts of self-deification (Hitler, Stalin, Mao). Ultimate reverence, bordering on worship, has been invested in such leaders, and in each instance that power has recognized no limits.

The secularizing tendency of the modern world has reflected this spirit. Nathan Rotenstreich earnestly assesses the peculiar character of modern atheism.

> The dictum "if there is a God how could I bear not to be God" expresses it to succinct perfection. Modern atheism is based not only on doubt of God's existence, or on the argument that God's existence cannot be demonstrated by rational means, but also on the view that God's existence as limiting man's expansion and autonomous power is an impediment to his dominion over all the world.[26]

The Covenant vs. Dr. Skinner

In at least three discernible ways a confrontation has emerged between the agada's view of human nature and the competing images of man in a technological age. First, the agada confirms the reality of human *freedom*. The concept of *yetzer* was not intended as a repudiation of man's power to choose between good and evil. Covenant man is held accountable because he has the power to obey or defy God. "All is in the hands of heaven except the fear of heaven."[27] The angel of conception determines many things, but not whether someone will be good or evil.[28] Indeed, the very meaning of human character depends on the assumption that virtue is at least in part an achievement, not a fateful gift. God Himself is not spared the risk of freedom.

> Rabbi Berachia said: "When the Holy One, Blessed be He, came to create man, He saw righteous and wicked arising from him. Said God, 'If I should create him, wicked men will spring from him. If I do not create him, how will righteous spring from him?' "[29]

Professor B. F. Skinner and other behaviorists regard this traditional notion of "freedom and dignity" as a pernicious illusion. A person's behavior, they claim, is not determined by a willing self but by genetic factors and "by the environmental circumstances to which he as an individual has been exposed."[30]

It is no more of a personal achievement for a man to choose the good than for a pigeon properly conditioned to dance a figure eight. Change the inner and outer environment and you will modify the behavior. Why does man not conform to our ideals? Because we have not yet created a social environment that reinforces such behavior. Theoretically we could and should make goodness as automatic as the salivation of Pavlov's dog in the presence of a bell.

Skinner would acknowledge that his view is no more provable than the agada's concept of human freedom and dignity. At first glance, however, the behaviorist's position is beguilingly seductive to modern man. After all, you and I have "rediscovered" the *limits* of human freedom. It is the mark of advanced societies to ask of a criminal not only whether he did it, but whether he had the power to choose between right and wrong. In courts of law guilt is qualified by the notion of "sickness."

In jurisprudence as in life, the line between limited freedom and determinism may be thin. Even the traditional agadists were aware of the *yetzer*'s threat to man's moral choice. But neither they nor we regard sin simply as sickness and virtue simply an instance of mental health. We praise and we blame. We *judge* a human life as if character were at least in part a personal achievement.

Even when the term *illness* (sickness) is appropriate, the concept of freedom remains intact. We admire a person for the way he *chooses* to deal with his illness. Does he recognize it? Does he seek therapy? Does he struggle to confront his demons and gain mastery over them? Emotional illness does not negate freedom or character, but tests each in another way. *Freedom is not the absence of limiting conditions. Freedom is our power to deal with the boundaries of life creatively.*

The Skinner alternative to freedom and dignity may beguile us on other grounds. After all, the religious view of man has not ushered in the messianic age. How many religious pageants of confession, repentance, and atonement have been enacted through the ages without radically elevating the quality of human life. Such gentle taunts may be capped by the question: Why not give the new social engineering a try? In truth, however, Skinner has offered thus far no concrete model of social engineering which would predictably resolve our major social traumas. He has not told us what schedules of reinforcement are required to remove racial prejudice, corruption in government, economic exploitation, or war. Even if he did, it might be necessary to reject his counsel on other grounds.

Suppose Skinner's world could be brought about. Would it be a dream come true or a nightmare? Anthony Burgess's *A Clockwork Orange* imagines Skinner's scenario. Alex is the leader of a teenage gang which has terrorized old and young with vicious acts of violence. Alex is caught, charged with second-degree murder, convicted, and imprisoned. The prisoner agrees to participate in an elaborate experiment of conditioning through visual, auditory, and electrical stimuli. The experiment succeeds. Within two weeks the vicious Alex automatically associates all thoughts of violence with terrifying, painful physical and emotional experiences. Alex is no longer capable of even fantasying the violence of his past. When the doctor in charge displays the "new Alex," the prison chaplain asks: "He ceases . . . to be a creature capable of moral choice?" The doctor replies: "These are subtleties. We are not concerned with motive, with higher ethics . . . only with cutting down crime."[31] The chaplain elsewhere replies: "When a man cannot choose he ceases to be a man."[32]

Lest we imagine that *A Clockwork Orange* is simply theoretical, we need only cite the words of Professor James McConnell of the University of Michigan, a Skinner disciple: "The day has come when we can combine sensory deprivation with drugs, hypnosis and astute manipulation of reward and punishment to gain absolute control over an individual's behavior."[33] Why institute such conditioning? "To learn how to force people to learn to love one another, to force them to want to behave properly."[34]

The news media have reported efforts in "behavior modification" at the Connecticut State Prison in Somers. Convicted child molesters were administered painful electric shocks while they watched slides of naked children. There was no shock administered when slides of naked women appeared. Dr. Dominic Morino, chief of mental hygiene, explained to newsmen that such therapy produces feelings of anxiety whenever the inmate thinks of a child as a sexual object. Those participating in the experiment were volunteers.[35]

As president of the American Psychological Association, Kenneth B. Clark suggested to his colleagues that society develop a drug which would biologically control man's evil impulse. A "peace pill," said Clark, is necessary in order to prevent the nation's leaders from precipitating a global catastrophe.[36]

If we take seriously the agada's image of man, we shall be exceedingly leery of this kind of technological messianism. Fortunately there are impressive dissenting voices within the scientific community itself. Dr. Peter Breggin, in his address to the American Psychiatric Association, offered this comment to his colleagues: "I do not deny that man's biology can limit or control him. I merely deny that man's most important personal and political problems can be understood or treated in terms of defective biology. It is the non-mechanistic, self-generating capacities of man which characterize him as a man."[37]

While it would be tempting to reshape man as a creature incapable of imaginatively devising evil, ours is a *human* adventure precisely because man has been given great power and freedom. Remove man's freedom and one is left not with persons but with oranges. Organic? Yes, but functioning like clockworks.

The root of man's dangerousness is the root of his dignity. Hence the rabbis can, in a brilliant paradox, suggest that even God called the evil impulse good. "Were it not for the *yetzer hara*," they said, "no man would build a house, take a wife, and beget children . . ." *Man, the creature uniquely conscious of his power to defy God's purposes, is summoned to harness his power and his temptation in the service of God.*[38]

I have outlined two ways in which the agada challenges the Skinner scenario. (1) Man's freedom is not an illusion but a self-conscious power to do good or evil. (2) Man's dignity requires that he remain a covenant partner who is capable of saying no to his Creator. His power to say no renders his yes all the more significant. Modernity juxtaposes two symbols, the "Skinner Box" and the covenant. The one assumes that man is essentially no freer than other animals and makes the ritual of conditioning the key to salvation. The other regards man as a creature uniquely endowed with power and freedom. Man hears the divine call. He heeds and defies it, acknowledges responsibility (guilt), and is capable of self-renewal. God wants to be served by a creature capable of defying Him. No technological shortcuts to redemption are acceptable which undermine man's essential freedom and dignity, even if we must face the prospect of confessing our guilt, seeking forgiveness, and celebrating our power of repentance for many years to come.

The technological possibility of reshaping man's moral nature is part of a broader issue. Should man use his recently gained and growing knowledge of genetics to reshape the "native endowment" of the human species? Suppose "genetic surgery" could correct subnormal intelligence or prevent a birth defect? Suppose we could effectively breed a different and superior geno-type? Even this latter possibility is hardly academic. Rand Corporation predicts that by the year 2005 an asexual form of reproduction called cloning may be feasible.[39] This procedure would enable us to program in advance the genetic endowments of human beings and create multiple copies.

The responsible use of man's power may not rule out all genetic surgery. As in conventional surgery, such procedures may constitute a partnership with God in fulfilling the intended promise of creation. *The scientist-technician is practicing a religious vocation when he acknowledges his power as the gift of God and employs it with accountability.* However, one must always ask: Is the risk of harm proportionate to the hope of benefit to the individual?: And do we know enough to answer the question?

When the genetic frontiersman begins to talk about radically reshaping man in a predetermined image (positive eugenics), the questions become even more awesome: Do we have enough wisdom to know which genetic traits are good or bad for the human adventure? Are there not many unknown variables? Is not the damage we may do irreversible?

The promethean mood of some genetic frontiersman suggests the admonition embodied in the rabbinic play on the words *urdu* ("have dominion") and *yardu* ("they shall descend"). God says to man: "If you use the power I give you responsibly, then *urdu*, have dominion! If you abuse it, *yardu*, let man descend from his special place in creation."[40]

On the issue of genetic engineering, Hans Jonas has made a significant distinction between reversible and irreversible intrusions upon human nature. He notes that attempts to reshape man through conventional education are fallible but at least reversible, whereas the genetic remaking of man in some image or assortment of images based on the values of a contemporary elite would alter with fateful finality the future of the human species. Jonas ends his plea with a contemporary agada.

We have not been authorized . . . to be makers of a new image (of man) nor can we claim the wisdom and knowledge to arrogate that role. If there is any truth in man's being created in the image of God then awe and reverence and yes, utter fear and ultimate metaphysical shudder ought to prevent us from meddling with the profound secret of what is man.[41]

The reference above to scientists as a contemporary elite suggests a third contrast between modernity and the agada's view of human nature. Biblical messianism contends that before "the end of days" there remains a radical disjuncture between power and righteousness. Those in authority live with the temptation to abuse power and normally succumb. Before the dawn of the Messiah the prophetic spirit is needed to speak truth to power. In the interim no king is immune to the arrogance of power.

From time to time men mistakenly suppose that by virtue of birth or intellectual gifts a certain group of individuals may transcend man's ambiguous relation to power. In our own age, the scientist-technologist-engineer, with his commitment to dispassionate truth, has been lifted by some to the pedestal of moral immunity. This notion is not only contrary to the biblical doctrine of power but contrasts sharply with the rabbinic understanding of such matters. Abaya said that the *evil yetzer* is strongest in scholars. He proceeds to relate an incident. He overheard a man and woman speak of journeying together. Abaya resolved to follow them "in order to keep them from transgression." He followed them only to discover that they parted company without having fulfilled his fantasies. Abaya confessed to himself: "If it were I, I could not have restrained myself." This realization depressed him, whereupon a certain old man (Elijah) came up to him and said: "The greater the man, the greater is his evil inclination."[42]

Neither rabbinic nor scientific wisdom renders one immune to the temptations of power. The candor of a Nobel scientific laureate has confirmed that science is a human enterprise with political overtones. James Watson, who shared the Nobel Prize for his work on the structure of DNA (the molecule of heredity), published a breezy account of that research project under the title *The Double Helix*. Watson records that one of the most joyous moments in the life of his research team occurred when they learned that Linus Pauling, a research competitor, had apparently followed a dead end![43]

Infinitely more sobering, of course, is the fact that some of the most vicious experiments on human beings in Nazi Germany were conducted by men with Ph.D.'s. In an age of technology no less than in the time of the Bible and Talmud, all men remain subject to the temptations of evil. Intelligence is no guarantee of moral purity. We have not outgrown the traditional concept: the greater the man, the greater his power to do good or evil.

In its image of man's nature, the tradition confronts the secular world with three ringing affirmations. (1) Man is free. (2) His freedom and dignity include the power to enhance or betray his covenant. (There can be no freedom to do good without the power to think and do evil.) (3) In premessianic days, before the *yetzer* has been fully tamed, virtue remains not only an achievement but a struggle from which *no* person is immune.

Hence we must confront our technological messianists with the question: Who will control the controllers?

Covenant Man and the Kingdom of God

Covenant man not only aspires to serve God with both *yetzers*, he prays and works for the day when the tensions and social conflicts of the present world will be overcome. He envisages a world where there are no Dachaus or Hitlers, a world in which persons will be masters of their *yetzer hara* and the earth will be full of the knowledge of the Lord.

The very concept of man in history, helping to bring about that which has never been, is itself, as we noted earlier, a Hebraic gift to human culture. Mircea Eliade has strikingly contrasted pagan myth and biblical agada. Pagan man believed that he could do nothing of value which had not already been done by the gods in primeval time. Biblical man is summoned to be God's partner in fulfilling the promise of creation. Pagan man finds fulfillment by persistent flight from the terrors of time. Biblical man seeks not to escape from the temporal world but to sanctify it.[44] Indeed man is summoned to "repair the world that it may become God's kingdom."[45]

Earlier I spoke of the prophetic goal for history as a day when nations shall learn war no more, when God will grant man a new heart, and when all will acknowledge His sovereignty. How shall this day be brought about? The tradition offers no formal *political* blueprint, but three dimensions of messianism are expressed: the turning of the people toward God, the formation of a community which takes seriously the values of Torah, and the divine initiative through either the advent of a messianic king or the direct manifestation of God's redemptive power. Let us consider each briefly.

The first path has already been discussed. Man is personally accountable for the quality of his life. He is free to serve or betray the will of God. Each man must seek integrity through the service of God with the fullness of his being. The kingdom of God begins in every human heart and in every man's wrestling with his *yetzer*.

Man is helped or hindered in his struggle by the quality of the community in which he resides. That brings us to the second dimension. If the standards (law) of a community affirm the sanctity of life, the resident of that community finds social support in his quest for decent personhood. Similarly, it is easier to combat the temptation to steal in a community where stealing is generally condemned and punished. It is easier to cultivate our power to love in a community where love is a social ideal. Conversely, a society whose laws and prevailing standards reflect moral insensitivity and unconcern for the disadvantaged is a society which diminishes human integrity.

Since the structure of laws, values, and conditions in a society may impede or enhance the fulfillment of our moral destiny, social change or political reform is itself an integral part of the good life. Communities need renewal. Thus the path to redemption is both personal and social.

A Jew who takes the covenant seriously will seek to sanctify God's world by personal deeds and by elevating the quality of his communal life. Certain individuals are singled out for their righteousness or their wickedness in biblical and rabbinic agada. Certain communities are singled out for good or evil. Notable among the evil communities were Babel, Sodom, and Jerusalem in the periods before the destruction of both Temples.

By observing the Torah, an individual and a community may contribute toward the repair of the world. The transcendent significance of man's individual and collective fidelity to God's commandments is dramatically expressed in the pages of agada.

> Rabbi Judah Ben Levi found Elijah and asked him: "When is the Messiah coming?" Elijah answers: "Go ask him." The rabbi asked: "Where may he be found?" Elijah: "Near the entrance to the city." Rabbi: "What are the signs?" Elijah: "He sits among the poor." The rabbi finds a beggar in the city whom he imagines to be Elijah and asks him: "When will the Messiah come?" He replies: "Today, if you will harken to God's voice." [46]

Another agada proclaims: "Great is tzedakah (charitable acts of righteousness) in that it brings the redemption nearer." [47]

We might conclude that the fulfillment of the goal of history depends only on man's individual and collective activity, that man has it in his power to compel the advent of the messianic age. Such is not the agada's perspective. While some rabbinic statements emphasize the human variable, others remind us that messianism is not simply a matter of man's individual and collective responsibility, but always requires divine initiative. If some agadists suggest that the new age will come when man has earned it, others view messianism as a divine response to human degradation and despair.

> In the footsteps of the Messiah insolence will increase and honor dwindle. . . . the meeting place (of scholars) will be used for immorality . . . the wisdom of the learned will degenerate, fearers of sin will be despised, and the truth will be lacking. Children shall shame the elders, and the elders shall rise up before the children. [48]

How reconcile the apparent contradiction? Emil Fackenheim states well the rabbinic paradox: ". . . man is free and morally responsible; and . . . he is dependent on the redemptive act of God . . . . He [the Messiah] will come when history has become good enough to make his coming possible, or evil enough to make it necessary."[49]

Man's task, through personal and social renewal, is to hasten the day, but man cannot compel the messianic climax of history. Man must struggle with his *yetzer* and seek to improve the community in which he lives. But man's deeds, though significant, are incomplete. His achievements are valuable but flawed. He must work diligently, but he must also prayerfully wait, for only God can bring the Messiah. Moreover, man must learn to live in a world to which the Messiah has not yet come, and he must beware of false Messiahs.

The Agada vs. the Secular Messianism of Our Age

From Roman times to the dawn of the modern era, the believing Jew took seriously the struggle with his *yetzer* and the need to elevate the standards of the Jewish community. But politics in the broader sense remained the domain of the Gentile. He lived as an exile in a kingdom of the Gentiles. He was divorced from the burden and joy of political power.

The modern era has catapulted the Jew into the realm of politics. Israel is ruled by a Jewish establishment, and in liberal Western societies the Jew is encouraged to regard himself as a citizen with a direct role in shaping the political destiny of the nations.

A medieval Jew believed that by observing the Sabbath and providing for the Jewish poor in a dignified manner he was fulfilling his divine vocation in the world. But that Jew had no role in regulating the general Sabbath observance or the charitable system of the surrounding Christian society. Today the Jew in Israel plays a role in determining Shabbat observance throughout his land and helps shape the welfare system by which all its citizens are served. Similarly, as a Jew in the United States I may seek to promote a structure of separation of church and state in the Sabbath observance of the total society, and I may "lobby" for a particular form of public assistance for all citizens of the land.

The political sphere of the modern Jew has been immensely broadened. Aside from prayer, the medieval Jew conceived of Torah observance and a concern for moral standards within the Jewish community as his only arsenal in "hastening the day." By contrast, the modern Western Jew has become deeply involved in the arena of political change within the larger society. Moreover, given the secularization of our time, he has been tempted to regard political activism as the sole means of redeeming the world. What contribution can agada's messianism make to an understanding of contemporary politics?

Some societies are more a reflection of basic Jewish values than others; therein is the rationale for political action. But all systems which men devise and all instruments of political power reflect the temptation and moral ambiguity of the human spirit. The *yetzer* is still with us whether we be revolutionary idealists, liberal intellectuals, philosopher kings, or scientific technicians. Some of the most high-sounding calls for ousting the establishment and ushering in the new order betray an ominous echo of power hunger among the challengers.

Our political acts are relevant to the fulfillment of history's goal, but no person, whatever his ideology, can claim to usher in the kingdom. A social dreamer or political activist must remain at best God's partner, not God's cosmic successor.

This perspective should not be used to justify the status quo. The cry of the oppressed ought give me no peace. The world can become more reflective of God's righteous will, and man as political creature has a role to play in making it so. But covenant man will ever acknowledge the limit of politics. The heady enthusiasm and destructive self-righteousness of some campus protest in the sixties led Patrick Moynihan to observe that "the crisis of our time is not political, it is in essence religious. It is a religious cry of large numbers of intensely moral, even godly people who no longer hope for God. Hence the quest for divinity assumes secular form but with an intensity of conviction that is genuinely new to our politics."[50]

A danger of our age is that those who have lost their faith in

God continue to believe in the Messiah. They believe that if only we enact a particular political program, or give enough power to this or that group, evil will melt away. They invest in human politics that ultimate trust which earlier generations reserved for God.

In the twentieth century, the most devastating example of messianic politics was the rise of Hitler. Germans on the right and left created a climate which helped elevate a man to power who believed he was the Messiah and could inspire that belief in millions of bewildered and desperate people. As survivors of the twentieth century, we have special reason to beware of messianic politics.

One of West Germany's major contemporary novelists was a young child when Hitler came to power. Günter Grass has written a novel entitled *Local Anesthetic*. The story has two principal characters, a forty year-old history teacher and his dentist. Much of this symbolic novel takes place in the dentist's chair.

The history teacher has total faith in education. He believes that if all men could go back to school and learn all there is to know about human needs and how to fulfill them, the millennium would come. The dentist reposes similar faith in technology. Behold the marvelous advances in preventive and therapeutic dentistry! They are a symbol of man's ultimate hope through science.

During much of the novel, the dentist is engaged in correcting the history teacher's bite. Finally it appears that the bite is corrected. Technology has triumphed! Ah, but we discover a double letdown. The dentist, who knows better, is revealed as a secret gobbler of sweets. He indulges this vice in the secrecy of his washroom. Meanwhile, his star patient is back in the chair. An abscess has developed beneath the history teacher's corrected bite. The dentist proceeds to clean out the abscess, but by now doctor and patient are forced to realize that whatever the "program," if we are counting on man's power and wisdom and goodness alone, "there will always be pain." Man may provide a local anesthetic. He can reform, reshape, and improve, but be he master technologist or master teacher or master politician, man cannot produce a Messiah.[51]

The insight of Günter Grass is echoed in some observations by sociologist Peter Berger:

> Most "lessons of history" are fraudulent. There are some "lessons" though that have considerable empirical foundations: most victories are ephemeral . . . few visions survive a single generation. Most important of all history is the arena of unintended consequences. This insight need not be paralyzing. Reality confronts us with demands that cannot be avoided even if we know that the consequences of our actions are beyond our control. Political morality does not demand visions, only that we act as best we can. The best political morality is informed by the heavy knowledge of the past. Its fruits are humility and compassion.[52]

Messianic politics is a poor substitute for religious hope. Such hope is grounded not only in man's potential under the covenant, but in God's redemptive love. Politics is no place for man-made Messiahs. We ought to see ourselves as faithful but fallible partners in the covenant of life. All our political efforts must stand under the chastening judgment of the Almighty. We are at best gropers toward the kingdom.

Politics is the arena of compromise and tolerance for ambiguity. Its fruits reflect our strength and our weakness, our clarity and our confusion. Religious faith should inform and cleanse our political vision, but politics cannot satisfy deepest hope.

Death: The Mark of Finitude

The covenant view of man's power and limits makes this additional assertion: To be human is to be mortal and to acknowledge that death is part of life. After Adam had eaten of the Tree of Knowledge, God says:

> Now that man has become like one of us, knowing good and evil, what if he should stretch out his hand and take also from the Tree of Life and eat and live forever? So the Lord God banished him from the Garden to till the soil from which he was taken. He drove the man out and stationed east of the Garden of Eden the cherubim and the fiery everturning sword to guard the way to the Tree of Life.[53]

Death is the boundary, the ultimate limit which compels man to admit he is not God. As God's covenant partner, man is summoned to share with his Creator the task of reshaping the world, but he also lives uniquely with the anticipation of incompleteness and death. "When the Lord created Adam, the angels mistook him for a divine being. What did the Holy One, Blessed be He, do? He caused a sleep to fall upon Adam, and all knew that he was but mortal man. Thus it is written: 'Cease ye from man in whose nostrils is the breath, for how little is he to be accounted'!"[54]

Although Adam's death is also regarded as punishment for his disobedience, both the Bible and rabbinic literature regard death—apart from Adam's sin—as man's encounter with his own creatureliness.

> Rabbi Hamma: "The first man was not worthy of death. Why was death decreed upon him? The Holy One, Blessed be He, saw that Nebuchadnezzar and Hiram would in the future regard themselves as divine. Therefore death was decreed upon Adam (and upon all men)."[55]

When the angels ask for an extension of Moses' life, they are told that death is "a decree which applies equally to all men," and when Moses himself entreats God to spare him on account of his righteousness, God says: "For all creatures death has been prepared from the beginning."[56]

Secular man may chafe at the image of a transcendent Creator, but he may not ignore the reality of his own finitude. Even the man who celebrates or mourns the "death of God" anticipates with far more certainty his own demise.

Alas, ever since the Garden of Eden man has fantasied ways by which he might outwit the Angel of Death. That fantasy has not left us. There are those who actively provide for the freezing of their corpses until such time as men have technologically transcended death. Medical technology has already demonstrated the power to extend the average life-span and to stay the hand of death. Oxygen may be fed directly to the lungs, chemical nutrients to the veins, catheters inserted into disabled organs.

Nevertheless, artificial support systems often appear to be prolonging death rather than extending life. Significantly, our culture has begun to reclaim the traditional concept that death is part of life. Death is a decree and a gift; it comes as conqueror or friend. Out of our love for man we must ask not only how to extend life, but how we may help persons to die with dignity.

The fantasy of deathlessness persists nonetheless. Professor Gerald Feinberg believes that as long as man lives with a sense of death, he can never be content. Feinberg concludes: "therefore I believe that a transformation of man into something very different than what he is now is called for . . ."[57] The professor envisages the creation of new beings, perhaps conscious machines who would not confront the limit of mortality. But would these creatures be human? The professor himself replies that they may be "humans, Martians, dolphins, or IBM 137,000."[58]

We may speculate on the impact of artificial organs or conscious machines on the concept of death, but as Feinberg himself implies, temporality is the price of humanity. An ageless person is a contradiction in terms. We used to say that the only alternative to aging is premature death. Even at best (or worst), technology may compel us to acknowledge that the alternative to aging and death is the loss of that mysterious and awesome complexity we call our humanity.

All of which brings us back to the declaration of the ancient psalmist: "Our years are like grass, in the morning it flourishes and groweth up and in the evening, it is cut down and withereth. . . . We bring our years to an end as a tale that is told. The days of our years are threescore years and ten, or even by reason of strength, fourscore years. . . . Teach us to number our days that we may get us a heart of wisdom."[59] Death is the price of human life. The consciousness of death is the mark of our personhood.

At the grave of a loved one I am bidden to recite "Praised Be Thou, O Lord our God, Ruler of the Universe, who dost form us in Thine image, who dost nourish and sustain us in Thy goodness, who causes us to die in accordance with Thy law and who hast implanted within us eternal life. Blessed are Thou, O Lord, Judge of Truth."

George Orwell said that the major problem of our time is the erosion of belief in personal immortality. Not coincidentally our culture has also made of death the new pornography. We find it easier to speak of sex than to talk of the end of our days. For all our technological bravado, we do not truly expect to outwit the Angel of Death, but we crave to deny our nothingness in a culture where images of human abidingness beyond the grave no longer seem intellectually or emotionally compelling.

Man's strategies for coping with the ineluctable reality of life vary. He may become a devotee of health foods and engage in elaborate cosmetic rituals. He may build monuments which will bear his name in perpetuity. He may pursue unbridled self-indulgence, as if pleasure will defer or at least lighten the long journey into night.

The problem of death exists not only for the middle-aged or the elderly, but for the young as well. During his senior year at Harvard, Steve Kelman wrote a book about the student rebellion on campus. Kelman pondered the anomaly of affluent, leisured, pampered students—an unquestionably privileged group—dubbing themselves an "oppressed class." Though himself a vigorous critic of our culture and a socialist, Kelman could not regard such rhetoric as a reasonable response to reality. His explanation:

> Students are today's idle rich; being idle, well fed and generally satisfied gives us a chance to do a great deal of solitary thinking and soul searching. . . . And many of us, like Hamlet, wind up "thinking too precisely on the events." Stop reading for a moment and don't think about anything else but death. The fact that at sometime you will be nothing. . . . it is only necessary to reflect on death to understand why some students view themselves as an oppressed class . . .[60]

The ultimate oppressor, Kelman suggests, is death. Social institutions call man to acknowledge limits. They are the surrogate of the ultimate limit, death. Some of the social ferment which erupted into violence in the sixties was fed not by a rational quest for social justice, but by a desperate yearning to escape from contemplation of the human end.

The special terrors of modernity have conspired to rob secular man of even his more intellectually respectable images of continuity. Thus the conviction that one endures through one's children, one's works, or a chain of personal influence—even this form of immortality has been challenged by the existence of nuclear weapons. Psychiatrist Robert Lifton notes that even without being used, the nuclear warheads challenge man's secular images of self-made immortality. "Who can be certain of living on through children and grandchildren, through teachings or kindnesses?"[61]

Covenant man acknowledged that death is part of human life and turned to God as the Guardian of Eternity. Whether I am a believer, an unbeliever, or a confirmed agnostic, I too must accept death as the end of my earthly pilgrimage. For transcendent hope I too must turn not to the promise of technology, with its fantasies of larger and better artificial support systems or a pill of eternal youth, and not to the work of our hands, but to the infinite God, who has summoned us to life and who "endows our fleeting days with abiding value."

Even in a secular age, an irrepressible longing for abidingness persists as do lingering intimations of our spirit transcending dust. No modern writer has chronicled the yearning and the intimations more movingly than Saul Bellow in *Mr. Sammler's Planet.* The old man, Sammler, stands at the deathbed of his younger nephew and benefactor, Elya Gruner. Sammler wonders about the destiny of man and muses: "Is God only the gossip of the living? Then we watch these living speed like birds over the surface of a water, and one will dive or plunge but not come up again, and never be seen anymore. . . . But then we have no proof that there is no depth under the surface."[62] Later Sammler says: "Consolers cannot always be truthful. But very often, and almost daily, I have strong impressions of eternity. This may be due to my strange experiences, or to old age. I will say that to me this does not feel elderly."[63] When his nephew expires, Sammler approaches the bed and recites a version of the *El-malay-rachamin,* "Remember, God, the soul of Elya Gruner."[64]

In an age of technology as in the age of the Bible, man remains a meaning-seeking creature called to covenant with a value-sustaining power greater than himself. Death remains for us as for our fathers the supreme reminder that we are junior partners in the covenant of life. We yearn for an ultimate validation of our life which may be bestowed only by the ultimate source of our being. We have not outgrown the confession of the psalmist: "Lord, let me know my end, how fleeting my life is. Surely every man stands as a mere breath, and now for what do I wait? My hope is in Thee."[65]

Covenant Man Is Everyman

It is said that the prophet Jeremiah and a companion once searched for the secret formula to create a golem. They tasted success. A robot suddenly appeared before them. Etched on its forehead were the Hebrew words *Adonoy, Elohim Emet* ("God the Lord is Truth"). Bearing a knife in its hand, the robot scratched out the first letter from the word *Emet*. Now the inscription on its forehead read *Adonoy, Elohim Met* ("God the Lord is Dead").[66]

This remarkable agada, which predates the technological age by centuries, embodies the fear that the new time of unprecedented human self-assertion will destroy the traditional image of man. Covenant man, so exquisitely limned in biblical and rabbinic agada, is at once uniquely empowered and existentially limited. He stands before the God who calls him into being, summons him for sacred partnership, and endows his finite labors with abiding worth. Can covenant man survive the promethean thrust of a technological age?

I have contended that agada continues to mediate an authentic image of man. It is no less true today than in the far reaches of the mystic past: the divine gift of dominion over nature is conditional. Man is accountable to God for his stewardship thereof.

The divine gift of freedom makes man potentially the most noble and most dangerous creature on earth. Man's freedom is God's supreme risk under the covenant. Man's power to serve God includes the capacity and temptation to betray the purposes of his Creator.

The messianic vision remains both a demand and a hope. Man is called to help redeem God's world, but the Messiah has not yet come, and many of the most pernicious pretenders find their way into the political arena. All man's systems are at best broken images of the kingdom of God.

The divine decree of death is man's ineluctable encounter with his own creatureliness. Implanted within him is a yearning for abidingness which rests ultimately on God's infinite power and love.

In the twenty-first century as in the first, agada presents the truest image of man's place in the universe. His awesome power and his littleness lend new cogency to the religious imagination of the sages. They perceived man as the crowning glory of creation—the creature for whom God prepared a world before summoning him to the divine banquet on the first Sabbath. But the agada also reminds man that even the gnats preceded him in the order of creation. Similarly agada envisages God exhorting each man to declare "for my sake was the world created," but does not permit him to forget that he is "but dust and ashes." Where may we find a profounder image of our grandeur and our littleness?

VIII · "Dost Thou Wish to Know Him?"
Some Concluding Remarks

Dost thou wish to know Him who spoke and by whose word the world came into being? Study agada, for through such agada you may understand the Holy One, blessed be He, and follow His ways.   (Sifre)

THERE IS A HASIDIC TALE about a man who each morning could not remember where he had put his clothes the night before. The difficulty became so acute that the man almost hesitated to go to bed. One evening he took pencil and pad, and while undressing he noted exactly where he put everything. The next morning he took the piece of paper and was able to find each article of clothing. When fully dressed, however, he sighed: "That's all very well. I know where all my clothes are, but where in the world am I?"

This story may be taken on two levels. The man may be so stupid, so distraught, so disoriented, that he does not even know his physical location—literally in what space he is standing. But the second level reflects a man's awareness of the deeper issue. He is not seeking to locate himself in space but to ask the "boundary question"—the question of life's meaning.

There are times when such boundary questions are, to say the least, inappropriate, even gauche. In the midst of a pennant-clinching game, if I stand next to a man who is frantically shouting encouragement to the pitcher, I ought not to ask him: "What is the

192

meaning of all this frenzy?" If I do he may well poke me, or at least assume that I have become mentally unbalanced. Such is not the time for the "deeper question."

On the other hand, from the perspective of a rabbi-agadist, there are "teachable moments" when religious questions touch a responsive chord. It may be a crisis situation, when the structures of life have crumbled and we feel especially exposed: illness, the encounter with death, a deep personal disappointment or defeat, a moment when we are temporarily dislodged from our firm niche in the pecking order of the marketplace, or a day of solitude on a sun-kissed lake. A rabbi may even find that certain seasons of the year present a greater openness to transcendence. During the High Holy Days, if I ask "Who are we, where are we," the congregation assumes I am not speaking of their physical location in the sanctuary but pointing to the story of their lives.

What of the future of agada? What of the future of Jewish faith? Will prayer in the synagogue survive beyond this or the next century? Will rabbis or their equivalent still seek to tell the life story of Jews by drawing on the ancient symbols of religious language?

Secularization is real. Many Jews feel more comfortable speaking of their commitment to the Jewish people than of their loyalty to the God of the covenant. Yet as we have argued in these pages, intimations of transcendence abide in the House of Israel. We are not prepared to institutionalize our religious doubts. Jews have not thronged to synagogues organized under the principle that "God is dead." Such extreme forms of "humanistic Judaism" have won no more than a handful of supporters among our people.

We still prefer to have the life-cycle events sanctified by religious symbolism. We continue to relish a sermon which effectively describes our life situation in the great stories drawn out of our people's heritage. We prefer a rabbi who affirms more rather than less of the tradition than we. The gestures of our ordinary life reveal traces of faith in a creative order, a sense of ultimate accountability, an inalienable hope in the promise of creation.

By such gestures we continue to acknowledge a rootedness in, and a yearning for, that dimension of life not adequately encompassed by the apostles of a postreligious modernity.

In *The Magic Mountain* Thomas Mann argues through one of his characters that a human being is a person who "consciously or unconsciously . . . seeks the final, the absolute . . . meaning in all his efforts and activities." If his culture responds to such questions with "hollow silence," a certain "laming of the personality is bound to occur."[1]

Comparable testimony is present in the annals of contemporary social science. A noted sociologist of religion, Robert Bellah, contends that "somehow or other men must have a sense of the whole if they are to live; they must have something to believe in and commit themselves to. . . . religion . . . is an imaginative statement about the truth (the worthwhileness) of the totality of human experience. The focus of such belief is unavoidably a reality transcending that which can be 'scientifically verified.' Men need to symbolize—to speak—of such a reality whether that speech is 'religious in a traditional sense or not.' "[2]

Agada is Judaism's classic "imaginative statement"—a collection of stories that evoke the Jew's perception of life as ordered and purposeful. These stories tell of God's creation of the world, His covenant with man, and His particular covenant with the children of Abraham. Within this symbolic framework the born Jew (and all others who feel so moved) are invited to perceive a world endowed with promise and an individual life imbued with abiding worth.

Our Life: A Significant Story

Let me review more specifically the unique symbolic power of agada. Through a great religious story, my individual life is linked to a transcendent drama. My little sojourn on earth is invested with scope and significance.

When, for example, the love of two persons is consecrated by the symbolism of agada they are reminded that such intimacy between man and woman is at the heart of life's meaning. Their love is placed in a cosmic frame. You will recall that the wedding benedictions begin by proclaiming God as creator of man, proceed to the affirmation of love as God's gift to His creatures, and then consecrate this couple to the task of building a "home in the midst of the people Israel" in order that they may transmit Torah from generation to generation.

On other liturgical occasions this same couple is invited, through agada, to share a people's history. They become partners to events which preceded their meeting and their lives by many centuries. At Passover they tell a story which binds their lives to bondage in Egypt and to a great liberation ("each Jew is obliged to regard himself as if he were going out of Egypt"). When the Torah is read in the synagogue, we are encouraged to feel that each generation stands anew at Sinai ("Praised be Thou, O Lord, who *gives* the Torah"). We are bonded to the God of the Universe as bearers of a special truth. Even so does the Bar Mitzvah or the Confirmand receive the Torah and feel part of a covenant people. The time will come to transmit the Torah to the next generation. Thus does agada grace our lives with a transcendent quality.

So often in life I encounter the yawning gulf between my vision and my powers. How easily I may be overcome by the sense of powerlessness and futility. While I feel moved to battle evil and labor for the realization of precious values, a tormenting question always threatens to paralyze my will by casting a spell of impotence: What am I? What can I truly hope to accomplish? What does it matter which path I choose? In the midst of this threat, agada invites me to be faithful to an apprehension of transcendent meaning. In covenant perspective my efforts *do* count; they are not futile gestures. My best visions are implanted by One who is active in history to redeem them and who summons me to a sacred partnership which lends abiding worth to my earthly pilgrimage.

To clarify this role of agada I might contrast it with a mass-media presentation of the news. In print and film we are deluged daily with images which purportedly tell the story of our lives. Despite the wizardry of the electronic industry (its capacity to capture the unsuspecting voice on a hidden tape, or relay a transatlantic conference via satellite, or project a live suicide attempt upon our TV screens), the mass media have not replaced the sensitive novelist as chronicler of the human adventure.

In defense of his art, Saul Bellow has observed that the weekly yield of the news media, for all its quantitative immensity, does not really speak to man's depths. "He [man] feels peculiarly contentless in his public aspects, lacking in substance and without a proper story. A proper story would express his intuition that his own existence is peculiarly significant. The sense that his existence is significant haunts him. But he can prove nothing. And the business of art is with this sense, precisely."[3]

Substitute the word *agada* for *art* and we have an eloquent articulation of the role of religious stories in a technological age. *At its best agada responds to man's intuition of his personal significance.*

Agada and the Sense of Community

Agada also enables this "intuition of significance" to be shared by mediating a sense of true community. Indeed the durability of religion's great stories is a measure of their capacity to transform deep private sensitivities into sharable experience and collective memory. The communicative power of a great agada is known to each of us. It bridges the so-called generation gap. Persons of all ages and backgrounds can tune in to a great story and respond with shock or a tingle of recognition. A preacher knows that stories will invariably intensify the attention level of his congregation. The great stories may be repeated again and again without losing their capacity to enthrall us.

Moreover there is something special about listening to such stories within a group. As I write these words I think of the spell which each year's recitation of the Abraham and Isaac narrative casts upon the assembled congregation during the High Holy Days. Although we know that in the end the sacrifice on Mount Moriah will not be demanded, nevertheless, the story affects us deeply. To feel part of a community is to be able to respond to its great stories with a sense of personal recognition and involvement.

It follows that worship is most successful when the liturgy mediates a sense of true community by empowering us to tell a significant story of our common life. Though we use the same liturgy, some worship services will be more evocative than others, depending on the experience we bring to the occasion.

Let me illustrate this point by reflecting on several worship occasions in my own congregation which were suffused with special vitality. The service held following President's Kennedy's assassination was one such event. Assembled to overflowing in the sanctuary, the congregation came not to hear a repetition of the TV or editorial coverage, but to share anxiety and to reconfirm hope. The daily liturgy's themes gave voice to our shared yearnings, and the "fit" of liturgy and experience lent special power and beauty to that hour of worship.

I also recall vividly a service held during a great Chicago blizzard. Most of us could not get to the regularly scheduled Sabbath service. A few could and did, each with his own story of braving the elements. Each of us felt the service took place only because of his presence. Each of us felt needed. We recited the customary prayers and affirmed the people Israel's public witness to God. On that occasion, however, we felt more poignantly the responsibility resting upon us. We were a symbol of a small people. The blizzard and the small attendance seemed to dramatize our vulnerability and our individual importance for the historic task of the Jew in the world. How fragile and how precious is man's power to bear witness to God. The blizzard we had braved was its own symbolic embodiment of Israel's pilgrimage and testimony in a turbulent world.

Those moments of worship are most genuine which evoke a sense of community and relate the symbols of faith to the visceral experiences of our common lives.

Agada: A New Way of Knowing

In addition to mediating a sense of sacred community and responding to our individual intuitions of significance, agada at its best possesses a unique power to bridge the gap between reflection and experience. C. S. Lewis, a great storyteller and lay-theologian, once asked why the narratives of a religious tradition are so much more durable than its formal theology and philosophy. Lewis offered this answer:

> Human intellect is incurably abstract. Pure mathematics is the type of successful thought, yet the only realities we experience are concrete—this pain, this pleasure, this day, this man. Now while we are loving the man, bearing the pain, enjoying the pleasure, we are not intellectually apprehending Pleasure, Pain, or Personality. . . . this is our dilemma—either to know and not to taste, or more strictly to lack one kind of knowledge because we are in an experience or to lack another kind because we are outside it. . . . You cannot study pleasure in the moment of nuptial embrace nor repentance while repenting, nor analyze the nature of humor while roaring with laughter.

How then resolve this dilemma between experiencing and understanding? Lewis responds: ''Myth [agada] is the partial solution. In the enjoyment of a great myth [agada] we come nearest to experiencing as concrete what can otherwise be understood as an abstraction. . . . Myth is the isthmus which connects the peninsular world of thought with the vast continent we really belong to.''[4]

The Einstein formula $E = mc^2$ symbolizes the order and unity of the universe, but in a way different from the biblical agada on that first page of Genesis. A mathematical formula objectifies the mystery of an ordered world. The Genesis agada enables us both to apprehend and taste life's unity.

The oneness of mankind is an abstraction we cannot directly experience. To be sure, Frank Borman, James Lovell, and William Anders may have come closest to doing so when, in late December 1968, they orbited the moon and *saw* planet earth from an angle never before accessible to mortal man.

Thanks to the wonders of TV, the astronauts' view of earth was transmitted to our home screens. The poet Archibald Mac-Leish beheld and was moved to exclaim:

> To see the earth as it truly is
> Small and blue and beautiful

In that eternal silence where it floats
Is to see ourselves
As riders on the earth together
Brothers on that bright loneliness
In the eternal cold—
Brothers who know now they are truly brothers.[5]

Even when vision is fortified with technology, the sense of unity still requires a poetic (agadic) consciousness. Long before *Apollo 8,* the cosmic brotherhood of man found expression in the Genesis agada. How fitting that the three astronauts concluded their telecast from outer space that day by taking turns reading from the first chapter of Genesis: "In the beginning God created the heaven and the earth . . . " No words could have matched the evocative power of the Genesis story at that moment in history. No story could more poignantly mediate our apprehension of *One* world.

Strategies for Reclaiming Agada

In the end our ability to relate to the world of agada depends on our making the story of Jewish faith the central narrative of our life. The struggle with agada is, in effect, a struggle with the faith claims of Judaism. For a variety of reasons alluded to in the introductory chapter, the believer who wishes to communicate and share his faith must encounter the stumbling blocks of a culture shaped by the scientific rationalism of at least two centuries. What strategies must a defender of the faith employ? The present volume may be seen retrospectively as a response to that question. Let us briefly retrace our steps.

One of the issues confronting modern man is the respectability of faith. He may discover a will to believe but feel compelled by the canons of sophistication to struggle against it. How pervasive is the modern temper's bias against the affirmation of meaning. That bias leads many to resist the deeper intuitions of the soul as dangerous illusions or as vestiges of childish innocence.

I am reminded of an accomplished medical researcher who

defensively admits that his laboratory environment impels him to see the world in an objective framework which leaves little room for the presence and activity of God. Yet outside the laboratory he finds himself wondering about certain mysteries that are beyond the competence of scientific reason, and he is involved in gestures of reverence (worship) which *seem* incompatible with the life of a research scientist. He professes to lead this double-life with some confusion and uneasiness.

The contemporary defender of the faith must respond to such uneasiness in many veterans of modernity. I have tried to suggest in (Chapter IV) that the premise of an essentially meaningless or godless world is as much a postulate of faith as the premise of meaning. The defender of Judaism must seek to explode those excessive claims of "reason" which inhibit man's power to respond to his "intuition of significance." Conversely, we must periodically rediscover that it is possible to take seriously the basic framework of agada without betraying the legitimate claims of scientific reason.

In my own quest for a reconciling vision, I have been helped by Buber's concept of two complementary orientations to reality: *I-It* and *I-Thou*. The first initiates us into the technological kingdom of dominion over nature. The second opens us to the discovery of our special bond to the Lord of nature and history. As Buber reminds us: "Without *It* man cannot live. But he who lives with *It* alone is not a man."

A second strategy enlisted in defense of the agadic world-view is the appeal to the intimations of transcendence which intrude upon us. We are often more religious than we profess. As we explore our "peak experiences," the ultimate premises of our moral imagination, our profound sense of a moral order in the universe, or that basic trust which is the ground of all great endeavor—we may discover traces of that transcendent reality whom our fathers envisaged as Creator, Giver of Torah, and source of redemptive power.

The task of the contemporary defender of faith is thus not only to help man feel less embarrassed by his will to believe, but more self-conscious of the religious experiences in his everyday life. This latter task I have attempted to outline in Chapter V of the present volume.

Thirdly, as we wrestle with the God of our fathers we need to discover that agada is not a rigidly confining spiritual straitjacket, but a resilient, elastic medium for the message of Jewish faith. The agada itself reflects the individual temperaments and idiosyncrasies of sages and seers in search for the gift of meaning. We encountered the flexibility of the agadic framework, for example, when we reviewed the many ways in which our forebears faced the problem of evil in a world governed by a God of power and love (see especially Chapter III and Chapter VI).

We also discovered that each generation both inherits an agadic legacy and reshapes that which has been given to it . Thus some agadists accentuated the personal image of the Messiah while others responded to the symbol of a messianic age. In our own time there are those who feel impelled to speak of God in the language of a technological world (energy, power) instead of the anthropomorphic symbols of earlier generations. I have found it necessary to reject the traditional agada's ethnocentric notion of God's special love for the people Israel, without, however, surrendering the concept of Israel's particular vocation in God's world.

In Chapter VI, I have argued that the traditional agada is generally more viable than some of its detractors allow, but that it is possible for each generation to make idiomatic and ideological changes without undermining the basic story of Jewish faith.

Are there no ground rules for agadic "reform"? Are there no limits beyond which one is trifling with the essential vision of Jewish faith? At what point does my revision of symbols constitute irresponsible irreverence?

Some answers to these questions have been implied in the preceding pages. I noted that for all its flexibility, the tradition did not countenance the premise of meaninglessness. *The underlying function of agada was, under all circumstances and conditions of life, to reaffirm God as Creator, Giver of Torah, and sustainer of hope.*

Similarly, as we noted in the introduction to this volume,

classical agada affirms the reality and interrelatedness of God, Torah, and the people Israel. The authentic Jew must wrestle with a three-dimensional covenant. One cannot responsibly speak of the meaning of Jewish existence (Israel) without speaking of God and of Torah. Any authentic Jewish theology must acknowledge that God, Torah, and Israel are inextricably interwined. Bold doubt is, as we have seen, no stranger to the world of agada. But Israel, if it remains Israel, must never cease to struggle for the gift of transcendent meaning. A synagogue whose liturgy affirms that God-talk is an anachronism has trespassed the bounds of agadic legitimacy.

Finally, I would suggest that responsible agadic revision ought seek to justify symbolic change by appealing not only to contemporary insights or new revelations, but to elements within the tradition itself. For all his radicalism, the observance of this ground rule has imbued Mordecai Kaplan's Reconstructionism with the mark of a Jewish quest for meaning. He has always strained to find within the tradition itself some ground for his symbolic revision thereof.

After the contemporary agadist has proclaimed the respectability of faith in an age of science, the intimations of faith in everyday life, and the malleability of religious symbolism, he must still seek to correlate the perceived realities in the human situation with the language of faith. He must persuasively suggest that even in a technological age, the classical agadic view of man's place in the universe has not lost its symbolic power or its essential truth. This I have attempted to argue in Chapter VII of the present volume.

After all these strategic overtures to the faith-questing Jew, he must be reminded of his need for significant Jewish experiences. Perhaps that is why the younger generation is returning to observances which received from its elders at best a tolerant shrug. The resurgence of elaborate Passover Seders (not ones in which liturgy is totally eclipsed by cuisine), the renewed observance of Havdalah (the ceremony separating the new week from the Sabbath), and Selichot (the midnight penitential service preceding the High Holy Days)—all mirror the yearning not merely to recall what our ancestors did and felt, but to do it ourselves and hopefully experience anew the grace of transcendence.

We come to the symbols of our heritage, however, after passing through the labyrinth of modern self-consciousness. Far more than our ancestors we know that we in part create the symbols by which we live. We make a distinction between the realm of *I-It* and *I-Thou*. We analyze in psychological and sociological terms the very rituals which we are bidden to embrace and respond to with the fullness of our being.

An analogy may help sharpen the difficulty. Before the age of Freud, Masters and Johnson, Drs. Ruben and Comfort—the dynamics and mechanics of human sexuality were less understood but more spontaneously encountered. It may well be that our age of scientific sexual awareness enables us to cure certain forms of barrenness, frigidity, and impotence, but it is also the case that excessive analysis *(I-It)* may impede spontaneity, full involvement, and joyful immediacy *(I-Thou)*. There is a price to be paid for the loss of innocence.

This challenging dilemma informs our religious quest as well. Harvey Cox phrased it thus: "The problem is how to reconcile a critical degree of self-consciousness with a burning desire for experience which is not spoiled by too much self-analysis. . . . We want to be coolly sophisticated yet not lose the simple directness we think is vital in human life."[6]

The challenge is real but hopefully not insurmountable. More crucial than all our strategy to revitalize our sense of Jewish sacredness is the need to re-experience for ourselves the evocative power of the great stories and ritual dramas binding the people Israel to an eternal God. Indeed, agadists through the ages have reminded us that when God offered the Torah to Israel, they replied: "We shall do and [then] we shall harken [more fully understand]." We need to participate in the Passover Seder to understand the power of agada (Haggadah). To put it otherwise—halacha leads us back to agada.

The Future of Faith

All strategies aside, the defender of the faith will continually return to the question posed at the beginning of this chapter. Does agada (a religious world-view) have a future? The formidable prognosticators are divided on the future of religion in an age of high technology. Philip Rieff has spoken of the emergence of "postreligious" man. Such a man will use technology to soothe his physical and emotional pain, extend his life-span, and fill his vacant hours with diverting pastimes. He may slough off all vestiges of faith as the infantile imaginings of an innocent past. In any case, he will be less inclined to ask the deeper questions if such questions intrude upon him: Why am I here? What is the purpose or meaning of my life? He will rationally conclude that such questions are unanswerable in any empirical way and therefore undeserving of his energy or perplexity. Indeed, to linger on such issues may be a symptom of neurosis.[7]

The authors of a Rand Corporation projection of the year 2000 appear to endorse the scenario of postreligious man. The word *religion* is not even found in the master index.[8] On the other hand, Andrew Greeley of the National Opinion Research Center, among others, ventures forth on a different projective limb. "Religion in the year 2000," writes Greeley, "will still provide at least a substantial component of the ultimate interpretive scheme or meaning system [for] the overwhelming majority of the population."[9]

Crucial to all such projections is an assessment of the long-range impact of technology on man's sense of the sacred. Almost a century and a half ago, a young Frenchman visited America as it first entered the industrial revolution. Alexis de Tocqueville speculated on the impact of the industrial age on man's quest for faith. Initially he predicted that the application of technology would reduce the hold of the churches on the minds and lives of their members. America would indeed lead the way in deflecting people from the pursuit of "pie in the sky" to the pursuit of an earthly salvation.

Nevertheless, man's production and consumption of various creature comforts will not content him because, said Tocqueville, "the soul has wants that must be satisfied, and whatever pains be taken to divert it from itself, it soon grows weary, restless and disquieted amid the enjoyments of sense." Since men must first enjoy bread in abundance before they discern that "man cannot live by bread alone," it follows that "the means which allow men up to a certain point to go without religion, are perhaps the only means we still possess for bringing mankind back by a long and roundabout path to a state of faith."[10] So spoke Tocqueville of the long-range impact of technology on faith. Now, a century and a half later, as we stand in the vanguard of the technological age, another Frenchman, Jean Revel, has visited America and reports seeing a "religious element" in America's current disquietude—"a need for sacredness."[11]

There are indeed impressive signs of the resurgence of powerful religious impulses, especially among the affluent, college-educated young. Within the Jewish community, colleagues confirm my own experience that today's younger generation is considerably more open to religious symbols and concerns than my own generation two decades ago. This certainly runs counter to the popularly held notion that sophistication must necessarily signal the diminution of religious concern. Tocqueville may well have scored another prophetic triumph.

I do not mean to conclude this foray into the world of agada by predicting stampedes to the synagogue, or a Jewish community in which faith has become a confident possession rather than an uneven quest, but only insist that in man's tomorrows, he will continue to tell stories which illumine the depth of his life. Such stories, whether told by biblical poet, neo-Hasid, folksinger, novelist, or rabbinic preacher, will point to the inexhaustible mystery at the heart of life and will affirm that beyond the mystery there is meaning.

Such stories will be told, and they will strike a responsive chord in the souls of many. Nevertheless, faith will remain a struggle and a quest, not an irresistible certainty. At least until the coming of the Messiah, the affirmation of life's meaning will not be unambiguously disclosed to human experience. That ambiguity is the price of God's transcendence and man's freedom.

In biblical agada, Moses asked to know God's name. He was told: "I am who I am." The so-called disclosure of God's name became, in reality, a confirmation of God's mystery. The ultimate Other in man's experience eludes our total understanding or control.

In the presence of the divine mystery, man remains free to deny as well as free to confirm the reality disclosed to the eye of faith. A contemporary agadist reminds us that it is God's plan to permit man leverage for both affirmation and denial. Rabbi Meir Simcha Hakohen of Dvinsk, Latvia, comments on the phrase "in the image of God created He him" (Genesis 1:27).

> The image of God is free intellectual choice, unforced free will. . . . He [God] said to Himself: "Let us make man in our image." This means that the Torah speaks in the language of men, saying: Let us leave man room to choose, that his acts may not be forced nor his thoughts imposed . . . that he may be able to act against his own nature and against what is right in the eyes of the Lord."[12]

Thus does the agada itself provide warrant to the assumption that Israel in the twenty-first century will become a congregation not of totally confirmed believers or totally confirmed disbelievers, but of men and women who continue to wrestle with the stories their fathers told and with the God their fathers affirmed. Freedom to deny will remain the price of freedom to affirm. Many of our great-grandchildren will be doing their share of both, and their mentors will declare:

> Dost thou wish to know Him who spoke and by whose word the world came into being? Study agada, for through such agada you may understand the Holy One, Blessed be He, and follow in His ways.[13]

Notes

CHAPTER I

1. Langdon Gilkey, "The Contribution of Culture to the Reign of God," in *The Future as the Presence of Shared Hope,* ed. M. Muckenhirn (New York: Sheed & Ward, 1968), p. 43.
2. Quoted in Jacob Katz, *Exclusiveness and Tolerance* (New York: Oxford, 1961), p. 170.
3. Arthur Cohen, *The Natural and The Supernatural Jew* (New York: Pantheon, 1962), p. 37.
4. Deuteronomy 29:9–14.
5. Deuteronomy Rabbah 2:35 (Vaetchanan).
6. Job 38:4
7. Midrash on Proverbs 31:10 f., 54b.
8. *Rabbi's Manual* (New York: Central Conference of American Rabbis, 1961), p. 73.

CHAPTER II

1. Genesis 12:1–3.
2. Genesis Rabbah 38:13.
3. See James Pritchard, ed., *Ancient Near Eastern Texts Relating to the Old Testament,* (Princeton: Princeton University Press, 1969), pp. 31 ff.
4. Yehezkel Kaufmann, *The Religion of Israel,* trans. and ed. Moshe Greenberg (Chicago: University of Chicago Press, 1960), pp. 38 f.
5. Mircea Eliade, *Cosmos and History,* (New York: Harper & Row, 1959), p. 104.
6. Isaiah 2:4.
7. Jeremiah 31:3.
8. Leo Baeck, *The Essence of Judaism,* trans. Victor Grubenwieser and Leonard Pearl, (New York: Schocken, 1948), p. 92.
9. See Pritchard, *Ancient Near Eastern Texts,* pp. 262 ff.
10. Genesis 15. See discussion in Nahum Sarna, *Understanding Genesis,* (New York: McGraw-Hill, 1966), pp. 128 ff.

11. II Kings 17:5 f.; see A. G. Lie, *The Inscriptions of Sargon II,* Pt. I (Paris, 1929), quoted in Pritchard, *Ancient Near Eastern Texts,* p. 195.
12. II Kings 25:27–30; cf. W. F. Albright, "King Jehoiachin in Exile," *Biblical Archaeologist* 5, (December 1942): 49–55, quoted in H. Orlinsky *Ancient Israel* (Ithaca: Cornell University Press, 1954), p. 121.
13. William H. McNeill, *The Rise of the West,* (Chicago: University of Chicago Press, 1963), p. 158.
14. Exodus 13:9.
15. Genesis 17:1 ff.
16. Exodus 19:3.
17. Ibid. 32:4.
18. Amos 5:21–24.
19. Jeremiah 33:10–11.
20. Hosea 2:16–17, 21–22, 25.
21. Ezekiel 36:20–24.
22. Isaiah 53:4f.
23. Ibid. 42:1, 4.
24. Ibid. 2:2–4.
25. Zechariah 8:20 ff.
26. Ibid. 14:9.
27. A.J. Heschel, *A Passion for Truth,* (New York: Farrar, Straus & Giroux, 1973), p. 257.
28. Deuteronomy 29:13.

CHAPTER III

1. Isaiah 40:1.
2. Ibid. 53:4 f.
3. Jeremiah 33:11; cf. 12:1.
4. Flavius Josephus, *The Jewish War,* trans. G. A. Williamson (Baltimore: Penguin Books, 1969), pp. 308 f.
5. Ibid., p. 309.
6. Ibid., p. 310.
7. Ibid., p. 350.
8. Abot de Rabbi Natan, chap. 4, ed. Solomon Schechter (Vienna, 1887; reprint ed., New York, 1945).
9. Mekilta Bahodesh, ed. Lauterbach, vol. 2, p. 194.
10. Babylonian Talmud, Yoma 9b.
11. Babylonian Talmud, Menachot 53b.
12. Midrash on Song of Songs 2:16.
13. Mekilta Bahodesh, p. 247.
14. Babylonian Talmud, Gittin 56b.
15. Ibid.
16. Pesikta Rabbati, Piska 30:4, ed. and trans. William Braude, vol. 2 (New Haven: Yale University Press, 1968), p. 597.
17. Midrash on Lamentations, introduction, no. 24, ed. Levin-Epstein (Warsaw, 1924).

18. Babylonian Talmud, Berachot 9b.
19. Exodus Rabbah 15:13; cf. Leviticus Rabbah 9:3, ed. Levin-Epstein (Warsaw, 1924).
20. Pesikta Rabbati 139a, ed. M. Friedman (Vienna, 1880).
21. Lamentations Rabbah 1:1, ed. Levin-Epstein (Warsaw, 1924).
22. Mekilta Piska, p. 113.
23. Jeremiah 31:2–6.
24. Psalm 33:20–22.
25. Pesikta Rabbati 106b.
26. Huston Smith, *The Religions of Man* (New York: Mentor Books, 1958), p. 234.
27. Elie Wiesel, *Night,* trans. Stella Rodway (New York: Hill & Wang, 1960), pp. 43 f.
28. Elie Wiesel, *The Gates of the Forest,* trans. Frances Frenaye, (New York: Holt, Rinehart & Winston, Inc. 1966), p. 225.
29. Ibid., p. 33.
30. Elie Wiesel, *Souls on Fire,* trans. Marion Wiesel (New York: Vintage Books, 1973), p. 107.
31. Ibid., p. 108.
32. Ibid., p. 111.
33. Commencement Address, Jewish Theological Seminary, June 4, 1967, in *Jewish Heritage,* Summer 1967, p. 55.
34. Armand L. Robinson, ed., *The Ten Commandments* (New York: Simon & Schuster, 1943), pp. xii f.
35. Babylonian Talmud, Sabbath 89a.
36. "Sacred Images of Man," *Christian Century,* December 11, 1957, p. 1473.
37. Ibid.
38. Babylonian Talmud, Sanhedrin 37b.
39. "Hymn of Victory of Merneptah," in *The Ancient Near East,* ed. James Pritchard (Princeton: Princeton University Press, 1958), p. 231.
40. I Maccabees 4:55 ff.
41. Babylonian Talmud, Shabbat 21b.
42. Ibid. 22b.
43. Genesis 32:25–28.
44. Abraham Joshua Heschel, *A Passion for Truth* (New York: Farrar, Straus & Giroux, 1973), pp. 302 f.

CHAPTER IV

1. Eliezer Berkovits, *Faith After the Holocaust* (New York: KTAV, 1973), p. 90.
2. Sam Kean, *Apology for Wonder* (New York: Harper & Row, 1969), p. 61.
3. I Kings 18:18–39.
4. Genesis 1.
5. Loren Eiseley, *The Unexpected Universe* (New York: Harcourt, Brace & World, 1964), p. 135.

6. Bertrand Russell, "Mysticism and Logic," quoted in David Edwards, *Religion and Change* (New York: Harper & Row, 1969), p. 265.
7. Walter Lipmann, *A Preface to Morals,* quoted in Edwards, *Religion and Change.*
8. Archibald MacLeish, *J.B.: A Play in Verse* (Cambridge: Houghton Mifflin, 1956), pp. 152 f.
9. *Union Prayerbook,* vol. 1 (New York: Central Conference of American Rabbis, 1940), p. 314.
10. Friedrich Nietzsche, *Thus Spake Zarathustra,* trans. Thomas Commons (New York: Modern Library, 1927), pp. 291 f.
11. Avot 6:2.
12. Jean-Paul Sartre, *Existentialism,* trans. Bernard Frechtman (New York: Philosophical Library, 1947), p. 58.
13. Sigmund Freud, *Totem and Taboo,* trans. James Strachey (1913; reprint ed., New York: Norton, 1962).
14. Sigmund Freud, *Moses and Monotheism,* trans. Catherine Jones (1939; reprint ed., New York: Vintage Books, 1955).
15. *Authorized Daily Prayer Book,* ed. Joseph Hertz (New York: Bloch, 1948), p. 129.
16. Sigmund Freud, *New Introductory Lectures on Psycho-Analysis,* trans. W. J. H. Sprott (New York: Norton, 1933), p. 222, quoted in Richard Rubenstein, *The Religious Imagination* (New York: Bobbs-Merrill, 1968), p. 11.
17. E. Fackenheim, "Elijah and the Empiricists," in *The Religious Situation* (Boston: Beacon Press, 1969), p. 858.
18. Martin Buber, *I and Thou,* trans. Ronald Gregor Smith (New York: Scribner's, 1937).
19. Alfred North Whitehead, *Science and the Modern World* (New York: Macmillan, 1926), p. 286.
20. *I and Thou,* p. 34.
21. Martin Buber, *Between Man and Man,* trans. R. G. Smith (Boston: Beacon Press, 1955) p. 16.
22. Charles H. Townes, in *Zygon,* September 1966, p. 207, quoted in Roland Gittelsohn, *Wings of the Morning* (New York: Union of American Hebrew Congregations, 1969), pp. 185 f.
23. Quoted in ibid., p. 188.
24. Genesis 9:12 f.
25. Psalm 13:1–3.
26. *Chicago Tribune,* August 15, 1971, p. 1.
27. Psalm 8.
28. Martin Buber, *Eclipse of God* (New York: Harper, 1952), p. 135.
29. Ibid., p. 70.
30. Harold Schilling, *The New Consciousness in Science and Religion,* p. 227.
31. Martin Buber, *Moses* (1946; reprint ed., New York: Harper Torchbooks, 1958), p. 75.
32. Ibid., p. 77.
33. Schilling, *New Consciousness in Science and Religion,* p. 228.
34. Eiseley, *Unexpected Universe,* p. 55.

CHAPTER V

1. The term is taken from Peter Berger's *A Rumor of Angels* (New York: Doubleday, 1969).
2. Genesis 1:1 f.
3. Babylonian Talmud, Sanhedrin 38a.
4. Nathan A. Scott, *The Wild Prayer of Longing* (New Haven: Yale University Press, 1971), p. 72 f.
5. John Hayward, "The Uses of Myth in an Age of Science," *Zygon,* June 1968.
6. Ludwig Wittgenstein, quoted in Michael Novak, *Belief and Unbelief* (New York: Macmillan, 1965), p. 42.
7. Abraham Maslow, *Toward a Psychology of Being,* 2d ed. (Princeton: Van Nostrand, 1962), p. 71.
8. Ibid., pp. 81 f.
9. Ibid., pp. 87 f.
10. Harvey Cox, *Feast of Fools* (Cambridge: Harvard University Press, 1969), p. 28.
11. Babylonian Talmud, Sanhedrin 38a.
12. Ibid.
13. Genesis 9:5 f.
14. Sanhedrin 37a.
15. Allen Wheelis, *The Moralist* (New York: Basic Books, 1973), p. 116.
16. Ibid.
17. Martin Buber, *The Knowledge of Man,* trans. Maurice Friedman and R. G. Smith (New York: Harper & Row, 1965), p. 132.
18. Genesis 4:10.
19. Joseph Conrad, *Lord Jim* (Cambridge: Houghton Mifflin, 1958), p. 69.
20. Yoram Kaniuk, *Adam Resurrected,* trans. Seymour Simckes (New York: Atheneum 1971).
21. Arthur Miller, *After the Fall* (New York: Viking, 1964).
22. Saul Bellow, *Henderson the Rain King* (Greenwich: Fawcett, 1968), p. 24.
23. Ibid., p. 267.
24. Saul Bellow, *Herzog* (New York: Viking, 1964) p. 231.
25. Ibid., p. 314.
26. Saul Bellow, *Mr. Sammler's Planet* (New York: Viking, 1969), p. 316.
27. Union Prayerbook, vol. 2 (New York: Central Conference of American Rabbis), pp. 146 f.
28. Eugene Borowitz, *The Masks We Wear* (New York: Simon & Schuster, 1973), p. 202.
29. Bernard Malamud, *The Assistant* (New York: Noonday Press, 1957), p. 229.
30. Babylonian Talmud, Shabbat 88a.
31. Mekilta, Bahodesh, ed. Lauterbach, vol. 2, pp. 234 ff.
32. Ernest van den Haag, *The Jewish Mystique* (New York: Stein & Day, 1962), pp. 52 f.
33. Jean-Paul Sartre, *Anti-Semite and Jew,* trans. George Becker (New York: Schocken Books, 1948), chap. 3.

34. Emil Fackenheim, *Quest for Past and Future* (Bloomington: University of Indiana Press, 1968), p. 19.
35. Ibid.
36. Loren Eiseley, *The Unexpected Universe* (New York: Harcourt, Brace & World, 1964), p. 117.
37. Exodus 15:11, 18.
38. Psalm 22.
39. *Union Prayerbook,* vol. 2, p. 56.
40. Isaiah 28:12.
41. *Worldview,* July 1972.
42. Robert Bellah, *Beyond Belief* (New York: Harper & Row, 1970), p. 201.
43. Huston Smith, *Condemned to Meaning* (New York: Harper & Row, 1965), pp. 46–57.
44. Psalm 90:17.
45. Martin Buber, *Knowledge of Man,* p. 62.
46. Smith, *Condemned to Meaning*, p. 55.
47. Ibid.

CHAPTER VI

1. J. F. Handelsman, "The Creation," *Playboy,* September 1971, p. 188.
2. Ibid., p. 189.
3. Babylonian Talmud, Sanhedrin 38b.
4. Babylonian Talmud, Baba Metzia 59b.
5. Roland Gittelsohn, *Man's Best Hope* (New York: Random House, 1966), p. 109.
6. Exodus 3:14.
7. Gershom Scholem, *The Kabbalah and Its Symbolism* (New York: Schocken, 1965), p.89.
8. Genesis 1:26 f.
9. Leviticus 19:2.
10. Mekilta Shirata, ed. Lauterbach vol. 2, p. 25; cf, Babylonian Talmud, Shabbat 133b.
11. *Chicago Daily News* (5th of a 10-part Series) by Benjamin Spock, based on the book *Raising Children in a Difficult Time.*
12. Psalm 90:4.
13. Gittelsohn, *Man's Best Hope,* pp. 11 f.
14. Psalm 145:17.
15. Frederick Plotkin, *Judaism and Tragic Theology* (New York: Schocken, 1973), p. 62.
16. Steven Schwarzschild, "Speech and Silence before God," in *Understanding Jewish Prayer,* ed. Jakob Petuchowski (New York: KTAV, 1972), p. 84.
17. Mordecai Kaplan, *The Meaning of God in Modern Jewish Religion* (1937; reprint ed., New York: Jewish Reconstructionist Foundation, 1947), p. 76.
18. Ibid., pp. 72 f.

19. Ibid., pp. 79, 80.
20. Sifre 144a.
21. Henry Slonimsky, *Essays* (Chicago: Quadrangle, 1967), p. 15.
22. Ibid., p. 63.
23. Babylonian Talmud, Yoma 69a.
24. E. Berkovits, *Faith After the Holocaust* (New York: KTAV, 1973), p. 125.
25. See the account of Luria's view in G. Scholem, *Major Trends in Jewish Mysticism* (New York: Schocken, 1941), pp. 244–86.
26. André Schwarz-Bart, *The Last of the Just* (New York: Atheneum, 1960), p. 353.
27. Babylonian Talmud, Berachot 33b.
28. Shubert Ogden, *The Reality of God* (New York: Harper & Row, 1964, chap. 1.
29. Mekilta, Bahodesh, vol. 2, pp. 234 ff.
30. *Kuzari* I:95.
31. Kaufmann Kohler, *Jewish Theology* (New York: Macmillan, 1928), p. 328.
32. Sifre 134b.
33. Mark Twain, *Concerning the Jews* (1897; reprint ed., New York: Harper & Brothers, 1934), p. 26.
34. Deuteronomy 14:2.
35. Isaiah 42:6.
36. Leviticus Rabbah 36:4.
37. *Union Prayerbook* (New York: Central Conference of American Rabbis, 1940), p. 42.
38. Zechariah 14:9.
39. Psalm 11:1, 5.
40. Ezekiel 20:33 ff.
41. *Authorized Daily Prayer Book,* ed. J. Hertz (New York: Bloch, 1948), pp. 145 f.
42. S. Schwarzschild, "The Personal Messiah: Towards the Restoration of a Discarded Doctrine," *Judaism* 5 (1956).
43. Pittsburgh Platform, Plank No. 5, in Gunther Plaut, *The Growth of Reform Judaism* (New York: World Union for Progressive Judaism, 1965), p. 34.
44. Ibid., p. 97.
45. *A Passover Haggadah,* ed. Herbert Bronstein (New York: Central Conference of American Rabbis, 1974), p. 93.
46. I Kings 21:1–29.
47. Babylonian Talmud, Menachot 45a.
48. Malachi 4:6.

CHAPTER VII

1. See *High Holiday Prayer Book,* ed. Philip Birnbaum (New York: Hebrew Publishing Co., 1951), p. 972.
2. Genesis Rabbah 17:4.
3. Psalm 8:3 f.

4. Psalm 24:1.
5. Psalm 100:3.
6. Genesis 11:4.
7. Tanhuma, Genesis 8b–9a.
8. Quoted in Roger L. Shinn, *Man: The New Humanism* (Philadelphia: Westminster, 1967), p. 153.
9. Babylonian Talmud, Hagigah 13a.
10. C. P. Snow, "The Moon Landing," *Look,* August 26, 1969, p. 72.
11. Ecclesiastes Rabbah 7:28.
12. Quoted in Ralph Burhoe, *Science and Human Values in the 21st Century* (Philadelphia: Westminster, 1971), p. 170.
13. Deuteronomy 30:19.
14. William Faulkner, Quoted from Nobel Prize Acceptance Speech, Stockholm, Sweden, December, 10, 1950.
15. Robert Gordis, *A Faith for Moderns* (New York: Bloch, 1950), pp. 191f.
16. Richard Rubenstein, *Eros and Morality* (New York: Harper & Row, 1970), p. 73.
17. Deuteronomy 30:11 ff.
18. *Union Prayerbook,* vol. 2 (New York: Central Conference of American Rabbis, 1948), p. 342.
19. Jerusalem Talmud, Berachot, chap. IV, 33b–34a.
20. Mishnah, Berachot 9:5.
21. Martin Buber, *Good and Evil* (New York: Scribner's, 1953), p. 97.
22. Ibid.
23. Genesis 3:7.
24. Isaiah 14:14.
25. Genesis Rabbah 42:3.
26. Nathan Rotenstreich, *Tradition and Reality* (New York: Random House, 1973), p. 324.
27. Babylonian Talmud, Berachot 33b.
28. Ibid., Nidah 16b.
29. Bereshit Rabbah 8:4.
30. B. F. Skinner, *Beyond Freedom and Dignity* (New York: Knopf, 1971), p. 101.
31. Anthony Burgess, *A Clockwork Orange* (New York: Ballantine Books, 1965), p. 226.
32. Ibid., p. 84.
33. James V. McConnell, "Criminals Can Be Brainwashed Now," *Psychology Today,* April 1970.
34. Ibid. For additional examples, see T. Roszak, *Where the Wasteland Ends* (New York: Doubleday, 1972), appendix to chap. 7.
35. *Chicago Sun Times,* January 2, 1974.
36. Jim Warren, "Peace Pills for Presidents?" *Psychology Today,* October 1973.
37. Cornish Rogers, "Bio-Medics, Psychology and Laissez-Faire," *Christian Century,* October 31, 1973.
38. Genesis Rabbah 9:7.
39. Paul Ramsey, *Fabricated Man: The Ethics of Genetic Control* (New Haven: Yale University Press, 1970), p. 106.

40. Genesis Rabbah 8:12.
41. Hans Jonas, "Contemporary Problems in Ethics from a Jewish Perspective," in *Judaism and Ethics,* ed. Daniel J. Silver (New York: KTAV, 1970), p. 47.
42. Babylonian Talmud, Sukkah 52a.
43. James Watson, *The Double Helix* (New York: Atheneum, 1968), chap. 22.
44. Mircea Eliade, *Cosmos and History* (New York: Harper & Row, 1954).
45. *Authorized Daily Prayer Book,* ed. Joseph Hertz (New York: Bloch, 1948), p. 553.
46. Babylonian Talmud, Sanhedrin 98a.
47. Ibid., Baba Bathra 10a.
48. Mishnah, Sotah 9:15.
49. Emil Fackenheim, *Quest for Past and Future* (Bloomington: University of Indiana Press, 1968), p. 90.
50. *Panorama* magazine, *Chicago Daily News,* October 18, 1969.
51. Günter Grass, *Local Anesthetic* (New York: Harcourt, Brace & World, 1969).
52. *Worldview,* September 1972, p. 4.
53. Genesis 3:22 ff.
54. Isaiah 2:22.
55. Genesis Rabbah 9:5; cf. Babylonian Talmud, Baba Bathra 75b.
56. Sifre 141a; Tanhuma B.; Wa'ethanan 6a.
57. Gerald Feinberg, *The Prometheus Project,* quoted in Ramsey, *Fabricated Man,* p. 155.
58. Ibid., p. 159.
59. Psalm 90:12.
60. Steven Kelman, *Push Comes to Shove,* Houghton Mifflin, 1970, p. 164.
61. Robert Lifton, "Protean Man," in *Religious Situation* (Boston: Beacon Press, 1968, p. 827.
62. Saul Bellow, *Mr. Sammler's Planet* (New York: Viking Press, 1969), p. 239.
63. Ibid.
64. Ibid., p. 316.
65. Psalm 39:4, 7.
66. Gershom Scholem, *The Messianic Idea in Judaism* (New York: Schocken, 1971), p. 338.
67. Babylonian Talmud, Sanhedrin 38a.

CHAPTER VIII

1. Thomas Mann, *The Magic Mountain* (New York: Vintage, 1969), p. 32.
2. Robert Bellah, *Beyond Belief* (New York: Harper & Row, 1970), pp. 206, 244.
3. Saul Bellow, "Machines and Storybooks," *Harper's,* August 1974.
4. C.S. Lewis, *God in the Dock: Essays in Theology and Ethics,* ed. W. Hooper (Grand Rapids: Eerdmans, 1970), pp. 65 f.

5. Archibald MacLeish, ''Voyage to the Moon,'' *New York Times,* July 21, 1969.
6. Harvey Cox, *Feast of Fools* (Cambridge: Harvard University Press, 1969), p. 144.
7. Philip Rieff, *Triumph of the Therapeutic* (New York: Harper & Row, 1966), esp. chap. 8.
8. Herman Kahn and Anthony Weiner, *The Year 2000* (New York: Macmillan, 1967).
9. Andrew Greeley, *Religion in the Year 2000* (New York: Sheed & Ward, 1969), pp. 168 f.
10. Alexis de Tocqueville, *Democracy in America,* trans. Henry Reeve (New York: Oxford University Press, 1947), p. 343.
11. Jean Revel, ''Without Marks for Jesus,'' *Saturday Review,* July 24, 1971.
12. Quoted in H.H. Ben Sasson, *Jewish Society Through the Ages* (New York: Schocken, 1971), pp. 341 f.
13. Sifre 83a.